Using

Prodigy

Using
Prodigy

Michael Miller

Using Prodigy

Copyright© 1995 by Que® Corporation

Library of Congress Catalog No.: 95-71430

ISBN: 0-7897-0323-8

97 96 95   6 5 4 3 2 1

Interpretation of the printing code: the rightmost double-digit number is the year of the book's printing; the rightmost single-digit number, the number of the book's printing. For example, a printing code of 95-1 shows that the first printing of the book occurred in 1995.

Screen reproductions in this book were created using Collage Plus from Inner Media, Inc., Hollis, NH.

Composed in *ITC Century, ITC Highlander,* and *MCPdigital* by Que Corporation.

Credits

President
Roland Elgey

Publisher
Stacy Hiquet

Publishing Director
Brad R. Koch

Editorial Services Director
Elizabeth Keaffaber

Managing Editor
Sandy Doell

Director of Marketing
Lynn E. Zingraf

Senior Series Editor
Chris Nelson

Acquisitions Editor
Beverly M. Eppink

Product Director
Benjamin Milstead

Production Editor
Heather Kaufman Urschel

Assistant Product Marketing Manager
Kim Margolius

Technical Editor
Jerry Dunn

Technical Specialist
Cari Skaggs

Acquisitions Coordinator
Ruth Slates

Operations Coordinator
Patty Brooks

Editorial Assistant
Andrea Duvall

Book Designer
Ruth Harvey

Cover Designer
Dan Armstrong

Production Team
Steve Adams
Angela Bannan
Becky Beheler
Brian Buschkill
Jason Carr
Chad Dressler
Bryan Flores
DiMonique Ford
Jason Hand
Damon Jordan
Clint Lahnen
Kaylene Riemen
Bobbi Satterfield
Craig Small
Kelly Warner
Todd Wente

Indexer
Kathy Venable

To my grandmothers, Alice and Clara: You are both an inspiration. I hope I'm going as strong as you two are when I'm in my eighties!

About the Author

Michael Miller is Director of Strategic Planning for Macmillan Computer Publishing, an eight-year veteran of the computer publishing industry, and author of more than a dozen computer books. Among his previous books are *Using CompuServe*, Second Edition, *Easy Internet*, *OOPS! What To Do When Things Go Wrong*, and *Real Men Use DOS*. His job at MCP is to help the publishing staffs at Que and other MCP business units focus on upcoming trends in the computer hardware and software markets.

Acknowledgments

Thanks to Roland, Stacy, Brad, Bev, and the rest of the Queballs for keeping this one going through the numerous (and seemingly arbitrary) changes at P*.

We'd like to hear from you!

As part of our continuing effort to produce books of the highest possible quality, Que would like to hear your comments. To stay competitive, we *really* want you, as a computer book reader and user, to let us know what you like or dislike most about this book or other Que products.

You can mail comments, ideas, or suggestions for improving future editions to the address below, or send us a fax at (317) 581-4663. For the online inclined, Macmillan Computer Publishing has an Internet site at **http://www.mcp.com** (World Wide Web) through which our staff and authors are available for questions and comments.

In addition to exploring our forum, please feel free to contact me personally to discuss your opinions of this book: I'm **bmilstead@que.mcp.com** on the Internet.

Thanks in advance—your comments will help us to continue publishing the best books available on computer topics in today's market.

Benjamin Milstead
Product Development Specialist
Que Corporation
201 W. 103rd Street
Indianapolis, Indiana 46290
USA

Contents at a Glance

Using Prodigy for News, Weather, and Sports

Using Prodigy for Work

Using Prodigy at Home

Index

Table of Contents

What's new about New Prodigy

see page 27

Answering common questions

see page 53

Part II: Using Prodigy to Communicate with Others

E-mail etiquette

see page 68

Ten tips for better BB use

see page 85

Part III: Using Prodigy with the Internet

What the Internet is— and what it isn't

see page 112

*How Internet
e-mail differs
from Prodigy
e-mail*

see page 120

*Miller's list
of the best
Web starter
pages*

see page 150

How information is stored on the Net

see page 170

Part IV: Using Prodigy for News, Weather, and Sports

More news than you'll know what to do with

see page 182

Flip through the pages of an online magazine

see page 208

*Rate your
goods online
with Consumer
Reports*

see page 210

see page 210

Part V: Using Prodigy for Work

20   Retrieving Financial Information

*Keeping
track with
stock quotes
and charts*

see page 220

*Planning the
perfect trip
with Prodigy*

see page 240

All the famous people, all the famous news

see page 284

A bulletin board just for homeowners

see page 306

Looking it up online: Prodigy's two encyclopedias

see page 320

Playing games on the Internet

see page 337

Introduction

Prodigy is like a giant electronic community. You wander down the virtual main street and find all sorts of shops, large and small, general and esoteric. And as you walk, you run into all sorts of interesting people to talk with. All manner of social interaction can be yours, just for the asking.

But with Prodigy, you don't have to lace up your shoes, put on your jacket, and do the walking. All you have to do is pull up a chair to your computer and punch a few keys. Nobody cares how you're dressed, or if you've washed your hair today. In fact, no one will even notice you're there, unless you want them to.

It's just more convenient to do all that stuff in one place. And what place could be more convenient than your own home, on your own computer— with Prodigy?

What's new with "New Prodigy?"

Since its introduction in the 1980s, Prodigy had offered the same interface, the same basic means of navigation, and pretty much the same features and services. During the summer of 1995, however, Prodigy announced a major upgrade to its service, called "New Prodigy." This upgrade entailed a state-of-the-art interface (much better than the now-outdated "Crayola" screens), easier navigation via hypertext links, many new features and services, and creation of interest groups that combined regular Prodigy features with related resources on the Internet.

Naturally, this book covers New Prodigy. In fact, if you're a long-time Prodigy user, you might need this book to show you everything that's new on New Prodigy of today!

What will you find in this book?

Let's take a quick look at the six major parts of *Using Prodigy* and see how they can help you be a better Prodigy user:

- **Part I: Getting to Know Prodigy.** This is where you learn Prodigy basics.

- **Part II: Using Prodigy to Communicate with Others.** This section tells you all about Prodigy's main communication features, including e-mail, bulletin boards, and Prodigy Chat.

- **Part III: Using Prodigy with the Internet.** Turn to this section when you want to use Prodigy to access all the resources of the Internet, including Internet e-mail, USENET newsgroups, FTP, Gopher, and the World Wide Web.

- **Part IV: Using Prodigy for News, Weather, and Sports.** Prodigy offers a variety of news, weather, and sports services; use this section to find the ones that are right for you.

- **Part V: Using Prodigy for Work.** If you want to improve your business skills—or just book your next travel plans—this section is for you, with sections on financial information, small business information, travel information, and computer-related information.

- **Part VI: Using Prodigy at Home.** Discover the hundreds of services that Prodigy has to offer for the entire family.

Although this book focuses on using Prodigy with Windows 95, it includes very useful information for Windows 3.1, DOS, and Mac users. Even though the examples are Windows 95-based, all the instructions—and recommendations—apply to users on all four platforms.

Conventions used in this book

The conventions used in this book have been established to help you learn to use Prodigy quickly and easily. Here are some of the conventions:

- Material you type appears in **bold type**. Bold type also indicates the Prodigy JumpWords you type to go directly to specific features and services, as well as new terms introduced in the book's text.

- The "hot keys" on menu items appears in <u>underlined type</u>.

- Screen messages and on-screen results appear in a `special typeface`.

- Key combinations use a plus sign (+) to separate the keys (Ctrl+S, for example). Press the first key and, while holding it down, press the next key. Release both keys at once.

TIP CAUTION **Tips and cautions give time-saving shortcuts, additional** information, and warnings about potential problems.

 Plain English, please!

Plain English sections define new terms and buzzwords.

 Q&A **What is Q&A?**

This is a special section to answer many common questions about Prodigy.

Navigating to specific Prodigy resources

While there are many ways to get to most Prodigy features and services (through the various Highlights screens, via your own personal "hot list," and so on), I'm choosing one particular way to direct you to Prodigy's resources—via **JumpWords**. These JumpWords are identified in the text in boldface type (like this: Jump:**highlights**). To use a JumpWord, press Ctrl+J and type the JumpWord in the Go To box. Prodigy then takes you directly to the service linked to that JumpWord.

Keeping up to date

Because Prodigy is constantly updating the features of its service, it's only natural that this book will, from time to time, cover a feature that has been changed or enhanced since the book was printed. Wouldn't it be nice if you could update this book anytime Prodigy changed anything?

Well, you can. I've created a special Web page just for you readers of *Using Prodigy*. This page will keep you up to date on any new Prodigy features, any changes to the Prodigy service, and correct any mistakes (heaven forbid!) that creep into the printed version of this book.

To access the *Using Prodigy* page, fire up Prodigy's Web browser (Jump:**www**) and go the the following URL: **http://www.mcp.com/people/ miller/prodtop.htm**. In fact, I recommend going there RIGHT NOW, just to see if I've posted anything important to your reading of the book.

In addition, feel free to let me know what you like and don't like about the book. My Prodigy e-mail address is **JESE31A**; my Internet e-mail address is **mmiller@mcp.com**.

Part I: Getting to Know Prodigy

1

Prodigy Basics for New Users

● **In this chapter:**

- ● **Navigate Prodigy with the toolbar and menus**

- ● **Jump from one section to another via hypertext links**

- ● **Go directly to sections via JumpWords**

- ● **Create your own personal hot list**

- ● **Display an A-Z index of Prodigy's resources**

- ● **Find additional resources with interest groups and More About boxes**

- ● **Learn how to print, copy, and save items from Prodigy**

Prodigy is as easy to use as pointing and clicking your mouse—provided you know what to point at!. . . . . ❯

Okay, Prodigy novice. You're installed and connected, and ready to start exploring the Prodigy service. Unfortunately, you don't have a clue about where to start. Well, don't fear, new Prodigy user. This chapter will get you up and running with all you need to know about essential Prodigy features.

If, on the other hand, you're an *old* Prodigy user (in terms of experience, not age!), you might want to skip this chapter and go directly to chapter 2, "The New Prodigy for Old Users."

Learning the Prodigy interface

When you first log on to Prodigy, you're taken to the Prodigy Highlights screen (unless you specify otherwise when you launch the program). This screen is kind of like the roadmap to the rest of the service, and is a great way to learn about how to use Prodigy.

Viewing the highlights

At this point you're looking at the *main* Highlights screen—there are other Highlights screens for other parts of the Prodigy service. These other screens function just like the main Highlights screen, however, so we'll take a look at its pieces and parts before we go traipsing off to the rest of the service.

As you can see on page 11, this screen consists of two basic parts (in addition to the menu and the button bar, which I'll discuss in a second): the feature items on the left, and the highlighted items in the scrolling list on the right. Let's take a brief look at each type of item.

The feature items on the left are those articles and services Prodigy is highlighting today. To view one of these items, just click on its icon. These items change daily.

 TIP Your cursor changes into a "hand" shape when it moves over a "live" item—either an icon or a piece of hypertext. Whenever you see your icon change to this shape, you can click on the underlying item to jump to its accompanying link.

Of more importance is the list of services on the right of the screen. These items, all underlined and in blue, are **hypertext links** to other parts of the Prodigy service. When you click on one of these links, you are transferred to the part of the service that the text is linked to.

 Plain English, please!

A **hypertext link** is a piece of text that is "linked" to another item elsewhere on Prodigy or on the Internet. Clicking on a hypertext link "jumps" you to whatever it is linked to. All hypertext links on Prodigy are underlined and in blue.

Pushing the right buttons

Okay, now that you're a couple of levels deep, how do you get back to the main Highlights screen? Well, it's as simple as clicking a button.

At the bottom of every Prodigy screen is a toolbar full of buttons. Clicking on one of these buttons performs a certain navigational function, as follows:

Icon	Function
	Highlights—returns you to main Highlights screen
	Back—when reading an article, returns you to previous page
	Forward—when reading an article, moves you to next page
	Menu—moves you back to previous screen
	Hot List—displays your personal hot list of favorite resources
	Web—launches Prodigy's Web browser to let you cruise the World Wide Web
	Mail—launches Prodigy Mail, for sending and receiving e-mail

continues

Icon	Function
Chat	Chat—takes you to Prodigy's Chat rooms
BBs	BBs—takes you to Prodigy's bulletin boards
Net	Net—takes you to Prodigy's Internet resources

TIP **You can add and remove buttons from the toolbar by selecting** Goodies, Tool Bar Setup. See chapter 3, "Customizing the Way Prodigy Looks and Acts," for more details.

The two most useful buttons are the Highlights button and the Menu button. When you click on the Highlights button you're always taken straight to Prodigy's main Highlights screen—from wherever you are in the service. When you click on the Menu button, you essentially "back up" a screen, which takes you to the screen you were viewing before you moved to the current screen.

So, if you want to move from your current screen back to the main Highlights screen, just click on the Highlights button. It's as simple as that!

What's on the menu?

Most all of Prodigy's commands are also accessible via pull-down menus. You can pull down Prodigy's menus by clicking on a menu item with your mouse, or by pressing the F10 key and moving to the menu item of interest.

Examining the Prodigy Highlights screen

Prodigy's Highlights screen is typical of what you see throughout Prodigy. Let's take a visual tour of what you find on this screen.

Title of page—this is the Highlights screen

Pull-down menus

Prodigy logo (on other screens, the title appears here)

Feature items—click on the logo to jump to the item

Tool bar—click on a button to perform a function

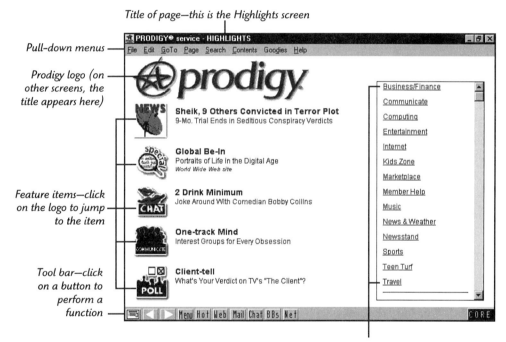

Hypertext links to other parts of the service—click on a link to jump to that part of the service

Navigating Prodigy

There are several ways to get from one part of Prodigy to another. Almost all involve some amount of pointing and clicking with your mouse.

Clicking and linking

A lot of what you see on-screen with Prodigy is somehow linked to another part of Prodigy. When you see your cursor change shape (from the normal arrow to a little pointing hand), that means that it's over something that's a hyperlink. The following items can be hyperlinked:

- Underlined blue text

- Icons

- Items in a scrolling list

 Plain English, please!

A **hyperlink** is a piece of text (also called **hypertext**) that is automatically linked to another document or part of Prodigy. Documents that contain hyperlinks are called **hypertext documents**.

And where do the hyperlinks take you? It all depends. Some take you to Prodigy's subsections (Chat, bulletin boards, etc.), some take you to specific articles or resources, and some even take you to resources out on the Internet! You really have to click on a link to find out where it takes you!

Jumping around

All that clicking is fine and dandy, but it could take you several clicks to get from one part of Prodigy to another. Isn't there any way you can "jump" directly from one place to another on the Prodigy service?

Yes, there is. Prodigy lets you use a **JumpWord** to go directly to other parts of the Prodigy service—and to enter Internet addresses to jump directly to places on the Net. You enter the JumpWord (or Net address) in a special navigation dialog box called the Go To box. To display the Go To box shown in figure 1.1, just press Ctrl+J.

Fig. 1.1
Press Ctrl+J to display
the Go To box, then
enter a JumpWord.

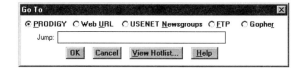

 TIP **You can also access the Go To box by pressing the F6 key, or by** pulling down the GoTo menu and selecting either Jump To or Navigate. In addition, you may want to add the "J" (for Jump) button to your Prodigy toolbar.

When the Go To box is displayed, make sure the PRODIGY option is selected, enter the proper Prodigy JumpWord, and then click OK. You'll automatically go to the area associated with that JumpWord.

Throughout this book I identify main features by their JumpWords. For example, I might tell you that Jump:**sports** takes you to the main Sports screen. You would type **sports** in the Go To box, click OK, and "jump" directly to the main Sports screen.

 CAUTION **Make sure you select the right type of resource before you click** the OK key—either PRODIGY JumpWord, Web URL, USENET newsgroup, FTP site, or Gopher site—or Prodigy might not jump you to where you think you're going! (But don't worry—you can get right back to where you were by selecting the Menu button on the toolbar.)

You can also use the Go To box to go directly to:

- Pages on the World Wide Web—enter the page's *URL* (shorthand for Web address); Prodigy automatically enters the **http://** part of the address

- Specific USENET newsgroups—enter the full name of the newsgroup

- FTP sites on the Internet—enter the full address for the site; Prodigy automatically enters the **ftp://** part of the address

- Gopher sites on the Internet—enter the full address for the site; Prodigy automatically enters the **gopher://** part of the address

TIP   **See Part III for more information on how to use these Internet** resources.

Q&A   ***When I enter a JumpWord, I get a No Match message. What did I do wrong?***

Essentially, you didn't enter a proper JumpWord. You may have entered a Web URL or newsgroup name with PRODIGY selected in the Go To box; that always causes trouble. You also may have simply entered the JumpWord wrong. Check what you typed and try again. Finally, it's possible that there is no JumpWord like the one you typed. If that's the case, click on the Closest Matches button in the No Match dialog box, and Prodigy will list the JumpWords that are spelled closest to what you typed.

Non-mouse navigation

What if you'd rather use your keyboard—can you navigate around Prodigy without clicking your mouse?

Well, you can do *some* things without your mouse, although that pesky two-buttoned rodent is necessary to take advantage of all of Prodigy's hyperlinks.

Function	Key combination
A–Z Index	F7
Action	F2
Backward	Page Up
Close open dialog box	Esc
Copy	Ctrl+C
Cut	Ctrl+X
Forward	Page Down
Go To	F6

Function	Key combination
Help	F1
Hot List	F3
Jump	Ctrl+J
Main Highlights screen	F5
Menu (return to previous screen)	Ctrl+M
Move to menu	F10
Next choice	Tab
Next Hot List item	F4
Paste	Ctrl+V
Previous choice	Ctrl+Tab
Print	Ctrl+P
Pull down Contents menu	Alt+C
Pull down Edit menu	Alt+E
Pull down File menu	Alt+F
Pull down GoTo menu	Alt+G
Pull down Help menu	Alt+H
Pull down Page menu	Alt+P
Pull down Search menu	Alt+S
Review	Ctrl+R
Save	Ctrl+S
Scratchpad	Ctrl+D
Snapshot	Ctrl+A
Tools	Ctrl+T
Undo	Ctrl+Z

Q&A   ***I live outside the U.S. Why can't I access all of Prodigy's features?***

Some of Prodigy's content providers only want their services used in the U.S. Some online retailers cannot ship outside the U.S. And, finally, some financial information is of interest only to Americans. For these reasons, some content is blocked to out-of-the-country Prodigy members.

If I leave Prodigy unattended, will I get billed for the inactive time?

To answer your question directly—YES! Prodigy bills you for all the time you're online. Fortunately, Prodigy also senses when you've been inactive for too long, pops up a dialog box warning you that you haven't done anything for awhile, and then automatically disconnects. This happens when you haven't interacted with Prodigy for at least 10 minutes.

Getting personal with your very own hot list

If you tend to frequent the same spots over and over, there's a way to create your own personal list of favorite Prodigy places. Prodigy lets you create a **hot list** of your favorite spots; you can then call up your hot list and jump directly to specific items on your list.

To display your hot list, just click on the Hot button on the toolbar or press the F3 button. You'll see a dialog box that looks similar to the one in figure 1.2.

TIP   If you're using Prodigy's Web browser, you can display the hot list by clicking on the Hot List button. You can even add specific Web pages to your hot list!

Jumping to any item in your hot list is as simple as displaying the list, selecting the item, and clicking on the Go button.

To add an item to your hot list, just jump to that page, display your hot list, and then click on the Add to List button.

You can also edit your hot list by using the Move Up and Move Down buttons (to rearrange the order of items in your list) and the Remove button (to delete an item from your list).

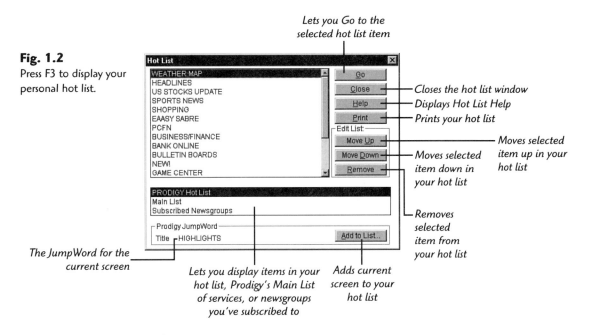

Fig. 1.2
Press F3 to display your
personal hot list.

Lets you Go to the
selected hot list item

Closes the hot list window
Displays Hot List Help
Prints your hot list

Moves selected
item up in your
hot list

Moves selected
item down in
your hot list

Removes
selected
item from
your hot list

The JumpWord for the
current screen

Lets you display items in your
hot list, Prodigy's Main List
of services, or newsgroups
you've subscribed to

Adds current
screen to your
hot list

TIP **You can jump sequentially through the items in your hot list**
(without needing to display the entire list) just by pressing the F4 key.

Searching for what you want

Creating a personal hot list is a good idea, but what if you have *no idea*
where you want to go? Fortunately, Prodigy lets you browse through an A to
Z list of everything it has to offer.

To display this A-Z index, just press the F7 key. You're presented with an
alphabetical list of everything available on Prodigy. You can scroll through
this list (by using the Next and Back buttons), or go to a specific point in the
list (by typing the first few letters of the topic in the Type to Move list box).

When you find the topic you want, highlight it and press the Go button. This
will jump you directly to that topic. In addition, you can add any topic to your
hot list by clicking on the Add To Hot List button.

And then, there's more...

While most of what's available on Prodigy appears right on-screen, there are often additional resources available. Prodigy gives you two ways to find these additional resources—through interest groups and special More windows.

Getting interested in interest groups

In addition to Prodigy's main services (bulletin boards, Chat, etc.—all discussed later in this book), Prodigy offers something called **interest groups**. An interest group is a collection of resources on a particular topic—resources that can include Prodigy services, Chat rooms, bulletin boards, USENET newsgroups, and World Wide Web sites. As I write this, Prodigy offers several dozen "major" interest groups, and literally hundreds of more specific "subgroups."

Prodigy's interest groups are actually pages on the World Wide Web. As you can see in figure 1.3, a typical interest group page starts with a feature article, but also includes dozens of links to related Web sites. In addition, the special Interact box lets you go directly to related Chat rooms and USENET newsgroups. Just click on any underlined blue text to link to related items.

Fig. 1.3
A typical interest group—note the Interact box that lets you go directly to related Chat rooms and newsgroups.

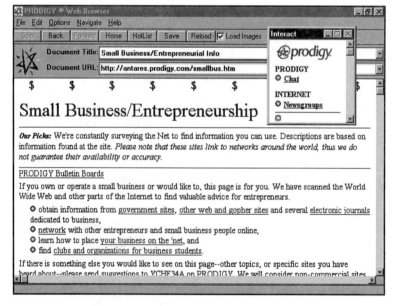

You can get to Prodigy's interest groups in a number of ways, including:

- Go directly to the specific interest group page by entering its URL (if you know it) into Prodigy's Web browser

- Go directly to the main Web-based interest group page (**http://antares.prodigy.com/mainpcoi.htm**) to see the complete list of interest groups

- Jump:**interest groups** to go to a general Interest Groups screen; this screen provides background info on interest groups, and lets you crank up the Web browser to access the Web-based list of interest groups

- Click the `Interest Groups A-Z` link on the main Highlights screen to see a Prodigy-based list of interest groups

 Plain English, please!

A **URL (uniform resource locator)** is an address for a site on the World Wide Web. See chapter 13, "Cruising the World Wide Web," for more information. **"**

Prodigy interest groups are great ways to discover resources related to what you're looking for. The grouping for both Prodigy-related resources and Net-based resources truly combines the best of both worlds—and fully integrates the wide world of the Internet with the normal Prodigy service.

 Q&A *Why can't I access Prodigy's interest group pages from my non-Prodigy Internet account?*

Use of Prodigy's interest groups are reserved for Prodigy members only. Prodigy only lets members access these pages; it blocks access to these pages from the rest of the Web.

Finding more about the current subject

Related to interest groups is another new Prodigy feature called **More About**. This feature lists a variety of resources related to the screen you're currently reading.

You can find More About options on just about any subsidiary highlights screen. For example, on Prodigy's Computing screen (Jump:**computers**), you'll see a hypertext link (underlined blue text) called More About Computing. When you click on that link, you're presented with the More About Computing box shown in figure 1.4.

Fig. 1.4
Finding out More About Computing.

To access a link in a More About box, just click on the appropriate button to show the list of links in that section, and then click on the desired link (underlined and in blue) in the list.

Using Prodigy tools

While you're cruising through Prodigy's various sections, you might find an article or screen that you'd like to keep for future reference. Fortunately, Prodigy lets you print, copy, and even save certain items to your hard disk.

Printing an item

Printing an item is as simple as pressing Ctrl+P. If you're reading an article, Prodigy can print that article automatically. If you're looking at a main screen, Prodigy can print the text from that screen. (Note, however, that Prodigy doesn't print any graphics from the screen—which can result in some strange-looking printouts!)

TIP **If you're using Prodigy's Web browser, it has a Print command that** prints the entire Web page—complete with graphics!

Q&A **Why won't my printer print a Prodigy item?**

Your printer is probably set up incorrectly. Select File, Print Setup to check your printer settings. Make sure you have the correct printer selected, and that it is configured properly.

Why doesn't my printout of a screen contain everything I saw on-screen?

Prodigy will only print main text items, so your printout won't include any graphics, icons, floating hypertext links, or contents of scrolling lists.

Shooting snapshots

Sometimes you want to take a "shot" of your current screen. You can then include this graphics file in another application—like including a screen shot of Prodigy in a Word report.

To take what Prodigy calls a **snapshot**, press Ctrl+A. Prodigy will ask if you want to take a snapshot of the entire screen or just the current area. If you select Entire Screen, the entire Prodigy screen is captured; if you select Area Only, you need to indicate the area you want to capture by drawing a "box" around it on-screen.

Click OK and you're asked whether you want to send the snapshot to the Windows Clipboard (where it can be pasted into another application), to the Printer (where it will be printed out), or to a File (where it will be saved in Windows bitmap format—with the BMP extension).

CAUTION **If you choose to print your snapshot, be prepared for a long wait.** Most printers take a long time to print out large graphics like this.

Choose your desired output and click OK. If you chose to save the snapshot as a file, you'll be asked to name the file and choose a directory to save it in. Prodigy will then take the snapshot, and proceed according to your instructions.

Copying and saving text

If you're reading an article on Prodigy, you can (in most cases) copy text from that article to place in other applications, or save that text in a disk file.

For example, you can copy text from a Prodigy article to insert into a Word document.

To copy an item you're reading, press Ctrl+C. This will display a Copy dialog box that contains all the text from the current item. Use your cursor to highlight the text you want to copy, and then click on the Copy button. This places the highlighted text in the Windows Clipboard. You can then change to another application and paste that text directly into any open document.

To save an item you're reading, just press the Save As button in the Copy dialog box. You'll be asked to name the file and choose a directory to save it in. Prodigy will then create a text file that contains the text you highlighted.

Q&A ***Why do some areas of Prodigy let me copy and save text, while others don't?***

This has to do either with the kind of item you're reading or with the copyright status of that item. In general, you can only save text-based articles, which means you can't save any graphics-related items. In addition, some content providers simply don't want you to copy their proprietary content; that would be in violation of that item's copyright.

All about Prodigy IDs

Prodigy is unique in that it allows access by multiple members of the same household, each with their own ID number. That way you can limit access to certain features to specific family members while allowing other family members full access to all features.

This works because Prodigy uses a master ID for each household. Each membership is assigned a six-digit ID number, along with a password. Each member uses the same "household" ID, but with a different suffix at the end. The main account member (let's say that's you) uses the suffix A. The rest of the family are assigned suffixes from B to F. That way Prodigy can keep track of each member in your household.

Let's look at an example. My "household" ID is JESE31. My personal ID, as the main account member, is JESE31A. If I were married, I could assign the ID JESE31B to my wife, and JESE31C, JESE31D, etc., to my children.

You can assign new IDs by Jump:**household member**. Click on the Add/Manage IDs button to display the Manage Household IDs screen. From here you can see the current status of all the IDs on your membership, as well as assign new IDs, remove old IDs (click Clear ID Info), and set access to Plus features for various family members.

Q&A

When I try to connect to Prodigy, nothing happens and I get an error message. What should I do?

Error messages are clues to deciphering the causes of various problems. When it comes to connection problems, there can be various causes, most of which have to do with the Prodigy software not being configured properly for your computer.

The more common error messages are CT 16, CT 25, and CT 29. They are generally caused when the Prodigy dialing number is busy, not answering, or your modem was unable to connect to Prodigy's modem for some other reason. The best solution is to try connecting at a later time.

If you continue to have problems, you may need to reconfigure your modem, which you do with Prodigy's Assist utility. See chapter 5 for more details on using Assist to debug modem problems.

After I connect to Prodigy, I receive an error message and get disconnected. How can I keep this from happening?

In this situation you'll typically see one of the following error messages: CM 4, CM 6, or LTM 33. These messages are generated when your computer doesn't receive any response from the Prodigy system. Usually this is caused by problems at Prodigy's end, or when another application on your PC is interfering with the Prodigy software. Try dialing again, and if the problem persists, close any other software running on your PC and then run the Prodigy software on your "clean" system.

If you see the OMCM9 error message, chances are you have call waiting on your phone line—and you just received an incoming call! You should disable call waiting before dialing Prodigy again. (You can do this by adding ***70** before the Prodigy dialing number.)

Other causes for this problem have to do with modem features such as flow control and data buffering. You may need to deactivate these features; contact Prodigy Technical Support at 1-800-PRODIGY for custom commands to disable the flow control and data buffering for your specific modem.

 Q&A ***I'm trying to connect to Prodigy through a hotel switchboard that requires me to dial 9 before the number. How do I change my setup to allow for this?***

Launch the Prodigy software and, when you see the Sign-On dialog box, click on the Set-Up button. When the Set-Up Options dialog box appears, enter a 9 in front of your Primary Phone Number. Click OK when you're done.

The New Prodigy for Old Users

In this chapter:

- **What is New Prodigy?**

- **Why did Prodigy change its look?**

- **What new features are available?**

- **How do I do my old tasks with New Prodigy?**

Hey! Prodigy looks different! . . . . ＞

I f you're a Prodigy user running Windows, sometime in August or September when you logged onto Prodigy you received an "automatic update" to your Prodigy software. By now you're probably used to that; Prodigy is constantly updating parts of its service via online upgrades.

But this update was different. For one thing, it took longer (because it was bigger). And, the next time you logged onto Prodigy, it looked different. *A lot different.* In fact, it even *worked* different.

What you experienced was the most major upgrade to Prodigy since its birth. As a result of this upgrade, you're now using what is called "New Prodigy." So, let's explore the New Prodigy and discover what it has to offer to you.

Why Prodigy changed its look

When Prodigy was launched in the mid-1980s, it had a pretty slick interface. In contrast to the text-based services of the time, it sported colorful graphics, and let you use a mouse to point-and-click your way through the service. In short, it was state-of-the-art for its time.

That time, however, came and went. Other online services, such as America Online and CompuServe, added even niftier graphical user interfaces (GUIs), and adapted themselves to the Windows environment. Their GUIs were true Windows interfaces and utilized all the features that Windows had to offer. In addition, they started linking related parts of their services together, which meant you could find all topics of a certain sort in a single place. In short, they progressed with the times.

Prodigy, however, did not. Prodigy's content began to stagnate. The old interface—affectionately dubbed the "Crayola" interface—was not adapted for true Windows use. What looked cool in the late 1980s looked dated in the mid-1990s. To put it simply, Prodigy got stale.

The management at Prodigy knew they had to do something. Development of a new interface and features started in the early 1990s. Some new features were phased in sooner than others; for example, Prodigy was the first online service to add Internet access and a World Wide Web browser. But the real changes had to wait until August of 1995, when New Prodigy was launched.

Actually, New Prodigy was phased in in bits and pieces. Prodigy's Internet tools were added late in 1994, and the new Prodigy Mail went live a month before the balance of the New Prodigy interface. Additional changes and enhancements are ongoing; when you get an automatic update upon connection, chances are some new piece of New Prodigy is being implemented.

At the time this book was written, not all Prodigy features had been updated to New Prodigy. Additional New Prodigy features are being phased in over time.

TIP See the *Using Prodigy* **Web page at http://www.mcp.com/people/ miller/prodtop.htm** for up-to-date information about New Prodigy features.

Q&A *I wasn't able to download New Prodigy. How can I upgrade?*

If, for some reason, you weren't able to complete the upgrade online, you should call Prodigy to receive a copy of New Prodigy on disk. Call 1-800-PRODIGY to request a disk copy—or download a copy from Prodigy's Web site (**http://www.prodigy.com/**).

Do I need to upgrade my software to run New Prodigy?

No. If you were running the old Windows version of Prodigy, you have more than enough power to run New Prodigy. (Although, as always, a faster modem and more memory is recommended.)

What's new about New Prodigy

New Prodigy utilizes true Windows-based software. It adds many new features, and—like competing services—integrates related resources into common groups. Prodigy even goes beyond its competitors by moving to a true hyperlinked interface, based on the HTML language used to create World Wide Web pages. The bottom line: New Prodigy cooks!

New Prodigy has been positively received by the online community, especially among newer users accustomed to the Windows interface and WWW-type hyperlinks. More experienced Prodigy users, however, seem to either love New Prodigy or hate it. The former group appreciates the added features and ease-of-use of New Prodigy. The latter group, apparently, just doesn't like change.

TIP **New Prodigy is currently only available for Windows users. While** there are plans to update the Mac version in 1996, no future updates are planned for Prodigy's DOS version. Some New Prodigy features, however, are built into the Prodigy service itself, and will be apparent to users on all platforms.

It looks better

So, what's new with New Prodigy? Let's start with its basic look and feel. Figures 2.1 and 2.2 show the main Highlights screen under the old Prodigy and under New Prodigy. As you can see, the graphics are more sophisticated with New Prodigy. In addition, the old clunky buttons have been replaced by a scrolling list of hypertext links. It looks better and offers more functionality.

Fig. 2.1
The old Prodigy Highlights screen.

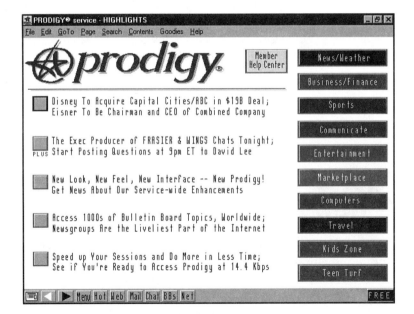

Fig. 2.2
The New Prodigy
Highlights screen.

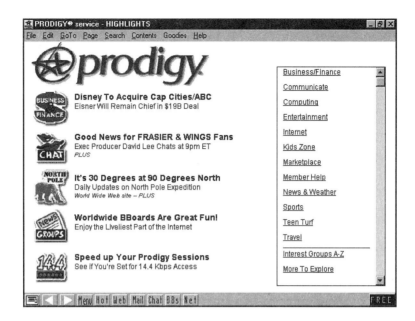

 **Plain English, please!**

> A **hypertext link** is a piece of text that is linked to another item, either on Prodigy or on the Internet. Clicking on a piece of hypertext "jumps" you to the linked item. In Prodigy, hypertext is always underlined and in blue. **"**

Prodigy calls this new interface "Webcentric," because it's based on HTML, the language used to create Web pages. In fact, if you're used to cruising the World Wide Web, you'll be right at home with New Prodigy.

It links to more information

One of the most important features of New Prodigy is its ability to hyperlink to additional information.

One of the key uses of hyperlinking is in what Prodigy calls **interest groups**. An interest group is a Web page that groups together all available resources on a given topic. For example, if you go to the Movies interest group, you'll find hyperlinks to Prodigy entertainment news, Prodigy Chat rooms, Prodigy bulletin boards, USENET newsgroups, and World Wide Web sites—all in one place (see fig. 2.3)!

In addition, New Prodigy has added a **More About** feature, seen in figure 2.4. This is an interest group-like listing of additional resources (both on Prodigy and on the Net), with hyperlinks to each resource. More Abouts are available for most major topics.

Interest groups and More Abouts break down the walls between Prodigy and the Internet. By letting you access content on the Internet—and making it relatively seamless—Prodigy gives you a lot more content than you had before. That's more bang for your buck, folks!

Fig. 2.3
A New Prodigy interest group; click on the underlined text to link to related resources.

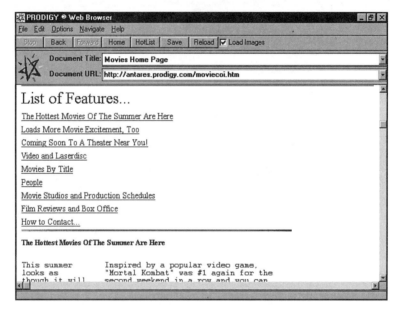

Fig. 2.4
Find out More About related resources—both on Prodigy and on the Net.

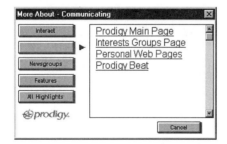

It adds some new features

In addition to all this "resource grouping" and hyperlinking, there are quite a few other features found in New Prodigy. These features either make it easier for you to perform old tasks, or add resources to what was previously available.

Let's look at New Prodigy's major new features:

- Complete Internet access, including an integrated World Wide Web browser

- Enhanced Prodigy Mail system, with a true Windows interface, built-in spell checker, ability to attach files, ability to do cc's and bcc's, and multimedia capabilities (for sound and picture files)

- A Go To window that allows you to jump to Web sites and USENET newsgroups—in addition to normal Prodigy JumpWords

- A hot list of favorite resources—including Internet resources—that replaces the old Path command

In addition, Prodigy took the opportunity to change some of its sections during this update. The old Reference section was eliminated as a separate section; its contents were shifted to other topic sections. And the Home/Family/Kids section was split into two new sections, Kids Zone and Teen Turf.

It takes away some old features

In true "out with the old, in with the new" fashion, New Prodigy also eliminated some little-used features from the old Prodigy. Here's what goes away with the New Prodigy:

- Macros (the new software just won't recognize all the old macros you may have created)

- The Path command (replaced by a new hot list for favorite resources)

- Ads (replaced by ad *buttons* that use less "real estate" than the old bottom-of-screen advertisements)

How to do old things the new way

While New Prodigy is essentially just an update to what worked best in the old Prodigy, there are some things that work a little different. Let's look at some of the major operational changes that come with New Prodigy.

No more Crayola buttons

Remember all those big clunky buttons on the Highlights screen and throughout the service? Well, they're gone, for the most part. And, for the most part, they've been replaced by hypertext links. Where you used to see a garishly colored button, you now find a piece of blue, underlined text. Click this text to jump to the linked section, just the way you used to click the big ugly button.

An enhanced path

In the old Prodigy you could create a path that included your favorite parts of the service; you could then "travel" that path, from topic to topic, just by invoking the Path command.

With New Prodigy, the Path command is replaced by a hot list. The hot list works much the same as the old Path command, but lets you include Internet resources as well as Prodigy resources (see fig. 2.5). You can even jump sequentially through all items in your hot list, just like you could with the Path command (just press the F4 key). In fact, Prodigy automatically added all your path items to your hot list when it upgraded you to New Prodigy.

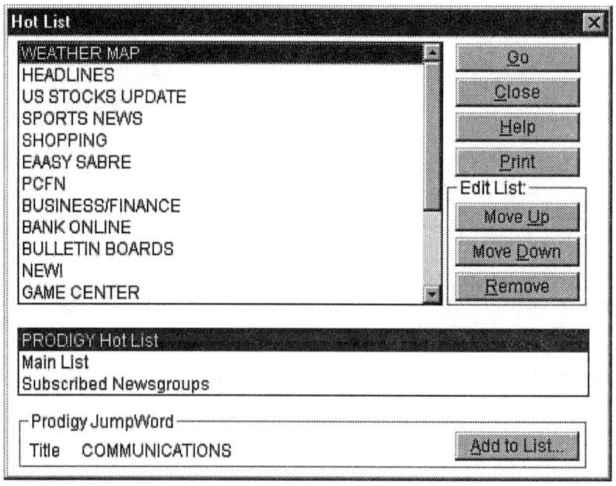

Fig. 2.5
New Prodigy's new Hot List replaces the old Path command.

More jumping

In the old Prodigy, you used JumpWords to go to specific parts of the Prodigy service. Well, the JumpWords are still there, but now you enter them in a new Go To window. (You can still use Ctrl+J to bring up this window, or you can use the new F6 Navigate command.) The big difference in the Go To window is the ability to jump direct to USENET newsgroups, World Wide Web pages, Internet FTP sites, and Internet Gopher servers—in addition to the regular Prodigy JumpWords (see fig. 2.6). In this case, the change is definitely an enhancement.

Fig. 2.6
Use the new Go To window to enter JumpWords and Internet addresses.

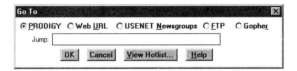

Mightier Mail

New Prodigy's Mail system is a tremendous enhancement over the old e-mail system. Prodigy Mail is now a true Windows program, which means all your Windows operations work within Mail. Prodigy also added a slew of new features to Mail, including a built-in spell checker, the ability to include separate files as attachments, the ability to carbon copy (cc) and blind carbon copy (bcc) additional recipients, and the ability to transmit and playback multimedia picture and sound attachments. Oh yeah, the interface looks a lot prettier, too.

Different buttons on the toolbar

Finally, New Prodigy made some basic changes to the old toolbar. There are now buttons for new features like the Hot List (Hot), the Web browser (Web), and the Internet section (Net).

All the old buttons are still available; you can add them back to your toolbar by selecting Goodies, Tool Bar Setup.

Q&A *I don't like New Prodigy. How do I get the old Prodigy back?*

There really isn't any easy way to "backgrade" your Prodigy software. Even if you were to reinstall your old Prodigy software, the Prodigy service would just automatically upgrade it to New Prodigy the next time you logged on.

Is New Prodigy slower than the old Prodigy?

Initially, New Prodigy appeared slower on some computers (generally older machines with less memory). However, Prodigy initiated some changes to New Prodigy to speed up the operation, such as painting all the text for a screen before the graphics (so you can read and act on a screen before it's fully painted). These changes make New Prodigy as speedy as the old Prodigy, and every bit as fast as competing online services.

3

Customizing the Way Prodigy Looks and Acts

● In this chapter:

- How to change buttons on the toolbar

- How to change Prodigy's screen fonts

- How to change which screen you see when you sign on

- How to change Prodigy's sounds

- Where you can find utilities for Prodigy

Change the look and feel of Prodigy by giving it your own personal touch . . . . ▶

rodigy—"straight out of the box," as it were—is pretty easy to use. But there are some little things you can do to make your time with Prodigy a little more effective and a little more efficient. That is, you can customize Prodigy so that it looks, sounds, and acts pretty much the way you want it to. Read on and I'll tell you how you can personalize Prodigy to make it work better for you.

Changing the toolbar

Prodigy's default toolbar includes buttons for the Highlights screen, Backward and Forward paging, return to previous menu, your hot list, the Web browser, Prodigy Mail, Chat rooms, BBs, and Net resources. But what if you don't use one of these features, and you want to dedicate a button to something else, like the Jump command? Fortunately, Prodigy lets you customize your toolbar to your heart's content.

To customize Prodigy's toolbar, select Goodies, Tool Bar Setup from Prodigy's pull-down menus. When you do this, you see the Tool Bar Setup screen shown in figure 3.1.

Fig. 3.1
Use this screen to customize the buttons on your toolbar.

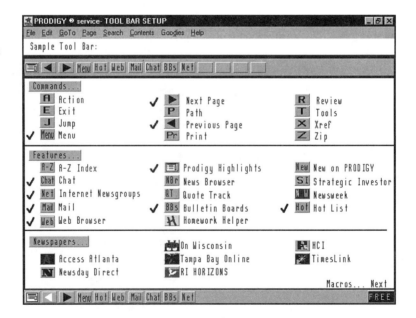

Your current toolbar is shown at the top of this screen. The buttons on the current toolbar have check marks next to them. All the other buttons on this screen represent commands you can add to your tool bar. As you can see, you can add buttons for essential Prodigy commands, for Prodigy features, and for the extra-fee newspapers available on Prodigy.

Deleting a button from the toolbar is pretty simple. Just go to that button in the button list, and click it. The check mark next to it will disappear, and the button will be removed from the toolbar at the top of the screen.

 CAUTION   **Deleting a button in the middle of the toolbar leaves a hole in** the toolbar; the buttons do not automatically rearrange themselves to fill the gap.

To add a new button to the toolbar—or to replace an existing button—follow these steps:

1 In the button list, click on the button you want to add.

2 On the sample toolbar at the top of the screen, click on the button you'd like to replace.

Voila! The button you selected takes its place on the button you clicked on in the sample toolbar. Select File, Save from the pull-down menu to save your new toolbar, and use your normal navigation methods to move to another screen.

Note that Prodigy's default toolbar comes with 10 buttons "preprogrammed." Your toolbar can have up to 14 buttons, which means you can only add four new buttons before you have to "reprogram" the existing buttons.

 TIP   **If you're like most users, you'll want to add these commonly used** buttons to the toolbar: Jump, Print, and Exit.

Changing the Highlights screen

By default, Prodigy displays the main Highlights screen when you first sign on. You can, however, select other screens to display as the first screen on your system.

Jump:**change highlights** to display the screen in figure 3.2. All possible initial screens are displayed. By default, the PRODIGY screen (what we call the main Highlights screen) is set as the sign-on screen. To select a different screen for sign-on, just click on its button. You'll see a dialog box with the options to View This Highlights Now or Make This Your Highlights. Click the latter button to see this screen when you sign onto Prodigy.

Fig. 3.2
Changing Prodigy's
sign-on screen.

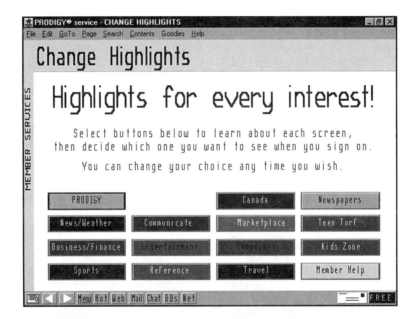

Changing the way Prodigy *sounds*

So far we've talked about changing the way Prodigy *looks*. There's also a way to change the way Prodigy *sounds*.

If you have a sound card in your PC system, you're probably already hearing the "voice of Prodigy." This is a synthesized voice that welcomes you to Prodigy, alerts you when you have new mail, says good-bye when you leave, and makes other comments when other events occur. You can, however, change the sounds you hear—and you can even turn them off!

Begin by selecting Goodies, Sounds. This displays the Sounds dialog box. As you can see, there are five main Prodigy sounds—for Signing On, Signing Off, New Mail, Inactivity Message, and Instant Messaging. You can test any of these sounds by clicking on the appropriate Test button.

To change a sound, click on its main button. For example, to change the Signing On sound, click on the Signing On button. You'll see a Sound Options dialog box, which gives you the following options:

- Use a Wave File—Select this option to change the .WAV file associated with this event (you'll have to choose from other .WAV files installed on your hard disk).

- Use PRODIGY Beep—Select this to replace the "voice of Prodigy" with normal Windows beeps.

- Use No Sound—Select this to turn off sounds for this event completely.

When you're done changing these sounds, click on the OK button to register your changes.

Frankly, I kind of like the default voices. When I'm not quite sure which beep means what, a friendly voice telling me exactly what's going on makes a lot of sense.

 Q&A ***How do I change the phone number I use to connect to Prodigy?***

Launch the Prodigy software and, when you see the Sign-On dialog box, click on the Set-Up button. When the Set-Up Options dialog box appears, if you know the new phone number, enter it as your Primary Phone Number and click on the Redial button.

If you don't know the new number, activate the Dial the PRODIGY Phone Directory option and click on the Redial button. Now you'll see the Dial the PRODIGY Phone Directory dialog box. Change any pertinent information and then click the OK button. When you initiate your connection, instead of dialing your regular Prodigy phone number, the software dials a special 800-number (1-800-775-7714) for the Prodigy Phone Directory.

Enter the area code and first 3 digits of the phone number you'll be dialing from, and then click on the Start Search button. Prodigy displays a list of possible phone numbers; click on the correct one and the Prodigy software will be automatically configured to use this number in the future.

 You can also dial Prodigy's voice number (1-800-PRODIGY) and maneuver through their voice-mail system to find your local dialing number.

 Be sure to have your modem manual handy whenever you have to dial Prodigy technical support!

Supercharge Prodigy with Add-On Programs

● **In this chapter:**

- **How add-on software saves you time and money**

- **Compose e-mail offline with E-Mail Connection**

- **Browse bulletin boards on your own time with Bulletin Board Note Manager**

- **Use Journalist to compose a newspaper with the news you select**

These three programs automate common Prodigy tasks and cut down on the amount of time—and money—you spend online . . . . ●

Prodigy is a great service. No doubt about it. But what if—by simply installing an add-on software program—you could make Prodigy even better? Would this interest you?

If you are interested in enhancing your Prodigy experience, then this chapter is for you: I tell you about three add-on programs that can make Prodigy more efficient—and lower your monthly Prodigy bills!

Why should you add new software to Prodigy?

Prodigy, as you know it, works just fine, thank you. So why should you bother installing even more software to work with Prodigy?

Well, ask yourself the following questions. Would you like to:

- Reduce the time—and money—you spend online?

- Use Prodigy at your own pace?

- "Personalize" the information you receive from Prodigy?

If you answered yes to any of these questions, read on. I'll tell you about the following three add-on programs for Prodigy:

- **E-Mail Connection**, which lets you read and compose e-mail messages offline

- **Bulletin Board Note Manager**, which lets you read and compose BB messages offline

- **Journalist**, which lets you select the type of news you want to read—and then goes online to Prodigy to automatically compose your own personal newspaper

The one common factor to these programs is that they let you do most of your work offline, on your time—and without running up your monthly Prodigy bill. They will then go online for you, much faster than you could yourself, and they do it automatically.

This chapter is meant to be an introduction to these programs, not a full-fledged tutorial. So read on, and I'll tell you all about them!

Better mail with the E-Mail Connection

If you read ahead to chapter 8, "Sending and Receiving Electronic Mail," you learn how to use Prodigy's online e-mail system. E-mail, of course, is short for "electronic mail," which lets you send electronic messages to other computer users on the Prodigy service and throughout the Internet.

The only problem with Prodigy's standard e-mail is that you have to do all your work online. That means that the Prodigy meter is running while you stare into space thinking of just the right words for a new e-mail message, and while you want to leisurely peruse the latest messages in your Inbox.

E-Mail Connection fixes this problem. With E-Mail Connection (EMC, for short) you do all your composing and reading offline, without having to log onto Prodigy. And that, my friends, cuts down on your time online—which lowers your monthly Prodigy bills!

EMC lets you do anything you can do with regular Prodigy e-mail. The neat thing is, EMC does all these things *automatically*. You compose your messages offline, and then determine when you want to send the new messages in your Outbox (or receive new ones to your Inbox). EMC automatically connects to Prodigy, sends all the messages in your Outbox, and retrieves any waiting messages. After it completes its tasks, you can read your new messages offline, on your own time.

Figure 4.1 shows you the main EMC screen. You use the buttons across the top and the icons along the side to proceed from task to task.

When you want to compose a message, all you have to do is click on the Compose button. You'll see a Draft message window. Enter the address of the recipient (either manually or from your Prodigy address book), type a subject line, and then start composing your message. When you're done writing, click on the Send button and this message is deposited in your Outbox. To send the messages in your Outbox, click on the PRODIGY icon and either Connect immediately or Schedule a time to connect.

Go to the
next message

Go to the
previous message

Search saved messages
for a specific message

Reply to the
current message

Print the
current message

Forward the current message
to another recipient

Delete the
current message

Fig. 4.1
The E-Mail Connec-
tion for Prodigy.

Compose a
new message

View the
contents of
your Inbox

View the
contents
of your
Outbox

Connect
EMC to
Prodigy
now, or
schedule
a future
connection

View the
contents
of your
address
book

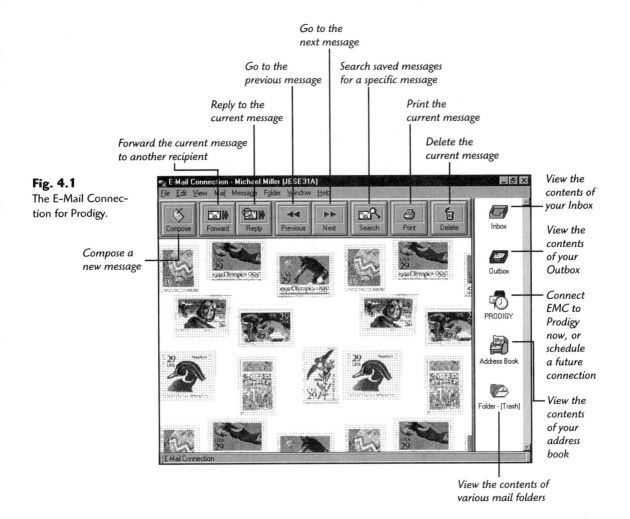

View the contents of
various mail folders

Retrieving new messages is as easy as clicking on the PRODIGY icon, and
then clicking on the Connect button. (You can also schedule an automatic
connection at a future time.) EMC automatically connects to Prodigy, checks
for new e-mail messages, saves them in your Inbox, and then disconnects—
just like that. Click on the Inbox icon to view your new messages; double-
click on a message to read it.

With E-Mail Connection you won't waste your online time reading and
composing messages. I find EMC essential, since I hate being under the gun
when I write messages online with Prodigy's normal e-mail system. This way

I can compose all my e-mail messages on my own time, and then upload them to Prodigy in one bunch.

You can download a copy of E-Mail Connection directly from Prodigy (Jump:**emc**). The cost is $14.95.

Automate Prodigy bulletin boards with Bulletin Board Note Manager

In chapter 7, "Sharing Special Interests on Bulletin Boards," I tell you more about Prodigy bulletin boards. For now, let's just say that Prodigy BBs are online "clubs" where you can exchange messages with other members about interests you have in common. Using a BB consists of going online, reading messages, and leaving your own messages. The downside of this is that you do all your reading and writing while you're online with Prodigy—with the meter running. Wouldn't it be nice to do most of these time-consuming BB tasks offline, without racking up additional Prodigy bills?

A new utility for Prodigy called **Bulletin Board Note Manager** (BBNM) lets you do just that. BBNM lets you download and upload notes and replies, so you can do the actual reading and writing of notes *offline*.

The way it works is simple. You begin by selecting the boards and topics you're interested in (see fig. 4.2). Then BBNM connects to Prodigy and automatically downloads the contents you specified. When it's done, it automatically disconnects from Prodigy—letting you read and reply to these new notes at your leisure.

Like E-Mail Connection, Bulletin Board Note Manager saves you online time and money by letting you do your reading and replying offline. My only problem with the program is that it's a little hard to learn. However, once you get it figured out, it's a snap to have it do all my online BB work—I can then read the notes I want to read, when I want to read them.

You can download a copy of Bulletin Board Note Manager directly from Prodigy (Jump:**bbnm**). The cost is $19.95.

Fig. 4.2
Reading notes offline
with Bulletin Board
Note Manager for
Prodigy.

*Use the toolbar to select which
boards and topics to view—and to
compose new messages and replies*

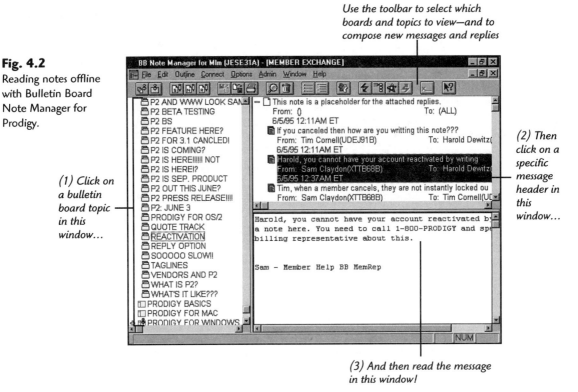

*(1) Click on
a bulletin
board topic
in this
window...*

*(2) Then
click on a
specific
message
header in
this
window...*

*(3) And then read the message
in this window!*

Create a personalized newspaper with Journalist

Prodigy offers a lot of different news services, as you'll see in chapter 20, "Reading the Daily News." In fact, there's *so much* news available on Prodigy that it can be a bit overwhelming. Wouldn't it be nice if you could just read the news you want to read—and nothing more?

Believe it or not, a software program called **Journalist** allows you to build your own personalized newspaper, using all the news capabilities available on Prodigy. With Journalist you get just the news you want, in the format you want—nothing more, nothing less.

Journalist is a Windows-based program that works alongside Prodigy. You use Journalist to construct a template that reflects your "perfect" newspaper—the different types of news you want to read, in the exact places on the page you want to see them. Constructing a newspaper model with Journalist is kind of like dragging frames around a word processing or desktop publishing program; you then tell Journalist what kinds of news to put in which frames. (Actually, when you first install Journalist, a setup "wizard" leads you through step-by-step instructions for creating your personalized newsletter.)

Once you have your template constructed, you schedule Journalist to automatically dial into Prodigy, retrieve the latest news, and assemble your personalized newspaper. You can then view the newspaper on-screen, as shown in figure 4.3, or print out a hard copy on your printer.

Fig. 4.3

Journalist automatically creates a newspaper with the types of news you request, formatted into a newspaper you can read on your computer screen.

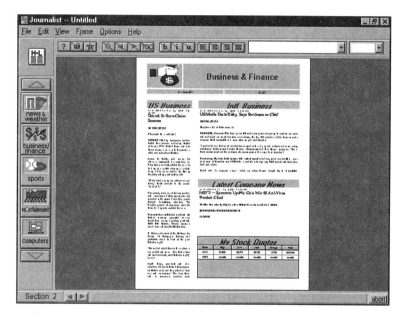

I think Journalist is a great program. It makes it quite easy to get the news you want from Prodigy—quickly and automatically. You can order Journalist directly from Prodigy (Jump:**journalist**). The cost is $29.95, plus shipping and handling.

Getting Help with Prodigy

● **In this chapter:**

- **Learn to use Prodigy's built-in Help system**

- **Go online for extended help and support**

- **Get answers to common Prodigy questions**

- **Use Assist to automatically correct connection problems**

- **Talk to a real-life human being at Prodigy's technical support department**

The nice thing about an online service such as Prodigy is the amount of help and support available—most of it online! . . . . ➤

Prodigy is fairly easy to use. It's easy to figure out most things you need to do. But every now and then even the most competent users run into a problem they can't solve. When that happens, it's time to discover Prodigy's various types of user help.

Using Prodigy's built-in Help Hub

Like most Windows programs, Prodigy comes with its own built-in Help system. This system resides on your hard disk, *not* online, so it's always available to you.

There are two main components to Prodigy's Help system, and they're both located on the program's Help menu. These components offer you specific Help for the current Prodigy page, and more comprehensive Help for all aspects of Prodigy software.

If you need help with the current screen, just pull down the Help menu by selecting Help, This Page. (You can also just press the F1 key.) This displays a HELP message that tells you about the current screen.

If you want to learn more about the features of the Prodigy software—and the Prodigy service—then you want to access what Prodigy calls Help Hub. **Help Hub** is nothing more than a normal Windows-based Help system, with information about various Prodigy features.

You can access Help Hub by pulling down Prodigy's Help menu and selecting Contents. This displays the Help Hub Contents screen; click on a topic to display a further list of items related to that Help topic (see fig. 5.1). Once you find the specific topic you're interested in, click on it and you'll see a screen full of information and helpful hints.

Most Help topics include "how to" information, along with a section titled "Good to Know." This section presents additional tips and tricks that you can use to make Prodigy more efficient and effective.

Fig. 5.1
The contents of
Prodigy's Help Hub.

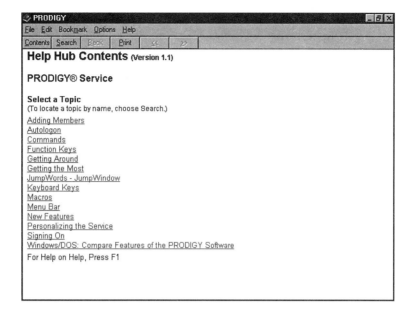

Getting more help online

Sometimes, though, you need more help than what is available with Help Hub. Fortunately, Prodigy has a complete Member Services center available online for all your support needs.

Jump:**help** to access the Prodigy Member Help screen, shown in figure 5.2. From here, you can:

- Access Prodigy's Chat rooms for real-time help and support (I recommend the P* Chat Camp room in the Member Services Help area)

- Go to the Member Help Bulletin Board (with great topics like Prodigy Basics, Member Services, P* Technical Help, Internet/Web Browser, and Member Utilities)

- Order Prodigy Membership Kits for friends and family

- Read about new Prodigy features in the What's New! section

- Learn about the latest goings-on in the Prodigy News section

Fig. 5.2
Prodigy's Member Help
screen.

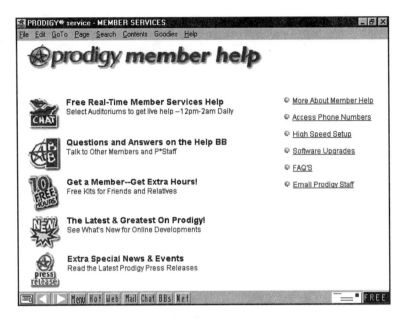

This isn't the only support available online, however. For example, if you want information about your Prodigy membership, Jump:**member informa-tion**. You'll see a list that lets you do things like add a member, change board access, change personal information, and get specific information about your account.

For the most complete listing of online Prodigy support information, however, click on More About Member Help. From here you have direct hyperlinks to just about every help-related resource available on Prodigy (and on the Internet). Figure 5.3 shows you the kind of help available from the More About—Member Help list.

Fig. 5.3
Linking to additional
Help resources.

If you can't find the answers to your questions in any of these spots, Jump:**ask us**. This screen lets you e-mail Prodigy's technical support staff, report service errors, and offer suggestions for future improvements to the Prodigy service. Reporting a problem here almost guarantees a personal response—via return e-mail, of course.

 TIP   **You can also find support information in the following USENET** newsgroups: **prodigy.usenet.help**, **prodigy.test**, **prodigy.chat**, and **prodigy.announce**.

Answering common questions

Chances are, the problems you're having aren't unique. It's likely other Prodigy members have experienced similar problems—and figured out the correct solutions.

Prodigy's Common Questions area (Jump:**common questions**) contains a comprehensive database of the most common problems faced by Prodigy users. You'll find answers to questions grouped by the following topic areas:

- Account/Billing
- Security Info
- Technical
- Using Prodigy (and, no, this isn't about any problems you might have with this book!)
- Offline Products (like Bulletin Board Note Manager, E-Mail Connection, and Journalist—all discussed in chapter 4 of this book)
- Online Features

Click on any of these topics and you'll see a list of the most frequently asked questions and answers about these topics. Because these are questions about the most common Prodigy problems, this is a good place to start your troubleshooting trek.

When you can't figure it out yourself, call Prodigy technical support

When all else fails, talking to a real live human being about your problems can often save the day. Fortunately, Prodigy has a toll-free number available 24 hours a day, 7 days a week, 52 weeks a year just for your support needs. So when you can't solve your problems through any other means, dial **1-800-PRODIGY (1-800-776-3449)** and talk to an expert.

Diagnose connection problems with Assist

Some of the most common Prodigy problems have to do with connecting to the service. If you're having trouble connecting, you won't even get the opportunity to avail yourself of Prodigy's online support services. How do you get help when you can't even get connected?

When you install your Prodigy software, you also install a special utility program called **Assist**. This program can help you diagnose and fix most connection-oriented Prodigy problems.

To launch Assist, use Windows' Start button to open the Prodigy menu group and then click on the Assist icon. Assist will then launch in a special DOS window. (Assist is a DOS-based program, but it runs just fine under Windows.)

You can use Assist in two modes: Regular and Expert. Most problems can be found using the Regular mode, so when you see the Welcome screen, simply click on the Continue button. At this point you'll be asked to supply any "error code" that Prodigy gave you when you failed to connect. (If you didn't receive an error code—or didn't take note of it—it's okay to select the Don't Know button.)

From this point on, follow the on-screen instructions. Assist checks your Prodigy phone number, dial tone, and modem settings, and attempts to correct your problem automatically. Note that this procedure takes a few minutes, and involves a bit of beeping and ringing from your modem.

If this doesn't fix your problem, you may need to select Assist's Expert mode. With Expert mode you can manually reconfigure Prodigy to recognize your specific hardware/software setup. Click on the appropriate option and follow the instructions from there.

If you're using Windows 95, you probably have to reboot your computer into DOS mode to use Assist's Expert mode; it won't be able to access everything it needs on your system while running within Windows 95.

To exit from Assist, simply pull down the File menu and select Exit. Alternatively, you can also exit Assist by pressing the Esc key.

Assist can fix most connection problems automatically. If you experience connection problems, you may need to place a call to Prodigy's technical support line (**1-800-PRODIGY**).

Part II: Using Prodigy to Communicate with Others

Sending and Receiving Electronic Mail

● **In this chapter:**

- Send and receive e-mail messages

- Reply to messages and create new messages

- Attach files to your messages—including pictures and sounds

- Send multiple copies of the same message to different people

- Manage the contents of your Address Book

- Search for the addresses of other Prodigy members

E-mail is the "killer app" of the online communications industry, and Prodigy's e-mail is the most popular part of the Prodigy service! . . . . ▶

Thinking of Prodigy as an electronic small town, it makes sense to envision an electronic version of the venerable post office, where electronic citizens can send electronic mail to other electronic citizens, who in turn receive their electronic messages in electronic mailboxes. Well, that's exactly how Prodigy's electronic mail system works.

Save stamps with Prodigy e-mail

When you Jump:**mail**, you're taken to Prodigy Mail, Prodigy's "electronic post office." This is actually a separate section of Prodigy; you jump into it, do your business, and then jump out.

CAUTION **You can't "toggle" back and forth between Prodigy Mail and** other parts of the Prodigy service; you must exit Prodigy Mail completely before you attempt any other online tasks.

While there are a lot of things you can do with Prodigy Mail, using it is as easy as pointing, clicking, reading, and typing.

Q&A *I'm done using Prodigy Mail. How do I get back into the regular Prodigy service?*

You first need to close Prodigy Mail by choosing File, Exit. Then you can jump to other parts of Prodigy like you normally do, using the buttons at the bottom of the Prodigy screen.

Receiving e-mail messages

When you Jump:**mail**, you're taken to Prodigy Mail's Mailbox (see fig. 6.1). The Mailbox is essentially an "inbox" for incoming e-mail messages. If you have e-mail messages, they're listed here. (If you have Prodigy's voice option turned on, you'll also receive a voice message any time you receive new mail.)

To read a message, all you have to do is highlight the message you want to read and then click the OPEN button. The text of the message is displayed in the bottom window.

TIP **You can also open a message by double-clicking on it.**

Displays additional info on message sender (and allows you to add sender to your address book)

Opens the message   *Prints the message*   *Retains the message (for 14 days)*   *Write new message*   *Forward this message to another user*   *Next message*   *Looks for new messages to retrieve*

Saves the message to disk   *Deletes the message*   *Toggles message text full-screen*   *Reply to this message*   *Previous message*   *Opens Address Book*

Fig. 6.1
Browsing through incoming e-mail in the Mailbox.

Attachments to messages

Status icons

Toggles attachment views in list window

Messages received

Message text

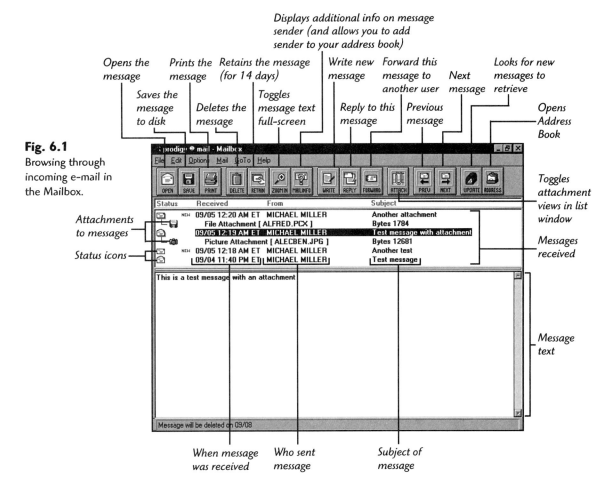

When message was received   *Who sent message*   *Subject of message*

When you look at the list of e-mail messages in your Mailbox, you see one or more icons next to each message. These icons tell you the status of your messages, and here's what they mean:

Icon	Message Status
▤	Unopened message
▤	Previously opened message
⚥	Retained message (held for 14 days before deleting)
🗑	Deleted message
💾	Message has a separate file attached
📷	Message includes an image file
🔊	Message includes a sound file
CC:	This is a carbon copy (cc) of a message sent to someone else
BLIND CC:	This is a blind carbon copy (bcc) of a message sent to someone else
⚑	Message has urgent priority
▤NEW	Message was marked "return receipt requested" (sender is automatically notified when you open the message)

Q&A   *I know someone has sent me new mail, but it doesn't show up in my Mailbox. Why is that?*

Mailbox sometimes needs to be "updated" to display recently received messages. Just click on the UPDATE button to refresh the list of messages received.

Replying to e-mail messages

Let's say you read a message, and you want to reply to the sender. Click the REPLY button to jump to the Reply window shown in figure 6.2. The sender's e-mail address is automatically inserted in the To: field, and the original message appears in the bottom window. All you have to do is type your new text in the top window, and then click the SEND button when you're done.

 TIP It's considered proper e-mail etiquette to "quote" the original message in a reply. Just highlight the text you want to quote, and then choose Edit, Copy. Now position your cursor where you want to insert the quote, and select Edit, Paste.

Fig. 6.2
Replying to an e-mail message.

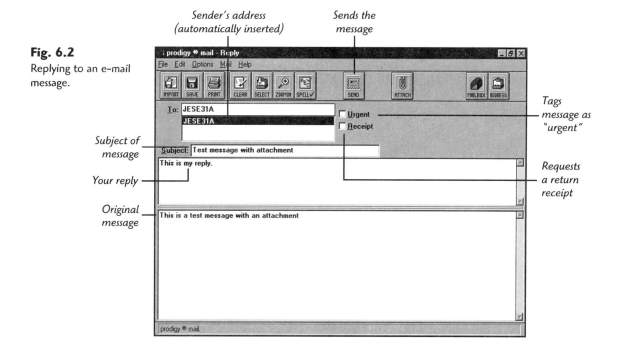

Sender's address (automatically inserted)

Sends the message

Tags message as "urgent"

Subject of message

Your reply

Original message

Requests a return receipt

Creating new e-mail messages

Creating a new message is a lot like replying to a message, except you don't have an original to reply to. Begin by clicking on the WRITE button, you'll see the Write window shown in figure 6.3.

Now you need to select a recipient. There are two ways to do this:

- Type the recipient's Prodigy address in the To: field

- Choose a recipient from your Address Book

An **Address Book** is simply a list (that you create) of people's e-mail addresses. If you find yourself writing frequently to someone, add her name to your address book so you don't have to type it in all the time.

To choose a name from the Address Book, click on the SELECT button. When you see the dialog box shown in figure 6.4, highlight a name from the left-hand list and click on the Send To button. This will add the recipient to the TO/CC list on the right-hand side of the dialog box. When you finish adding recipients, click the OK button; these names automatically are added to the To: field in your e-mail message.

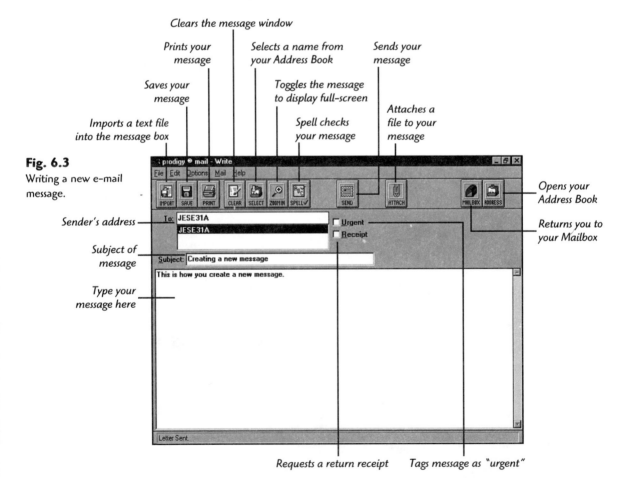

Fig. 6.3
Writing a new e-mail message.

Clears the message window

Prints your message

Selects a name from your Address Book

Sends your message

Saves your message

Toggles the message to display full-screen

Imports a text file into the message box

Spell checks your message

Attaches a file to your message

Opens your Address Book

Sender's address

Returns you to your Mailbox

Subject of message

Type your message here

Requests a return receipt

Tags message as "urgent"

CAUTION **When you add a recipient via the Address Book, only their nick-** name appears in the To: field; their Prodigy address is hidden (but still there!).

Now type a subject line in the Subject field, and then type the text of your message in the message window. When you're done, click on the SEND button and Prodigy automatically sends the message.

Fig. 6.4
Selecting a name from the Address Book.

Names in your Address Book

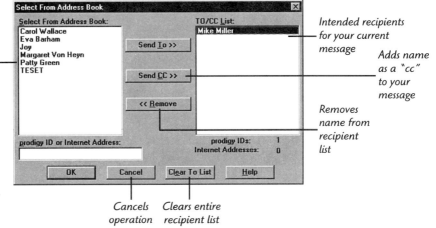

Intended recipients for your current message

Adds name as a "cc" to your message

Removes name from recipient list

Cancels operation *Clears entire recipient list*

Q&A ***Why didn't a recipient receive a message I sent?***
The most common cause for "undelivered mail" is an incorrect address. Make sure you have the right e-mail address for your recipient, and try sending another message.

TIP **Check your message for spelling errors before you send it by** clicking on the SPELL button.

TIP **If you want your recipient to treat your message with high** priority, click the Urgent box. If you want to be notified when your message is received, click the Receipt button.

Attaching files to messages

Sometimes you want to use e-mail to send a file to another user. You can send just about any type of file via e-mail, from word processing documents to graphics files. Prodigy will attach the file to your e-mail message, and your recipient will receive it along with your message.

CAUTION   **You can only send attachments to other Prodigy members. You** cannot send attached files to anyone with a non-Prodigy address—including users on the Internet.

Attaching a file is easy. When you're composing your message, just click on the ATTACH button. You're prompted to supply the name of the file you want to attach; click OK and Prodigy automatically attaches it to your current

Managing your Address Book

Prodigy's Address Book is where you store frequently used e-mail addresses. You can add addresses from your Address Book directly into new e-mail messages.

From time to time you probably want to update your Address Book to either add new names or remove old ones. To do this, click on the AD-DRESS button to display the contents of your Address Book.

To add a new entry, click the Add Entry button and, when the Address Entry dialog box appears,

enter the nickname and e-mail address for your new entry. (You also need to indicate whether this new entry is a Prodigy ID or an Internet address.)

To edit an existing entry, highlight that entry and click on the Change button. When the Address Entry dialog box appears, make your changes and then click OK.

To delete an entry, simply highlight that entry and click on the Delete button.

Updating your
Address Book.

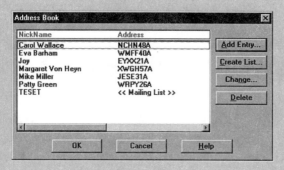

e-mail message. (You can attach multiple files to a single message, as well.) When you click the SEND button, the attachment is sent along with your e-mail message.

TIP **The ATTACH button turns yellow when a message has an attachment** (normally it's gray).

When you receive a message with an attachment, it appears subsidiary to the main message in your Mailbox. You'll probably want to save the attached file to your hard disk; to do this, double-click on the file. You'll be prompted by a Windows Save As box; select where you want to save it and click OK.

Q&A ***I sent an attached file to a friend but he didn't receive it. What went wrong?***

Your friend probably wasn't a Prodigy member. Unfortunately, you can't send attached files to anyone on the Internet, or anyone who's a member of another online service, like CompuServe or America Online. You can only send attachments to other Prodigy members.

Making your e-mail multimedia

Prodigy allows you to attach sound and picture files to your e-mail messages. This way you can send actual audio greetings to your friends and family— along with a picture of yourself (or anything else)!

You attach these files the same way you attach other types of files—click on the ATTACH button and select the specific file to attach. The big difference comes when you go to read the message; Prodigy lets you view or listen to these attachments as you read the message itself!

TIP **Prodigy automatically handles picture files in the .JPG format, and** sound files in the .WAV format.

You still need to save the sound or picture file (by double-clicking on it in your Mailbox). After the file is saved, however, Prodigy asks if you want to preview the downloaded picture (or hear the downloaded sound). Click the Yes button and you'll see the picture (or hear the sound) automatically.

Q&A *I clicked to hear the downloaded sound, but didn't hear anything. What gives?*

Chances are you either don't have a sound card on your system, or it isn't working properly. Check out your system before you try to play another sound file.

Q&A *When I view a picture file, it doesn't look right. What am I doing wrong?*

You're not doing anything wrong—it's your computer. You're probably trying to view a picture saved at a high resolution on a PC equipped for lower resolution video. The only thing you can do about this is replace your video card (and possibly monitor) with one of a higher resolution.

Sending multiple copies to a mailing list

There's one more neat thing you can do with Prodigy Mail. If you regularly send a single message to multiple recipients, you can create a **mailing list** of those recipients. The next time you need to broadly distribute a message, you only have to select one "name" for your recipient.

CAUTION   **You can only create up to two different mailing lists in your** Address Book—and each list can only have up to 20 different names.

To create a mailing list in Prodigy's Address Book, just follow these steps:

1 Click on the ADDRESS button to display the contents of your Address Book.

2 Click on the Create List button.

3 When the Create Mailing List dialog box appears, type a name for your list in the Mailing List Name field, and then Add names (from the left-hand list) to your mailing list (on the right-hand side).

4 When you're done, click OK.

When you want to send a message to the people on this list, just click on the SELECT button and choose the mailing list from your list of names. When you click the SEND button, it will automatically be sent to everyone on the mailing list.

TIP **See chapter 4 for information on Prodigy's E-Mail Connection** software that lets you handle e-mail tasks offline.

Looking up unknown addresses

In all these discussions about e-mail, I've assumed you know the address of the person you're mailing to. But what if you *don't* know the e-mail address of an intended recipient? Is there any way to look up e-mail addresses of other Prodigy members?

Jump:**memberlist** to display Prodigy's Member List service. This is a listing of Prodigy members and their e-mail addresses (i.e.—Prodigy IDs, and where they live [city and state]). The only catch is, Member List only lists those members who proactively add their name to the list! That means you might not be able to find the address of every single Prodigy member—only those that have added their names to the Member List.

If the person you want is listed, however, you can search by name (either first or last or both—or even parts of names) or by location (state first, then city). When the name you want pops up, you can then either write a message to this member, or add the name and address to your Address Book.

Suffice it to say, it behooves you to add your own name to the Member List if you want to be fully wired to the online community!

 Q&A *Why couldn't I find a member I was looking for in the Member List?*

Simple. That member did not add their name to the Member List. There is no way for you to look up Prodigy members who have not added their own names to the Member List.

 CAUTION **There is no way at present to look up the address of anyone on** the Internet.

E-mail etiquette

Let's get one thing straight from the start—no one gives out prizes for the best written e-mail messages. So, there's no need to spend a lot of time making sure you're using the most correct grammar; no one will care that much, as long as what you're trying to say is clear and understandable.

You also should be economical in your wording. Remember, you're paying for e-mail messages one character at a time, and if you're wordy, you just cost yourself money. You also cost your recipient time and money, because longer messages take longer to download and to read online—and the more time they spend online, the more money they also spend.

All that said, the nature of e-mail dictates a kind of formalized informality of language. Use short sentences, and abbreviate long (and common) words whenever possible. Try to "write for the screen;" this means trying to keep messages to a length that can be read in a single screen without having to use the scroll bars.

And, above all, remember that others are reading your messages. They can't hear the tone of your voice or look at your body language. That means they tend to take everything you write literally, no matter how you intend it. So, be aware of how others might interpret your words, and try to head off any misinterpretations ahead of time.

Using acronyms and abbreviations in e-mail messages

There are times when you can shorten your messages by abbreviating certain words and phrases. In fact, the world of online communications has built a core group of acronyms for common phrases that everyone understands. Feel free to use any of the following; you'll save space, everyone will know what you're talking about, and you'll look like a pro, IMHO.

- AKA (also known as)
- ASAP (as soon as possible)
- BTW (by the way)
- CIS (CompuServe Information Service)

- FWIW (for what it's worth)

- FYI (for your information)

- GD&R (grinning, ducking, and running)

- IMHO (in my humble opinion)

- IOW (in other words)

- LOL (laughing out loud)

- OTOH (on the other hand)

- PMJI (pardon me for jumping in)

- ROFL (rolling on the floor laughing)

- TLA (three letter acronym)

- TTFN (ta ta for now!)

Showing a little emotion in your correspondence

Because it's darned difficult (unless you're a very skilled writer) to put inflection or emotion in the written word, people will sometimes misunderstand the tone of what you're writing. The biggest misunderstanding comes when you're trying to be sarcastic and someone takes your words seriously.

The online community has developed, totally informally, a way around this problem. **Emoticons**, or "smileys," are little figures created by normal keyboard characters that, when looked at sideways, convey an emotion or tone.

As an example, the most common smiley is :-) . When you look at this emoticon sideways, you see a grinning face. Online users often put this smiley at the end of a sentence that shouldn't be taken too seriously. It communicates to the reader the light-hearted intention of the writer.

 TIP **If you can't see the smiling face, you're probably tilting your head** in the wrong direction! Try tilting your head to the left to view these smileys!

Naturally, after this whole emoticon thing got started, the online community got the bug big time. Here are just a few of the emoticons I've encountered over the past few years, some of them useful, some totally useless (but funny!):

Smiley	Means
:-)	Grinning
:-(	Frowning
:-o	Surprised
;-)	Winking
:-/	Skeptical
:-)'	Drooling
:-)8	Well-dressed (see the bow tie?)
8-)	Wearing glasses
*<|:-)	Santa Claus (see the hat?)
=:-)=	Punk rocker with a goatee

Sending e-mail across the Internet

The nice thing about Prodigy's e-mail system is that not only can you send and receive messages from other Prodigy members, but you can also send and receive messages from anyone on the Internet. The only thing you need to do is use the right Internet address for your recipient; Prodigy will automatically route it across the Internet to the intended recipient.

Internet e-mail addresses look quite a bit different from Prodigy's normal addresses. Unlike Prodigy's simple ID-based e-mail addresses, there are three parts to an Internet address: the *username*, an @ sign, and the *domain address*. (The domain address generally has two or more parts, each separated by a period.)

A typical Internet address looks something like this:

username@organization.domain

See chapter 11, "Sending Internet E-Mail," for detailed information on sending and receiving Internet e-mail.

Be careful when using smileys. Use too many and it looks a little too cute. Use obscure smileys and many people won't get your point. My advice is to stick to the basic ones, and use them sparingly—only in situations where you're likely to be misunderstood.

Getting quoted in a reply

There's just one more thing you need to know about e-mail etiquette—how to compose a proper reply to another message.

Because e-mail does not represent real-time communication—in fact, some people only read their messages once a week!—it's easy to read a reply to a message and completely forget what the original message was about. At times like this it helps to be reminded about what you're replying to.

This is why you will see, in many messages, a recap of the original message at the start of a reply. Usually, this "quote" from the original message is set off with angle brackets, like this:

```
>This is the original message, set off from
>the reply with angle brackets.
```

Your reply follows the quote from the original message, and is typed normally.

To quote from a Prodigy e-mail message, just highlight the text you want to quote, and then choose Edit, Copy. Now position your cursor in your reply where you want to insert the quote, and select Edit, Paste.

Sharing Special Interests on Bulletin Boards

● **In this chapter:**

- ● **What is a Prodigy bulletin board?**

- ● **How do bulletin boards work?**

- ● **Can I customize the way I use a BB?**

- ● **How to be a responsible BB user**

- ● **Save money with the Bulletin Board Manager**

*Share your special interests with other users on Prodigy's
bulletin boards* . . . . ▶

Prodigy contains a lot of useful information—weather, news, sports, and the like. But some of the most useful information you'll find comes from other Prodigy members. How do you get this information from other members? Well, the best way to find someone who has the information you need is through one of Prodigy's **bulletin boards**.

What is a bulletin board?

A Prodigy bulletin board is like a regular bulletin board, the kind you might find hanging on the wall of a special-interest club. (You remember these clubs from high school—Chess Club, Debate Club, Sewing Club, etc.) You walk into your clubhouse and find one of those cork bulletin boards. This bulletin board is there specifically for the use of club members. It's divided into sections, each for a different topic. And you can post notes—on paper, using a thumbtack—in any of the sections. Other club members read these public notes, and, if they want to, respond by posting a note of their own—or by dropping you a private letter.

 TIP **When I wrote this chapter, Prodigy had yet to change their** bulletin boards over to the New Prodigy look and feel. If Prodigy's bulletin boards look and work different than what you see in this chapter, go to the *Using Prodigy* Web page (**http://www.mcp.com/people/miller/ prodtop.htm**) for up-to-date instructions on the latest changes.

Prodigy has more than 75 different "clubs"—or, as Prodigy calls them, bulletin boards ("BBs" for short)—each devoted to a specific area of interest. Each of these bulletin boards is divided into multiple topic sections, for topics of interest within the main BB area. Users post electronic notes to each other—and all users can read all of these public notes. You can respond to a note with another public note, or respond privately via Prodigy e-mail.

 TIP **USENET newsgroups are kind of like bulletin boards, only they're** on the Internet. See chapter 12, "Reading USENET Newsgroups," for more information.

How to use Prodigy's bulletin boards

Using a Prodigy bulletin board is relatively easy. Prodigy has an entire section devoted to BBs (Jump:**bulletin board**). On the screen shown in figure 7.1, you can read all about BBs, search for BBs by topic (the Topics A-Z button), or choose from an alphabetical list of BBs (the Boards A-Z button).

Fig. 7.1
Prodigy's main BB screen—click on the Boards A-Z button to select from a list of BBs.

TIP **You can also go to a specific BB by using a JumpWord or by** clicking on the Boards A-Z button and choosing the board you want. Then you select the topic you want to read from the list presented. Within that topic, you select the subject you're interested in. Finally, you begin reading the individual notes within that topic.

When you're reading a note, you have several options available to you. You can:

- Read any replies to this note
- Read additional notes on this subject
- Change subjects and read notes on the new subject

- Change topics and select a new subject to read about

- Reply to this note with another public note

- Reply to this note with a private e-mail message

Of course, you can also create new notes on existing subjects—or even create a new subject within an existing topic.

 Plain English, please!

A **topic** is a subset of the main bulletin board topic area.

A **subject** is a specific area within the topic.

A **note** is a specific message within the chosen subject.

A **thread** is a series of notes and replies, all on the same subject.

Reading and replying to notes—a typical bulletin board session

A typical BB session goes something like this. You enter the BB and browse through the list of topics to find one that interests you. Let's say you enter the Books & Writing Board (Jump:**books bb**). When you click on the Choose a Topic button, you see list of more than a dozen topics. For this example, let's say that you're interested in nonfiction books, so you click on BOOKS/ NONFICTION, and then click on the Begin Reading Notes button.

 TIP   **When you first enter a BB, make sure you read the Guidelines &** Problem Note Alert, found at the lower left on most BB screens. These notes address issues specific to each BB.

You now see a list of subjects on this topic. This list is in constant change, because it's created interactively by your fellow Prodigy members. When a member has something interesting to write about, he creates a new subject and posts the first note on that topic. After a period of time (it varies from BB to BB), the old notes will be deleted, so you constantly see a stream of fresh notes and subjects. (Under the normal configuration, you only see those notes created since the last time you visited the BB.)

When you click on one of the subjects in this list, you're taken to the first note on that subject. If you want to read replies to this note, you click on the Read Replies button. If you want to read other notes on this subject (if there are any), click on the Next Note button. If you want to change subjects, either click on the Next Subject button or on the Subjects button—in the latter case, you see the list of all subjects again, and you can choose another subject from this list.

Q&A *I'm looking for a specific topic on a board, and I can't find it. Where did it go?*

Topics on Prodigy's BBs are very flexible. If a topic has "low traffic" (meaning few members are reading or writing on that topic), it will eventually be deleted and replaced with a potentially more popular topic. In fact, entire BBs can come and go as members' demands change. Click on the Boards A-Z button on the main BB menu to see the most current list of BBs, or on the Topics A-Z button to see the most current list of individual BB topics.

TIP **If you can't figure out what to do when you're reading a note, just** click on the Options button—it lists all the available options for this note (Select a new Subject, Return to Main Menu, Reply publicly to this Note, etc.).

If you want to reply to this note with another (public) note, click on the Reply button. You see the Reply screen—just type your reply and click OK when you're done to post the note to the BB.

If you prefer to reply privately, click on the E-Mail Reply button. You see a similar Reply screen, but when you click OK this time, the message is automatically sent as a private e-mail message.

Q&A *Why can't I find any replies to a note a posted in a previous session?*

This will happen if you haven't visited a BB in a while, and you're only reading notes posted in the past couple of days. To view older notes, change the date in the upper-right corner of the BB's main menu to the date you last visited this board.

Of course, it's also possible that nobody replied to your note.

TIP **From time to time some bulletin boards create temporary topic** areas for special guests. These guests are generally celebrities or experts in an area of interest to BB members. When these guest topics appear, you can leave a question (via a note) for the guest, who will then—if you're lucky— answer it in another public note.

Creating a new note

Creating a new note is as easy as replying to an existing one—you just do it on a different screen. To create a note, you have to go back to the BB's main screen. Make sure you have a topic selected, and then click on the Write a Public Note button.

CAUTION **In some BBs, the Write a Public Note button won't be visible until** you've selected a topic on this BB.

Now you see a list of available subjects, like that shown in figure 7.2. You can choose to add your note to one of the existing subjects, or to create a new subject by clicking on the Add a New Subject button.

Fig. 7.2
Choose a subject from this list, or choose to add a new subject with your note.

Whichever you choose, you're presented with the blank note window shown in figure 7.3. If you chose an existing subject, the SUBJECT box is already filled in. If you chose to add a new subject, you need to type the name of the new subject in the SUBJECT box.

Fig. 7.3
Writing a new note—fill in the blanks!

Fill in the recipient's ID here—or type ALL

Fill in the subject name here

Type your note here

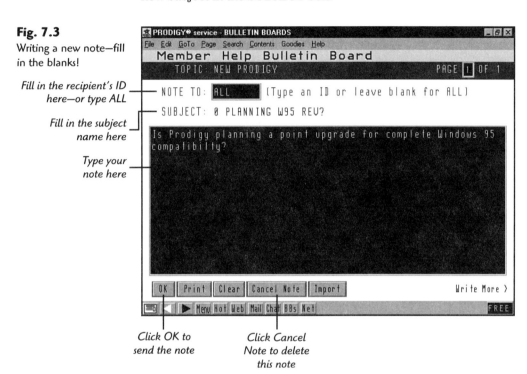

Click OK to send the note

Click Cancel Note to delete this note

You also need to select who you're addressing the NOTE TO. This will be an individual member's Prodigy ID—or you can address the note to ALL, to make sure everybody on the board reads it. (I recommend the latter for most new notes.)

Now you can start writing the note. If you need to use more than one page, click on the next page button to start the new page. When you're done, just click OK and the note will be posted automatically.

Entering a bulletin board

When you jump to a BB, you see its main screen. This screen displays highlights or notices for the BB, as well as buttons for all the main BB operations. From this screen you can choose the topic to read, set some board options, write a new note, and begin reading existing notes. In addition, many BBs have corresponding Chat sections, and you can access those sections from this main BB screen.

When you click on the Begin Reading Notes button, you're presented with a list of subjects for your chosen topic. Click on one of these subjects to begin reading the notes.

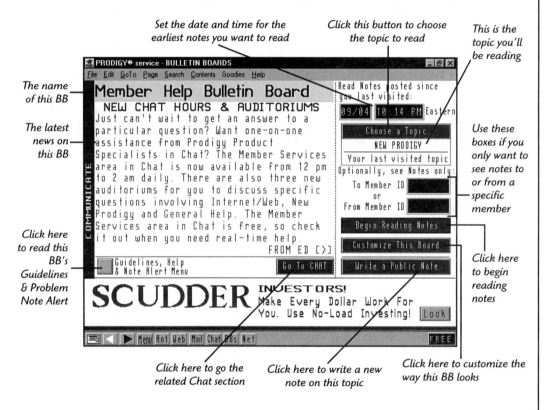

Set the date and time for the earliest notes you want to read

Click this button to choose the topic to read

This is the topic you'll be reading

The name of this BB

The latest news on this BB

Click here to read this BB's Guidelines & Problem Note Alert

Use these boxes if you only want to see notes to or from a specific member

Click here to begin reading notes

Click here to go the related Chat section

Click here to write a new note on this topic

Click here to customize the way this BB looks

If you click on the Begin Reading Notes button *before* you've chosen a topic, you'll be presented with the list of topics before the list of subjects is displayed.

Reading a bulletin board note

When you click on the Begin Reading Notes button, you're presented with a list of subjects for your selected topic. When you click on one of these subjects, this is what you see next—a note!

The note itself takes up the majority of the screen. But there's also other information— who sent the note, who they sent it to (and All is an appropriate posting), and when they sent it. From here you can read other notes, change subjects or topics, or reply to this note.

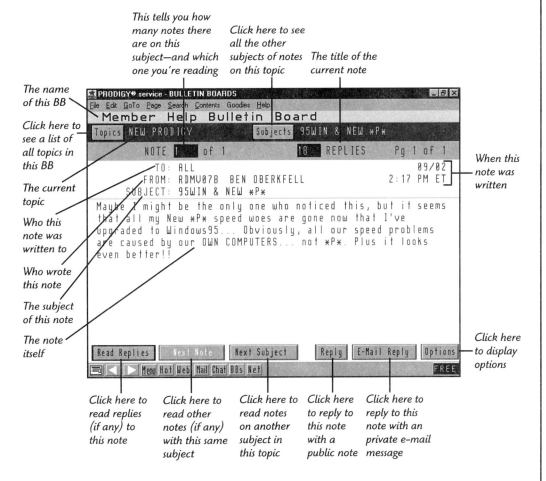

This tells you how many notes there are on this subject—and which one you're reading

Click here to see all the other subjects of notes on this topic

The title of the current note

The name of this BB

Click here to see a list of all topics in this BB

The current topic

Who this note was written to

Who wrote this note

The subject of this note

The note itself

When this note was written

Click here to display options

Click here to read replies (if any) to this note

Click here to read other notes (if any) with this same subject

Click here to read notes on another subject in this topic

Click here to reply to this note with a public note

Click here to reply to this note with an private e-mail message

When you're done reading notes, just click on the Menu button to return to the previous screen.

Quoting previous notes in your replies

When you reply to a note, it's good etiquette to insert a brief "quote" from the original note in your reply to refresh the reader's memory about what it is you're replying to. The easiest way to quote a note is to copy selected text from the original note into your reply.

Doing this, however, is a wee bit complicated. Follow these steps to insert quoted text in a reply:

1 While reading the original note, click on the Reply button to open a blank Reply Note window.

2 From the Reply Note window, click on the Review Original Note button.

3 When the original note is displayed, pull down the Edit menu and select Copy.

4 When the Copy window appears, use your cursor to highlight the text you want to copy, and then click on the Copy button.

5 Click on the Cancel button to close the Copy window, and then click on the top-left button to close the Review Original Note window.

6 In your Reply Note window, move your cursor to where you want to insert the quote, and pull down the Edit menu and select Paste text.

7 To let the next reader know that this text is a quote from another note, insert a right angle bracket (">") in front of each line of the quote.

When you're done, you have text that looks like this:

```
>This is a quote from
>another note.
```

By the way, because Prodigy's notes are by nature somewhat brief, don't copy the *entire* original note into your reply. Just the first few lines—or the most important few lines—will do.

TIP   **You can manage your BB notes offline—without incurring Prodigy** expenses—with a software program called Bulletin Board Note Manager. Read more about BBNM in chapter 6.

Customizing the way you use bulletin boards

You can customize several features of any particular bulletin board. When you click on the Customize This Board button on any BB's main screen, you see a screen that lets you change the following options (see fig. 7.4):

Fig. 7.4
Use this screen to customize the way you use BBs.

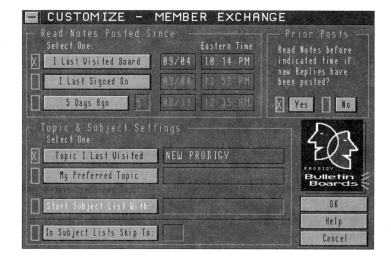

- Select the earliest notes you want to read. You can read notes posted since you Last Visited Board, since you Last Signed On to Prodigy, or notes posted in the past *X* number of days (you can select the number of days).

- Opt to read notes that were posted *prior to* the selected period if new replies to that note have also been posted.

- Instruct Prodigy to start up this BB with a specific topic—either the last topic visited or a preferred topic. (If you choose to start with a preferred topic, you can also select which subject within that topic you want to view first.)

- Set which subjects (by letter) are listed first. This is useful if you want to skip all subjects starting with non-alphabetic characters—just enter "A" in this box.

CAUTION When you change the options for a particular BB, this only affects this BB. It will *not* change the options for any other BB.

Q&A *I customized several boards, but now Prodigy won't let me customize any more—why?*

Prodigy will let you customize up to 17 boards. After that point, you have to use 'em as-is.

Can I restrict my children's access to certain bulletin boards?

There are some BBs that you might not want the younger members of your family to access. Fortunately, Prodigy lets you control access to any individual bulletin board. All you have to do is make sure that each member of your family has his or her own account number ("A," "B," "C," etc.), and then follow these instructions.

Go to the main BB screen and click on the Change Access button. You can then select the board(s) you want to block for specific members of your household. (Remember, the main account member has an ID ending with "A," and other members have IDs ending in other letters.)

That's all there is to it. When someone in your family goes to a BB that they don't have access to, Prodigy simply won't let them on it!

TIP If you can't figure out what to do when you're reading a note, just click on the Options button—it lists all the available options for this note (Select a new Subject, Return to Main Menu, Reply publicly to this Note, and so on).

Finding the right bulletin board for you

Now that you know how to use BBs, you're probably curious as to what kinds of boards are available on Prodigy. To find a specific bulletin board, just query Prodigy.

To do your searching on Prodigy, you can choose to search by either board *name* or board *topic*. To search by board name, Jump:**boards a-z**. You can either page through the available boards, or type the first few letters in the box at the top of the screen. Prodigy will then take you to the closest board in its list; click on the GO TO button to access that board.

To search by topic, Jump:**topics a-z**. You can search this list of topics until you find the one you're looking for; click on its button to access the related bulletin board.

Ten tips for better BB use

Bulletin boards are great ways to communicate with others who share your special interests. But to be a responsible BBer, you should follow the advice given in the following Tips for Better BB Use:

1 *Keep your notes short.* They're called *notes*, not *letters*, for a reason—they're supposed to be *short*. That said, for the benefit of those members reading your notes, try to limit yourself to one or, at most, two screens of text.

2 *Keep your notes on subject.* If you're responding to a note on a specific subject, don't all of a sudden change course and start writing about a totally different subject. If you want to change subjects, create a new subject with a new note.

3 *Look before you post.* Don't just jump into a BB and start posting notes willy-nilly. Check around to see what the culture of this board is, and what kind of notes are posted. That way you can better fit in with the BB's "regulars."

4 *Don't post stupid notes.* Reread tip #3. You don't want to post questions that have already been answered, or you run the risk of incurring the wrath of other board members—in the form of flames. (A **flame** is a nasty message from one member to another.) Remember, Prodigy has more than two million members—you don't want to embarrass yourself in front of that many people, do you?

5 *Don't flame other members.* As tempting as it may be at times, don't let other members get to you. No matter what another member might write, resist the urge to respond in a nasty fashion. You're better than that!

6 *Watch your language.* Very few boards have restricted access, which means young eyes could be reading every word you post. Remember, Prodigy is pretty much a family service, so don't post anything that you wouldn't want your kids reading. And if you don't watch your language, Prodigy *will*—because Prodigy automatically scans all notes for certain offensive words and phrases.

7 *Watch your children.* Conversely, if you let your children access Prodigy, you might want to monitor what BBs they read. Since you don't want your kids hooking up with unsavory "cyberstrangers," it's a good idea for your children to practice the same sort of stranger awareness online as they do out in the real world.

8 *Don't send duplicate messages.* Most members read multiple boards, and multiple topics and subjects within a given board. Posting the same note in several different areas (just to be sure everybody sees it!) will only result in you annoying your fellow members.

9 *Don't gratuitously self-promote.* That is, don't use Prodigy's bulletin boards for advertising purposes. That's what the classifieds (Jump:**classifieds**) are for.

10 *Keep private discussions private.* Remember, notes can be read by anyone and everyone. If you want to engage in a private discussion with another member, keep it private by using Prodigy e-mail.

8

Talking to Other Users with Prodigy Chat

● **In this chapter:**

- Learn how to prepare for a Chat session

- Choose a nickname and a Chat room

- Experience a typical Chat session

- Set up a private Chat room

- Participate in a special Chat event

- Discover uncensored Pseudo Chat

- Send Instant Messages to other members

More Prodigy members use Chat than any other Prodigy feature! . . . .

S mall towns are often buzzing with the latest gossip. People chat with fellow townsfolk everywhere they meet—at the beauty salon, at the supermarket, at the hardware store. Chat is just a way of life for most folks.

Well, that electronic small town we call Prodigy also has its forum for online "chats." Prodigy's Chat rooms let you get together with fellow members to talk about anything your heart desires—through your computer keyboards, of course.

What is this Chat thing, anyway?

Prodigy **Chat** is a service that lets you "talk" to other Prodigy members in real time. You type a message (normally in brief sentences), and it is instantly displayed to other members of your Chat room. Unlike other communications forums on Prodigy (such as bulletin boards or e-mail), Chat displays messages the moment they are sent.

Chat conversations take place in Chat rooms. A **Chat room** is kind of like one of those 900-number phone lines, where numerous people gather to talk about supposedly related topics. All the conversations in a Chat room are totally public, which means everyone can read what everyone else is "saying." Each room is typically limited to 25 members or less, though, to keep the conversations manageable.

There are three different kinds of Chat rooms:

- **Prodigy rooms** are public rooms created by Prodigy, each devised to cover a specific interest area.

- **Member rooms** are created by your fellow Prodigy members, and are generally fairly open as to topics; these rooms exist only while they're in use, and cease to exist when the last member leaves the room.

- **Auditoriums** are larger Chat rooms used for special events with featured guests.

Prodigy has literally hundreds of different Chat rooms. There are close to 50 different Chat areas, each covering a separate topic area. Within each area are numerous separate Chat rooms—created both by Prodigy and by Prodigy members.

If you feel like "talking" (through your keyboard), all you have to do is select a room, give yourself a nickname, and jump right in. You'll find that Prodigy Chatters are some of the friendliest people you'll ever meet—online or off!

Getting set up for Chat

Jump:**chat** to enter Prodigy's Chat area. As you can see in figure 8.1, the big Chat events are highlighted, and there are links that let you perform most normal Chat functions. Before you enter a Chat room, however, there are some preparations you need to make. Let's take a look at the "pre-Chat" niceties.

Fig. 8.1
Prodigy's main Chat screen.

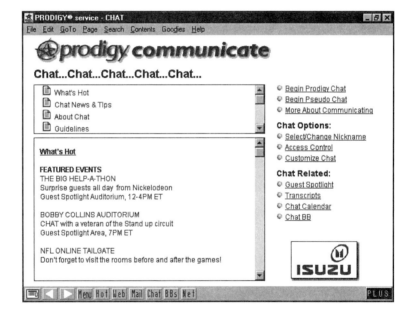

Choosing a nickname

While you can use your Prodigy ID during Chat sessions, most experienced Chatters give themselves a **nickname**. This nickname can be anything you want, and you don't have to use the same nickname two times in a row. Many Chatters create online "characters" to match their nicknames, and thus live out a fantasy life through their Chat sessions. Others just like to have their own "handle" (like in the old CB radio days) when they're in a Chat session.

To select a nickname, click on the Select/Change Nickname hyperlink. When the Chat Nickname dialog box appears, enter a new nickname (between 3 and 12 characters long) and click OK.

Setting other Chat options

Next, you can configure various aspects of Prodigy Chat to your personal liking. Click on the Customize Chat hyperlink to display the dialog box shown in figure 8.2.

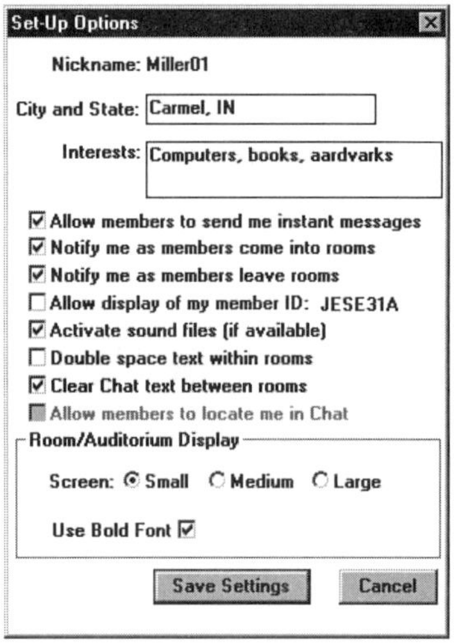

Fig. 8.2
Configure Chat options for your own personal tastes.

Once you make your choices, click on the Save Settings button. Now you're ready to choose a Chat room!

Choosing a Chat room

Your next step is to choose a Chat room—and then start chatting! Click on the Begin Prodigy Chat hyperlink to display the screen shown in figure 8.3.

This dialog box displays the available areas and rooms for your Chat session. Follow these steps to select a room:

1 Select the room type—Prodigy, Member, or Auditorium (if this is your first Chat session, stick with the official Prodigy rooms).

2 Select an area of interest.

3 Select a specific room within the area of interest.

4 Click the Go to Room button to enter the selected room.

It's as simple as that. There are other options on this screen, of course, and I'll discuss them later in this chapter. For now, though, let's see what happens when you actually enter a Chat room.

TIP **Click on the Guidelines button to read Prodigy's Chat guidelines.**

Types of rooms displayed: Prodigy, Member, or Auditorium

Available areas

Click here to go to the selected room

Fig. 8.3
Choose your Chat room from this screen.

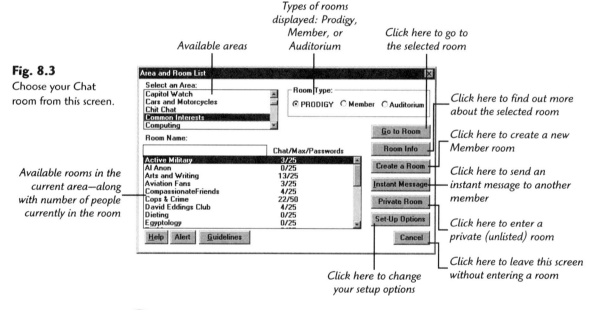

Click here to find out more about the selected room

Click here to create a new Member room

Available rooms in the current area—along with number of people currently in the room

Click here to send an instant message to another member

Click here to enter a private (unlisted) room

Click here to leave this screen without entering a room

Click here to change your setup options

Q&A *Can I limit access to Chat for various family members?*

Yes. From the main Chat screen, click on the Access Control button. When the Chat Enrollment screen appears, click on the Select Names button. From here, you can grant access to particular family members. Those members who *aren't* enrolled can't access Chat.

Examining the Chat window

When you enter a Chat room, you see a Chat window similar to that shown below. Let's take a look at the various parts of this window.

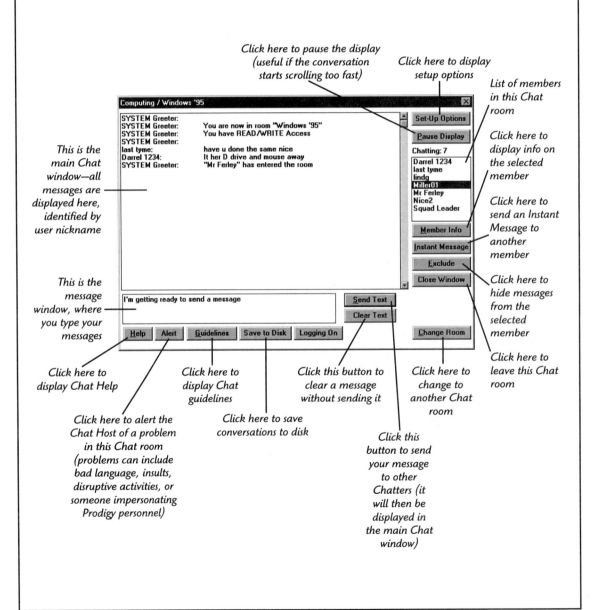

Click here to pause the display (useful if the conversation starts scrolling too fast)

Click here to display setup options

List of members in this Chat room

This is the main Chat window—all messages are displayed here, identified by user nickname

Click here to display info on the selected member

Click here to send an Instant Message to another member

This is the message window, where you type your messages

Click here to hide messages from the selected member

Click here to leave this Chat room

Click here to display Chat Help

Click here to display Chat guidelines

Click this button to clear a message without sending it

Click here to change to another Chat room

Click here to alert the Chat Host of a problem in this Chat room (problems can include bad language, insults, disruptive activities, or someone impersonating Prodigy personnel)

Click here to save conversations to disk

Click this button to send your message to other Chatters (it will then be displayed in the main Chat window)

A typical Chat session

Okay, so what's a typical chat session like? Well, when you first enter a room you're greeted by a message from the System Greeter. (This is automated, by the way!) Typically, one or more Chatters in the room will also greet you. Then all hell breaks loose!

As you can see from the following transcript, the typical Chat room has multiple conversations taking place, all simultaneously. (And you're entering in the middle of many of them!) It's difficult to follow all the threads, let alone participate in one. But, believe it or not, most Chatters participate in several conversations at the same time.

 **Plain English, please!**

A **thread** is a series of related messages. A thread starts with a single message, and all replies to that message (and replies to the replies) comprise the thread.

Here's a sample of what you can expect to find in a typical Chat room:

```
SYSTEM Greeter:    You are now in room "Internet Help"
SYSTEM Greeter:    You have READ/WRITE Access
Eugeneeeeeee:      And not to mention not very nice
Brandonv:          Sorry someone here picked up the phone
GoG8rs:            I have to go see about my account tomorrow
SYSTEM Greeter:    "Frannarf" has left the room
Wolfgame:          personal:  http://pages.prodigy.com/Hell/
                   wolfgame/
SYSTEM Greeter:    "Killer2" has entered the room
SYSTEM Greeter:    "CHREISTEINE" has left the room
GoG8rs:            Here they have the right to "SPY"
Killer2:           it says it just isan't there...
Wolfgame:          NetHelp: http://pages.prodigy.com/Confu-
                   sion/nethelp
Brandonv:          You do nethelp??
GoG8rs:            I want to play Descent :(((((((((
Brandonv:          and why in Confusion??
SYSTEM Greeter:    "esor725" has entered the room
SYSTEM Greeter:    "ladebak" has entered the room
SYSTEM Greeter:    "LOZZ" has entered the room
SYSTEM Greeter:    "pearlst" has left the room
ladebak:           Anyone wanna check out my newly-finished
                   Web page?
SYSTEM Greeter:    "Dr  Forbin" has left the room
Miller01:          What does everyone think of the Prodigy
                   personal web pages?
```

```
Eugeneeeeeee:       sux
ladebak:            I love them.
Killer2:            has anyone been on my site today?
Brandonv:           what is url ladebak
Killer2:            they rock!!! I have 5 pages!!!
Brandonv:           Can't live without them
SYSTEM Greeter:     "Baby Talk" has entered the room
Eugeneeeeeee:       no graphics
Eugeneeeeeee:       200k limit
Eugeneeeeeee:       no cgi
ladebak:            http://pages.prodigy.com/MA/ladebak
```

As you can see, people are constantly coming and going, sentence fragments are bouncing back and forth, and nobody complains about bad spelling. That's because you have to read, think, and type all at the same time—as well as try to follow multiple conversations—which is mighty difficult, to say the least.

That said, spending time in a Chat room is somewhat exhilarating. It's a great way to get the juices flowing, and you meet some mighty interesting people there. It's no wonder why Chat is the most popular area on the Prodigy service.

TIP **Many Chatters use Instant Messages to initiate private conversa-** tions away from the hubbub of a noisy Chat room. See the section on Instant Messages later in this chapter for more information.

Q&A *How do I keep from getting annoying messages from a particular Chat room guest?*

Just highlight that member's name in the Chat list, and then click on the Exclude button.

Setting up your own private Chat room

Okay, you've participated in your share of public Chat rooms. Why not create your own *private* Chat room, just for you and select online friends?

It's really quite easy to do just that. Just follow these steps:

1 From the main Chat screen click on the Begin Prodigy Chat hyperlink.

2 When the Area and Room list is displayed, click on the Create a Room button.

3 When the Create a Member Room dialog box appears, select a Chat area for your room (see fig. 8.4).

4 Give your room a name.

5 If you want all members to see your room listed, check the Listed option; if you want to keep it private, check the Private option.

6 Determine the maximum capacity of your room (15 members is the default).

7 Check the Display Participant Nicknames option to show nicknames in the room list.

8 If you want to restrict room entry or text submissions, enter passwords in the appropriate fields.

9 Click OK to create the room.

Fig. 8.4
Creating your own
private Chat room.

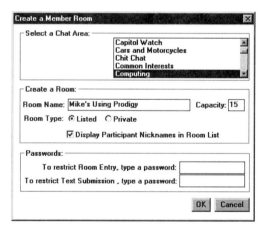

The next thing you know, a new Chat window appears for your newly created room. Now all you have to do is wait for someone else to show up!

TIP **You can use a private Chat room to conduct cross-country online conferences** with friends or business associates.

All about special events

In addition to the normal Chat rooms, Prodigy also holds a variety of **Chat events**. These sessions are generally with celebrities of one sort or another, or focus on major issues of interest to large groups of people. And the groups here can get *very* large; some Chat auditoriums permit hundreds of people to participate at the same time!

To keep things from getting too chaotic, however, all special events have a moderator. The moderator keeps things under control—and controls the flow of questions to celebrity guests.

Checking the Chat calendar

To find out what Chat events are scheduled in the coming month, click on the Chat Calendar hyperlink from the main Chat screen. You'll see a calendar with buttons for each week; click on one of the weekly buttons to display the Chat schedule for that week.

One recent week had over 40 special events scheduled on topics that included trivia games, wrestling, astrology, pets, the Internet, and collecting. Guests in that same week included *Hard Copy's* Terry Murphy, TV Producer Stephan J. Cannell, ESPN Anchor Craig Kilborn, Canadian Reform Leader Preston Manning, and actor Ray Walston. Prodigy also participates in occasional cross-service special events, like a recent event with rock megastar Michael Jackson that was "simulcast" on Prodigy, CompuServe, America Online, and the Internet.

Participating in a special Chat event

A special Chat event is much like a normal Chat session, only larger. The main difference is that the flow is pretty much one way. That is, members submit questions to the Moderator, who prioritizes them and passes them on to the guest. The guest then sends his responses, for all to read.

For popular guests, show up on time and get your question(s) in early. There are often more questions posed than can be answered in the allotted time. (For that reason, many moderators only allow single questions in a crowded Chat event.)

Adult Chat—and more—with Pseudo

Regular Prodigy Chat can get a little risqué, but it's periodically monitored to keep things within guidelines. If you want totally uncensored Chat, however, you need to enter a special area called **Pseudo**—where anything goes!

Unlike the rest of Prodigy (save for the Internet bits), Pseudo is totally uncensored. It contains explicit adult content, and is not recommended for members under the age of 18. In fact, if you think you might be offended by totally frank discussions about adult subjects, don't even think about entering Pseudo.

When you Jump:**pseudo** (or click on the Begin Pseudo Chat hyperlink) you're presented with an "enrollment" screen. You have to manually enroll any family members who you want to have access to Pseudo. Then you go through a variety of "nuisance" screens until you enter Pseudo proper.

The main Pseudo screen lets you access Pseudo's Chat rooms, bulletin board, and the Pseudo Forum. The Forum contains areas that cover topics like music (Pseudo Sounds), gay interests (Male Room), and tattoos and body piercing (Flesh Art).

Pseudo's main screen.

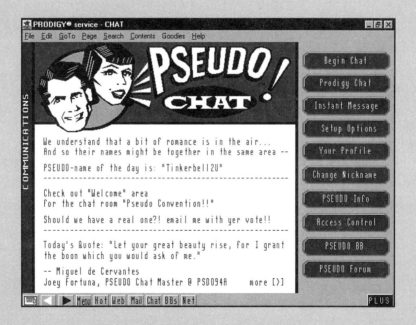

The interesting thing is, Pseudo Chat often has as much—if not *more*—traffic as does regular Prodigy Chat! And, while many of the conversations are indeed quite randy, a lot of members gather here primarily because none of the conversations are monitored (like they are on regular Prodigy Chat). So you'll find a lot of lively—and mature— discussions on a variety of topics, not just sex!

Instant Chat with Prodigy's Instant Messages

In addition to Chat rooms, Prodigy has another way to send real-time messages from one member to another. This feature is called **Instant Messages**, and you can access it from within Chat or anyplace else on the Prodigy service.

Prodigy's Instant Messages feature allows you to send a private message to any other members who happen to be online with Prodigy at this point in time. All you need to know is the nickname of the member you want to contact.

The most common place to send an Instant Message is during a Chat session. Typically, you find someone you want to have a private discussion with—away from the "noise" of the Chat room—so you send an Instant Message. You do this by clicking on the Instant Message button in the Chat window. When you see the Instant Message Center dialog box, type the recipient's nickname in the top left box, and then type your message in the top right box. Click on the Send Text button to send your message. Replies to this message (and any other messages—you can send multiple Instant Messages to multiple members) appear in the lower-right box.

Sending an
Instant Message

Instant Message Center

Send To: (nickname)

Darrel 1234

This is an instant message.

Send Text
Clear Text

Help | Delete | Save | Exclude | Member Info | Set-Up Options | Cancel

Exclude
Close Window

Send Text
Clear Text

Help | Alert | Guidelines | Save to Disk | Logging On | Change Room

To send an Instant Message from anyplace else on Prodigy, select GoTo, Instant Message from Prodigy's pull-down menu. You'll see the same Instant Message Center dialog box; fill in the boxes and send your message.

If you couldn't make it live, read the transcript

Prodigy makes transcripts of most major Chat events, and posts these transcripts online for your reading pleasure. Click on the Chat Transcripts button on the main Chat screen to see a list of recent transcripts.

A moderated special Chat event is much less chaotic than a normal Chat room because the moderator helps to keep everything organized. By the way, most celebrities seem to get a big kick out of meeting their public online like this—which is why the number of special Chat events keeps increasing!

TIP   **As if you didn't get enough conversation in the Chat rooms,** Prodigy also has a Chat bulletin board! Topics on this BB include technical questions, upcoming chat events, new member questions, and general chatter.

Advertising Your Personal Wares

● **In this chapter:**

● **How do I respond to one of Prodigy's classified ads?**

● **How do I place my own classified ads on Prodigy?**

● **How do I use Prodigy to help me find a new job?**

● **Finding a date with an online personal ad**

Online classified ads are a good way to find other members interested in buying what you have to sell . . . . >

If Prodigy is like a small town, then it should have a small-town newspaper, complete with classified ads. Well, Prodigy does have classified ads, in dozens of different categories. Browsing through Prodigy's classified ads is just like browsing through the classifieds section of a newspaper—except that you can respond immediately, online.

Using Prodigy to advertise online

Jump:**classifieds** to go to Prodigy's classified advertising section. As you can see in figure 9.1, Prodigy's Online Classifieds let you both read and place ads, as well as place and respond to online personal ads.

Fig. 9.1
The main Online
Classifieds screen.

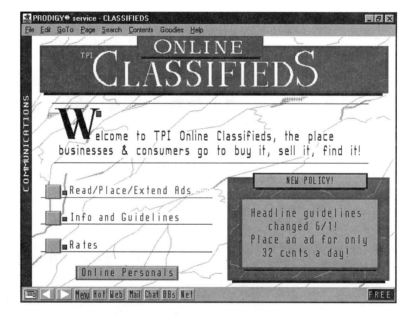

 TIP   **Prodigy's classifieds are run by a third party, Tele-Publishing (TPI)** of Boston. TPI's guidelines for propriety for the ad section mirror those of Prodigy.

Each classified ad costs $10 for the first 30 days, and an additional $10 for each additional 30 days, up to 90 days maximum. That's just for the first page, of course; additional pages cost $1 each, up to a six-page maximum.

Reading (and responding to) classified ads

Let's start by looking at some existing classified ads. Begin by going to the main Online Classifieds screen (Jump:**classifieds**) and clicking on the Read/Place/Extend Ads button. The next screen gives you the option of browsing ads, placing ads, or extending/removing ads; click on BROWSE ADS to proceed.

At the next screen, you need to click on the category of ads you want to browse. And, because it doesn't cost you anything (other than normal Prodigy connect-time charges) to browse the classifieds, feel free to browse to your heart's content.

Now you see a list of all the ads in the category you selected. You can either page through the ads, or search for ads that start with a certain set of letters. Either way, when you find an ad you want to read, just click on it.

Now you're reading an ad like the one in figure 9.2. From here you can go to the next ad (or the previous ad), print a copy of the ad, back up to the list of ads (the AD NAME LIST), or even back up all the way to the category list.

Fig. 9.2
Reading a classified ad.

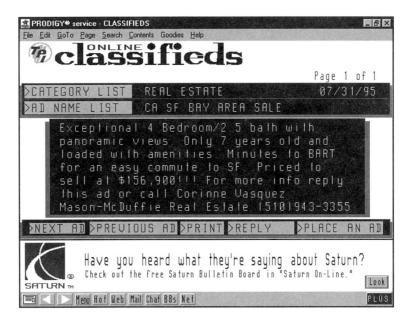

Of course, at some point in time you'll probably find an ad you actually want to respond to. Some ads make you respond via voice phone or postal mail; others, however, come with their own REPLY button. When you click on a REPLY button, you see a clean window in which you can write your reply. Just press the SEND button when you're done, and your reply (in e-mail form) will go out to the person or firm who placed the ad.

 TIP **Don't forget to include your e-mail address, postal address, or** voice phone in your reply!

Placing online classified ads

To place an ad, click on the Read/Place/Extend Ads button on the main Online Classifieds screen. The next screen gives you the option of browsing ads, placing ads, or extending/removing ads; click on PLACE ADS to proceed.

 TIP **You might want to review other ads before you place yours to get** a feel for how other people do it.

Next you'll see a list of available ad categories. When you click on the appropriate category, you'll see a terms/pricing grid, like that shown in figure 9.3. Click on the number of days you want to run the ad (30, 60, or 90) to proceed.

You'll now be asked if you want to receive replies to your ad via Prodigy e-mail. Answer NO if you don't want to get e-mail replies—but if you answer NO, make sure you include a phone number or mailing address in the body of your ad, or you won't get any replies! (I'd answer YES if I were you—it speeds up responses if readers can just click a button and send e-mail while they're highly interested in your ad.)

Now it's time to start writing the ad. Put a headline in the AD NAME field, and then enter your body text in the large area below. When you're done writing, click on SUBMIT AD to officially place the ad.

Fig. 9.3
The pricing grid for
Prodigy's classified ads.

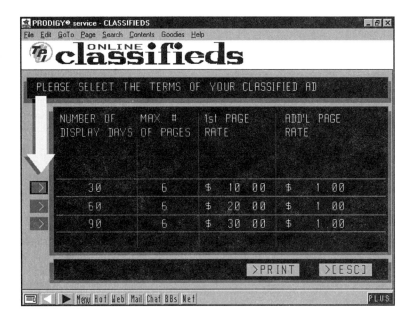

 TIP Remember that the $10 ad cost is just for a single screen; if your ad is long enough to go to multiple screens, you'll pay an additional $1 for each additional screen.

Finding jobs (and employees) online

Just as the classifieds in your local newspaper have a section for Help Wanted, so does Prodigy's Online Classifieds. To read Help Wanted ads, all you have to do is click on the Help Wanted category, and then browse—and reply to ads—exactly the same way you do with other ads in other categories.

There are some slight differences when it comes to *placing* a Help Wanted ad, however. In addition to the normal ad placement procedure, you're asked to provide the state the job is in, as well as what Prodigy calls a "job description." I tend to view the job description as a one- or two-word category for the job—like "Marketing" or "Outbound Sales."

After you get done with this, however, it's pretty much the same procedure to write and place the ad as I talked about earlier.

TIP   **Some people have success finding jobs from these online** classifieds; others don't. You might find that simply participating in appropriate bulletin boards, USENET newsgroups, and Chat rooms might bring more success. In any case, I wouldn't recommend limiting your job hunting to Prodigy—you cover more bets by using Prodigy to *supplement* your traditional job hunting activities.

Looking for love in all the online places: Prodigy's Online Personals

One swinging part of the new online classifieds is the Online Personals section. You access this section by clicking on the Online Personals button on the main Online Classifieds page. With Prodigy's Online Personals, not only can you place traditional personal ads, but also add voice greetings to your message.

Begin by clicking on the Place Extend Browse Ads button. Then click on PLACE ADS when the next screen appears, and choose one of the following categories:

- Men seeking women

- Women seeking men

- Men seeking men

- Women seeking women

With personal ads, you get a 30-day limit on your ad. The cost is $2 for the first 2 pages, and $1 for each additional page.

When you okay the term for your ad, you're prompted for your area code and "ad description." For these purposes, think of "ad description" as a one- or two-word headline that will grab the attention of potential beaus. Click CONTINUE and you're presented with the ad entry screen, which looks just like the classified ad entry screen. Enter the text of your ad, and then click on SUBMIT AD.

How to write an effective online ad

Whether you're advertising a household item, a piece of computer equipment, or yourself (for either job or personal purposes), there are some simple guidelines you can follow to create a more effective classified advertisement. Follow these tips to get the results you want—fast!

- *Keep the headline short and punchy.* Make the headline action-oriented and to-the-point. I use the phrase "whack 'em up side the head" to indicate the kind of impact a headline should have.

- *Use an "A" word.* Prodigy's classified ads are listed alphabetically—so if you want placement at the head of the pack, start your headline with one of the first letters of the alphabet. (Some advertisers actually start their headlines with characters—like the apostrophe—or numbers, since Prodigy alphabetizes characters and numbers ahead of letters!)

- *Keep it short.* You can use multiple screens if you want to, but I don't recommend it. Many buyers won't go to the effort of turning the page, so keep it all on one screen!

- *Cut to the chase.* You don't have much space, so get to the point quickly in your body copy. Many buyers won't read more than the first sentence, so make sure it grabs them as fast as possible.

- *List all relevant features—and only the relevant ones!* Potential buyers want to know certain essential things about what you're selling—age, size, etc.—so make sure you include them in all your ads. But make sure you don't list too many things; prioritize the "feature set" and include only the top-priority items.

- *Abbreviate when you can.* Again, you don't have much space to work with, so use abbreviations when appropriate (i.e, FWD for "front wheel drive"). Make sure you use common abbreviations, however; if potential buyers can't figure out what you're talking about, you're in trouble!

- *Sell benefits, not features.* Once you get beyond the basic "specs," make sure you talk about what the item for sale can do for the potential buyer, not just about what it is. For example, saying that a car has front wheel drive points out a feature; if you say "FWD for great snow handling" you've turned that feature into a benefit.

- *Include a price.* Look, they're gonna ask you the price, so get that out of the way first. At the very least, include a price *range*, or indicate that the price is negotiable—but include some sort of price, whatever you do.

- *Be honest.* Whether you're talking about the features of a snowblower or your own personal characteristics, be honest. Sooner or later the potential buyer will see the merchandise at hand and find out the truth, so don't start by misrepresenting what you're trying to sell.

TIP **Online Personals also lets you record a voice mail greeting, which** can then be accessed via a 900-number. If you choose to use the voice mail option, the cost of your Prodigy ad is free! TPI will e-mail you instructions for recording your voice ad after you place your regular ad.

Browsing through personal ads is equally simple. Just click on BROWSE ADS, select your category, and then scroll through the listed ads until you find ads in your area code. Click on the ad you want to read, and then use the REPLY button if you want to reply.

It's that simple, although I'm not sure these personal ads are all they're cracked up to be. First of all, the volume of ads is relatively small for any particular area code. Second, there's a better place to meet people on Prodigy, and that's the Chat section (discussed in chapter 8). You might want to quickly browse through these personal ads and then head over to the Chat section ASAP!

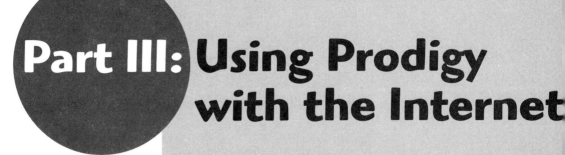

Part III: Using Prodigy with the Internet

10

A Little Bit about the Internet

● **In this chapter:**

- **What is the Internet?**

- **What can you do on the Internet?**

- **Exploring the Internet with Prodigy**

The Internet opens up online worlds beyond even what Prodigy itself has to offer . . . . ▶

Every time you pick up a newspaper or magazine or turn on your TV, you're bombarded with news stories about the latest thing in the world of personal computing—this thing called the **Internet**. Most of the stories are vague enough that you really can't tell what this Internet thing really is, but it sounds neat, and it sounds like it's something you want to get involved with. The problem is, you don't even know where to start. How do you find out more about the Internet, then, and—more important—how do you get connected to it?

The answers to your questions are here in this chapter. Read on and I'll tell you all about the Net (which is what we *Internauts* call it) and how you can use Prodigy to connect to it.

What the Internet is—and what it *isn't*

Let's start with what the Internet *isn't*. It isn't a thing. You can't touch it, or buy it in a box. It isn't even a *collection* of things.

The Internet is made up of hundreds of thousands of computers, each connected to all the other computers via the "wiring" of the Internet. The Internet itself really doesn't do any more than connect all these computers— all the things you can do are found on the computers that are connected to the Net.

Think of the Internet as kind of like a public utility—like the electric company. When you hook electricity up to your house, what happens? Does your house start to glow, does it spin, does it sprout a second story? No, when you hook electricity up to your house, *nothing happens at all*.

Nothing, that is, until you plug something into a wall socket. You can plug lots of things into your sockets—televisions sets, radios, vacuum cleaners, blenders, any other appliance you can think of. And after you plug in an appliance, you can start doing things—when you plug in your blender, you can make milk shakes or daiquiris or bread dough. Now, the electricity itself doesn't make your milk shake, but because you're hooked up to the electricity you have the ability to make milk shakes, if you want.

The Internet is just like the electric company. When you hook your computer up to the Internet, *nothing happens*. Your computer doesn't start to glow or spin or grow an extra disk drive. Nothing happens until you plug in an Internet "appliance." You can plug in an e-mail appliance to send messages, or an FTP appliance to download files, or a World Wide Web appliance to browse hypertext documents. All this is possible because you're connected to the Net, but the Net itself doesn't really do any of this.

How the Internet works

The Internet is really pretty simple. You start with a computer—*your* computer. It's on your desk, all by itself, truly a *personal* computer.

Next, you hook your computer up to a *network* of other computers. If you're at work, you may hook into the company local area network (LAN). If you're at home, you use your PC's modem to dial into and connect with Prodigy—which is itself a network comprised of you and a few million other Prodigy users.

But wait—you're not connected to the Internet yet—you're just connected to Prodigy, which is a kind of wide area network (WAN), sitting by itself and not connected to anything else. The final step, you see, is for the Prodigy network to tap into the big backbone that is the Internet—thus letting you (who are connected to the Prodigy network via your modem and local phone lines) piggyback onto the Internet.

Once you're connected to the Internet, you can connect to any one of the hundreds of thousands of other networks that are connected to the Net. Each one of these networks contains thousands of users (very few networks have millions of users, like Prodigy does!), giving you access to somewhere over *30 million* other computer users all around the world.

That's right, once you're connected to the Net, you can communicate with 30 million of your closest friends! You can send them e-mail, or share some cool files, or even read online documents they "publish" on something called the World Wide Web. In short, you can do just about anything you want to do—providing their computer networks allow it!

But don't get confused. The Internet isn't a commercial service, like Prodigy. It's only the connections between all those individual, *private* computers.

That means there's no one really running the Internet, no help desk, no technical support, no documentation. So what you find on the Net is uncensored, untested, and unwarranteed. Sometimes it doesn't even work all that well! So if you're comfortable with the sanitized, monitored world of Prodigy, think twice before you venture into the wild, woolly West of the Internet—you just never know what you'll find there!

Things you can do on the Internet

The Internet lets you do anything the computers on the Net will let you do. And most of the big computers on the Net—called Internet **host sites**—let you do a lot. Many of these host sites contain thousands of files for downloading, let you connect to online special interest groups (called **newsgroups**), send e-mail, and display hypertext World Wide Web documents. All you have to do is use the Internet to connect to these sites, and you're on your way to becoming an honest-to-goodness Internaut!

Communicate with others via e-mail and newsgroups

The first thing you can do on the Net is communicate with other Internauts. In fact, this is the one common use of the Net—talking to other Net users!

There are two main ways to communicate with other users on the Net. The first is one you're probably already familiar with—**electronic mail**. You can use the Internet to send e-mail to any of the 30 million other users on the Net, as well as to users of other online services, such as America Online or CompuServe. Chapter 11, "Sending Internet E-Mail," tells you how it works.

The second way to communicate with other Internauts is through something called a **USENET newsgroup**. A newsgroup is kind of like a Prodigy bulletin board, in that it's a virtual "place" for you to exchange messages with others who share your special interests. Chapter 12, "Reading USENET Newsgroups," tells you how it works.

Find and download files with FTP and Gopher

Another popular use of the Net is to find and download computer files. This sounds a little boring, but since any information you might be looking for is going to be stored in a file somewhere on the Net, it's important to learn how to do this. There are various ways to find files on the Net; you use whatever method is applicable to your task at hand.

Two of the most popular methods of downloading files from the Net are called **FTP** and **Gopher**. FTP stands for **file transfer protocol**, and is the fastest way to download files—*if you know exactly where they are.* If you don't know where to look for your files, you use the method called Gopher. Both of these methods are discussed in chapter 15, "Downloading Files with FTP and Gopher."

Browse hypertext documents with the World Wide Web

The neatest part of the Internet is kind of a subset of the Net called the **World Wide Web**. The Web (as we Internauts call it) consists of hundreds of thousands of online "documents" called **Web pages**. Each Web page sort of looks like a page from a book, complete with different types of text and graphics. The big difference is, the text on a Web page can be **hyperlinked** to other documents! That means that when you're reading one Web page, you're just a mouse click away from other related—and linked—information on another totally different Web page.

You browse these Web pages with something called a **Web browser**. You'll have to read chapter 13, "Cruising the World Wide Web," to learn more about the Web itself.

 TIP   **Prodigy lets you create your own personal Web pages. See chapter 14, "Creating Your Own Web Pages," for more details.**

Connecting to the Internet with Prodigy

You'll be pleased to know that you have fairly complete access to the Internet as part of your Prodigy membership. You access Prodigy's Internet services (Jump:**internet**) by clicking on the Communications button on Prodigy's Highlights screen, and then clicking on the Internet Forum button. From here you can click on buttons that take you to the World Wide Web browser, to USENET newsgroups, to Internet E-mail, or to FTP/Gopher services. You can also go to Prodigy's Internet Bulletin Board (Jump:**internet bb**) to learn more about the Net from your fellow Prodigy users.

The great thing about using Prodigy to access the Net is that you don't need to do anything new or extra. You don't have to establish a new account, or install new software, or learn to use a new program. No, all you have to do is Jump:**internet** and you have full access to Prodigy's Internet connection.

The rest of this book deals with using Prodigy to connect to the Internet—and doing all sorts of stuff once you get there.

Answers to the most common questions about the Internet

In the past year I've talked to a lot of Internet users (and potential users). I hear a lot of common questions, and thought I'd share them—and the answers—with you.

If I'm hooked up to Prodigy, am I also hooked up to the Internet?

If you have a Prodigy membership, you can access Prodigy's connection to the Internet (Jump:**internet**). Once you access one of Prodigy's Internet services (such as FTP or the World Wide Web browser) you are connected—via Prodigy—to the Net. But none of the other Prodigy services you use are part of the Internet—and no one from the Internet can access them without a proper Prodigy membership.

Can I use Prodigy to send e-mail to a friend of mine who has an Internet account?

Yes, you can. To send your friends e-mail, you need to know their Internet e-mail address, which probably looks something like **username@domain.name**.

What if I don't know my friend's Internet e-mail address?

Then you're out of luck. There's no general directory of Internet e-mail addresses—so you'll have to call up your friend and ask him for his address.

Why did I get so many nasty messages from other users after I posted a newsgroup article?

Nasty responses to a newsgroup posting are called **flames**. You get flamed when you do something that other users regard as in poor form, or just plain stupid. For example, if you're the two-hundredth guy to ask a common-sense question (like "what's this newsgroup all about?"), you won't make any friends—and will probably be flamed for your efforts. That's why it's always good to "lurk" in newsgroups for awhile before you start posting messages, to find out what's acceptable behavior and what isn't.

Why can't I access a certain site?

The most common reason you can't reach a particular Internet site is that it's too busy. An Internet site is just a computer, more or less like your own PC. When it gets too many people using it at one time, it slows down and then ultimately won't let anybody new sign on until one of the current users signs off. Some popular sites are just about impossible to access during busy parts of the day. Of course, it's also possible that any particular site has closed down, moved, or just terminated its access to the Internet.

Why is the Internet so slow sometimes?

The Internet is just a bunch of computers connected by a bunch of wires. When too many people use it (or use a particular computer site) at the same time, it gets a little overloaded—which translates into things slowing down. Try accessing a different site, or log on at a different time when things might not be so busy. In addition, some of the most popular sites have **mirror sites** that "mirror" their content and alleviate some of the traffic load.

How can I keep family members from accessing objectionable content on the Net?

The only way to restrict Internet access is to turn it all off. You can't just turn off access to a particular newsgroup, for example; you have to restrict access to Prodigy's entire newsgroup service. Remember, the Internet is totally unmonitored and uncensored, and contains lots of content that may offend some people some of the time.

Can I use Netscape (or Mosaic or any other third-party Internet software) with Prodigy?

Nope, sorry. Prodigy forces you to use its tools and interfaces; you can't use third-party Internet programs via Prodigy. This, of course, is one of the drawbacks of Prodigy's Internet service, and why some users opt for a separate account with a true Internet Service Provider. (Note, however, that Prodigy has signed an agreement with Netscape to replace Prodigy's current Web browser with a new browser based on Netscape. Look for this some time in early 1996!)

Should I give my credit card number over the Internet?

No, no, no! (Or at least not yet.) The Internet is an unsecured environment, which means that a talented hacker can grab messages willy-nilly—which could include your credit card number. Until secure credit transactions are in place—which should be sometime in 1996—you should avoid sending sensitive credit information over the Net. (To put things in perspective, however, it's just as easy for a "phone phreak" to steal credit card info from a cellular phone call as it is for a "cracker" to grab the same info from the Internet.)

Can anyone on the Internet gain access to the files on my personal computer?

No—your personal computer is protected from the Net via "firewalls" in place at Prodigy. You can get out, but no one else can get in.

Can I create my own personal Web page?

Yes, you can. See chapter 14, "Creating Your Own Web Pages," for detailed information on using Prodigy's Web Page Creator.

11

Sending Internet E-Mail

● **In this chapter:**

- **How is Internet e-mail different from Prodigy e-mail?**

- **How do I send e-mail to someone on the Internet?**

- **What is an e-mail mailing list?**

You can use Prodigy's e-mail system to send electronic mail to anyone connected to the Internet . . . . ▸

Т he most used feature of the Internet is electronic mail. Practically all of the 30 million people connected to the Net use e-mail to communicate with other users. And because Prodigy is connected to the Internet, you can send e-mail directly from Prodigy to any other user connected to the Net. It's as easy as using regular Prodigy e-mail!

How Internet e-mail differs from Prodigy e-mail

Internet e-mail is a lot like regular Prodigy e-mail. Internet e-mail messages are text messages sent electronically, and you use Prodigy's e-mail center to compose, send, and receive them. You don't have to learn any new techniques or codewords or anything; you send and receive Internet e-mail pretty much the same way you send regular Prodigy e-mail.

 TIP **See chapter 6 for more information about Prodigy e-mail.**

The big difference between Internet e-mail and Prodigy e-mail is in the addresses. You see, Internet e-mail addresses look quite a bit different from Prodigy's normal addresses.

When you send e-mail to another Prodigy member, all you have to know is their member ID. This ID is used when you address your Prodigy e-mail; Prodigy knows to send that piece of mail to the person who owns that ID.

Unlike Prodigy's simple ID-based e-mail addresses, there are three parts to an Internet address: the **username**, an **@** sign, and the **domain address**. (The domain address generally has two or more parts, each separated by a period.)

A typical Internet address, then, looks something like this:

> ***username@organization.domain***

Let's look at the three parts of an Internet address in a little more detail.

- *username* is the Internet username of the recipient. Many Internet usernames consist of the user's first initial and last name. Others, though, can get a bit bizarre. In truth, there are few conventions on how to create a username, so be prepared for just about anything!

- @ separates the username from the domain address.

- *organization.domain* is referred to collectively as the **domain address**. Typically, the domain address identifies the user's Internet service provider. That provider can be a commercial service, or a university, or a government branch, or a large corporation. Every provider will have a unique domain address.

 TIP **A domain address can have more than two parts, as long as each** part is separated by a period. For example, look at the domain address for the computer science department at Indiana University: **cica.indiana.edu**. Believe it or not, some domain addresses can be two or three times this length—with six or seven parts, all separated by periods!

As an example, my Internet address is **mmiller@mcp.com**.

My username is *mmiller*, and the domain address of my Internet provider is *mcp.com*. (The *mcp* in the domain address stands for *M*acmillan *C*omputer *P*ublishing, the parent company of Que that has its own Internet domain.) Put them together, and you have my complete Internet address.

Receiving e-mail from the Internet

The easiest part of Internet e-mail is *receiving* it. It's easy because *you* don't have to do anything other than look in your Prodigy mailbox (Jump:**mail**)— Internet e-mail messages are received there just like regular Prodigy e-mail messages.

However, someone sending you e-mail from the Internet needs to know a thing or two. First, they have to know your Prodigy ID. Then they have to know how to turn your Prodigy ID into a proper Internet address.

Your Prodigy ID by itself is unrecognizable by the Internet, for the simple reason that it includes no domain address. The Net doesn't know where you are without this vital information.

So the folks at Prodigy got their own domain address, **prodigy.com**. Now the Internet looks at this domain address, and views all of Prodigy as a single computer site.

Knowing this, if someone on the Net wants to send e-mail to you, all she has to do is to make sure the address line includes your username (which is your Prodigy ID), followed by Prodigy's domain name (prodigy.com). This way the e-mail flows first to the domain (Prodigy), and then to you within that domain.

So, your Prodigy address (as someone on the Internet would view it), looks like this:

> *myid*@**prodigy.com**

Using my Prodigy address (**jese31a**) as a real example, to e-mail me from the Net, you use this address:

> **jese31a@prodigy.com**

Q&A *A friend on the on the Internet sent me an e-mail message and I didn't get it. What went wrong?*

He probably forgot to include the **@prodigy.com** after your Prodigy ID. For example, if your Prodigy ID is **myid**, any Internet e-mail sent to you should be addressed like this: **myid@prodigy.com**.

Sending e-mail to users on the Net

With Prodigy, e-mailing to someone on the Net is as simple as entering their Internet address where you would normally enter a Prodigy ID in a normal Prodigy e-mail message (Jump:**mail**).

So, to send e-mail to someone on the Net, all you have to know is the recipient's Internet address—enter that address in the TO: field. Figure 11.1 shows a sample message addressed to my personal Internet address, **mmiller@mcp.com**.

Fig. 11.1
Addressing a Prodigy
e-mail message to
my Internet address.

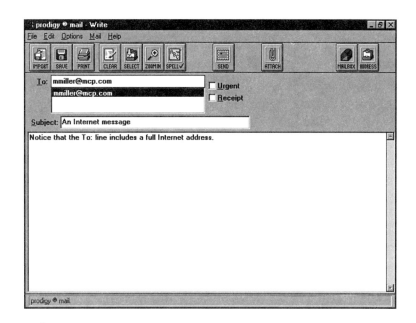

TIP   You can store complex Internet addresses in Prodigy's e-mail
Address Book, as discussed in chapter 6.

Q&A   *I sent e-mail to a friend on the Internet and he didn't
receive it. What went wrong?*

Most returned e-mail is due to an incorrect address. Make sure you type the
address correctly—and remember that an Internet e-mail address is more
complex than a Prodigy e-mail address.

Q&A   *I sent e-mail to a friend on CompuServe via the
Internet and he didn't receive it. What did I do wrong
this time?*

CompuServe addresses change when you access them via the Internet.
CompuServe addresses generally consist of two numbers separated by a
comma, like this: **12345,1234**. When you send mail to CompuServe
via the Internet, the comma changes to a period and you add
@compuserve.com to the end of the address, like this:
12345.1234@compuserve.com.

CAUTION **Internet e-mail has to be text only, which means you can't use** Prodigy's new multimedia e-mail features in a message going to someone on the Internet.

Sending e-mail over the World Wide Web

There's one more way to send Internet e-mail from Prodigy. When you're using Prodigy's Web browser to cruise the World Wide Web (see chapter 13, "Cruising the World Wide Web"), you'll find that some Web pages have e-mail hyperlinks. You can click on these links to send e-mail to the Webmaster for that Web site.

When you click on an e-mail hyperlink, a special Send Internet E-Mail Message dialog box is displayed, with the To: box already filled in. Just add a subject line and compose a message, and then click the Send button to send the message. It's as easy as that—and you don't have to leave the Web and go back to Prodigy's normal e-mail system to send the message.

Using the Internet to send e-mail to America Online, CompuServe, and the Microsoft Network

While Prodigy doesn't talk directly to its competitors in the online services field—America Online, CompuServe, and the Microsoft Network—you can use the Internet to send e-mail to friends you have that are members of these services.

You need to know the ID for their particular service, and then add the proper domain name. For CompuServe, add the domain name **compuserve.com**; for America Online, add **aol.com**; for the Microsoft Network, add **msn.com**. With CompuServe you also have to remember to change the comma in the user ID to a period—for example, the CompuServe ID **12345,1234** changes to **12345.1234**.

Let's look at my personal CompuServe address as an example. My CompuServe address is **73207,2013**. To send me e-mail via the Internet, then, you address it to: **73207.2013@compuserve.com**.

Now let's look at my personal America Online address, which is **MillerM522**. To send me e-mail via the Internet, you address it to: **MillerM522@aol.com**.

Finally, let's look at my personal Microsoft Network address, which is **MLM**. To send me e-mail via the Internet, you address it to: **MLM@msn.com**.

Making new friends with e-mail mailing lists

There's one more thing about Internet e-mail you need to know about. That thing is an Internet **mailing list**.

Internet mailing lists are like Prodigy forums, except that all messages are sent via e-mail. Sometimes, messages are grouped by a **list manager** (the guy who runs the mailing list) into a single, large e-mail message. Other times, each message is sent separately to all list subscribers—which can result in a *lot* of e-mail messages!

Just like Prodigy's bulletin boards, each mailing list focuses on a specific topic of interest. Unlike forums, the lists are not arranged in any sort of order; in fact, they're most often managed by interested individuals, on their own time.

 **CAUTION** **Since you have to pay Prodigy while your read your e-mail, receiv-**ing a lot of mailing list messages can be a costly affair. Don't get caught by surprise by a big Prodigy bill caused by reading too many mailing list messages!

There are all sorts of mailing lists available on the Internet—several thousand in total, ranging from a *Beverly Hills 90210* fan club to a list devoted to chemical engineers. To obtain a master list of all current mailing lists, send an e-mail message to **listserv@ubvm.cc.buffalo.edu**. Leave the subject of this message blank, and enter *only the following* as the body of the text:

list global

After you've determined which lists you're interested in, you need to *subscribe* to that list. To subscribe to an Internet mailing list, you have to send an e-mail message to the manager of that list, noting that you want to become a member. This message needs to have the word **SUBSCRIBE** in the subject field. Then, for the body of the text, enter *only the following:*

subscribe *listname yourname*

Note that *listname* should be the name of the mailing list, and *yourname* should be your real name, *not* your Prodigy ID. The list manager will get your e-mail address from the message's header information.

After you send your subscription request, you should begin receiving mail from the list within two or three days.

TIP   **To cancel a subscription to a mailing list, simply send an** "unsubscribe" message to the mailing list manager. Type the word **SIGNOFF** in the subject field. Then, for the body of the text, enter *only the following:*

    signoff listname yourname

12

Reading USENET Newsgroups

● **In this chapter:**

- **What is a newsgroup?**

- **What kinds of newsgroups are there?**

- **How do I subscribe to newsgroups?**

- **How do I read and reply to newsgroup articles?**

- **How do I compose my own newsgroup articles?**

If you like Prodigy bulletin boards, you'll love USENET newsgroups! . . . . ▶

Prodigy has about 75 bulletin boards; each bulletin board is divided into dozens of separate topics related to the main topic. That results in several thousand separate topics available for public discussion.

However, that number pales next to what's available on the Internet. There's a part of the Internet called **USENET** that offers what are called **newsgroups**. These newsgroups are similar to Prodigy's bulletin boards. The big difference, however, is in the sheer number—there are more than 10,000 newsgroups available on the Internet, covering every type of topic imaginable!

What is a newsgroup—and how does it work?

In many ways, a newsgroup is like one of those clubs you probably joined back in high school—you know, like the Chess Club, or the Debate Club, or the Sewing Club. Those clubs were places where people with similar interests could go to hang out with others with the same interests.

A newsgroup is kind of like an online club. Users who share a special interest congregate online to talk about the topic at hand, via electronic messages (called **articles**). You read messages from other users, add your comments, or post your own messages.

Does this description sound familiar? It should—a USENET newsgroup is very similar to a Prodigy bulletin board.

There are some differences between bulletin boards and newsgroups, however. Take a look at table 12.1.

Table 12.1   Differences between Prodigy bulletin boards and USENET newsgroups

Feature	Prodigy Bulletin Boards	USENET Newsgroups
Number available	75	12,000+
Contains multiple topics	Yes	No
Contains multiple messages (or "notes")	Yes	Yes
Moderated	Yes	No
Messages are grouped into topics (or "threads")	Yes	Yes
Messages are called...	Notes	Articles

The main difference between bulletin boards and newsgroups, however, is the culture. Whereas Prodigy bulletin boards tend to be relatively friendly places where newcomers are welcome, USENET newsgroups can be a bit insular and downright hostile to "newbies." In fact, it's quite common for old Internauts to "flame" newbies mercilessly; if you're new to a newsgroup and overstep your bounds, you're likely to see some of this behavior.

 Plain English, please!

A **flame** is a very nasty message sent to someone who annoyed another member. It's not uncommon to see flame wars between two newsgroup members in a feud. 🙬

Remember, too, that USENET is not part of Prodigy. Even though you can access USENET newsgroups via Prodigy, these groups exist on another network, and follow different rules than what you're used to with Prodigy. There are subtle differences in terminology and etiquette, and you'll need to master these or get flamed as an Internet "newbie" from that awful non-Net world of Prodigy.

(Yeah, they can get a little testy on the Net—which is something you'll have to get used to!)

What kinds of newsgroups are there?

With more than 10,000 newsgroups available, there's a newsgroup devoted to just about any topic you can think of. Are you a David Letterman fan? There's a newsgroup for you. Are you interested in Microsoft's release of Windows 95? There's a newsgroup for you. Do you want to place an online personal ad? There's a newsgroup for that, too.

Just like Prodigy bulletin boards, USENET newsgroups have their own type of organization. When you look at the name of a newsgroup, you see something that looks like this:

first.second.third

The first part of the name is called the hierarchy. Think of this as the major topic area, like the way Prodigy's bulletin boards are grouped. The second part of the name is like a topic on a Prodigy bulletin board, a subtopic related to the major topic. The third part of the name denotes another level of topic detail, and any subsequent parts (there can be an infinite number of parts) just break the topic down further.

 TIP   **Not all newsgroup names have three parts. At a bare minimum,** two parts are required (hierarchy and subtopic). Some very narrow-interest groups, however, go to four or even five levels to best describe their focus.

For example, a newsgroup in the *recreational* section discussing the *art* of the *cinema* is called the **rec.arts.cinema** group.

Newsgroup netiquette

One thing you need to know about USENET newsgroups—they generally don't like naive beginners (whom they call "newbies"). Most newsgroups are kind of "old boys clubs," and it's tough to break in and become one of the gang.

When it comes to newsgroups, it pays to look before you leap. That means you should **lurk** a bit; just read the articles and get a feel for the culture of a newsgroup before you make your first posting.

When you do post your first articles, try not to ask repetitive questions or flame other subscribers. Be nice, be patient, be polite, and be concise.

Another important thing to remember is that blatant advertising is not acceptable. Even moderate self-promotion is often frowned on.

There are dozens of different hierarchies in USENET. The following table lists some of the more popular USENET hierarchies.

Table 12.2   USENET hierarchies available on Prodigy

USENET hierarchy	Topics
alt	Alternative topics; generally related to areas that inspire a lot of different opinions
comp	Computer-related topics
misc	Miscellaneous topics
news	Topics related to netnews system administration
rec	Recreational topics
sci	Scientific topics
soc	Topics related to social issues
talk	Conversational and controversial topics

Subscribing to newsgroups

To participate in a newsgroup, you first need to **subscribe** to that group. When you subscribe to a group (which, unlike a magazine subscription, doesn't cost you anything) it automatically appears on your "short list" of newsgroups you can access easily from Prodigy's newsgroup section. (If you didn't subscribe to a "short list" of groups, you'd have to scroll through all 10,000 newsgroups every time you wanted to browse through just one!)

Begin by going to Prodigy's USENET Newsgroups screen (Jump:**newsgroups**), shown in figure 12.1.

From the main newsgroup screen, click on the Explore Newsgroups hyperlink. You'll see a window like that in figure 12.2. This window lists those newsgroups you're currently subscribed to. (If this is your first time in the newsgroup section, you'll find that you're automatically subscribed to a few Prodigy-specific newsgroups.)

Fig. 12.1
The main USENET newsgroup screen (Jump:**newsgroups**).

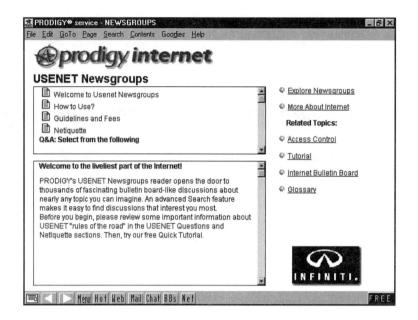

Fig. 12.2
A list of the newsgroups you're currently subscribed to.

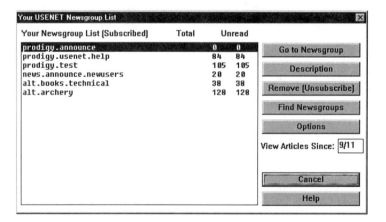

Subscribing to new newsgroups is a simple four-step process:

1 Click on the Find Newsgroups button.

2 When the Find a Newsgroup dialog box appears (see fig. 12.3), you have three different ways to find the newsgroups you want. You can look for the newest groups (Latest Newsgroups added), scroll through all 10,000+ groups (All available Newsgroups), or search for specific groups (Search Newsgroups for text pattern below). Select the method you want, and click the Find Now button.

Fig. 12.3
Here's where you
find newsgroups to
subscribe to; select a
search method and
click the Find Now
button.

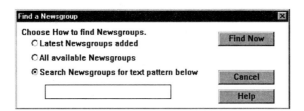

3 When the dialog box listing available newsgroups appears, select the newsgroup you want and click on the Add to Your Newsgroups button. The group will automatically be added to your list.

4 When you're done adding new groups, click on the Cancel button; you'll be returned to the Your USENET Newsgroup List window and the new groups will appear in your list.

If you want to **unsubscribe** to a newsgroup, just highlight the group in the Your USENET Newsgroup List window and click the Remove (Unsubscribe) button. The group will be automatically removed from your list.

TIP **USENET newsgroups are not a part of Prodigy, and as such are** unmoderated and may contain material offensive to some people. If you want to limit access to USENET newsgroups, click on the Access Control button on the USENET Newsgroups screen and follow the instructions that follow.

Q&A *Why can't I find a certain newsgroup with Prodigy's newsreader?*

Prodigy doesn't allow access to all 10,000+ newsgroups. Not that Prodigy censors newsgroups (they most adamantly do not), they don't offer every obscure newsgroup available, either. A lot of newsgroups are location-specific or company-specific, and thus aren't intended for widespread use. Prodigy obviously doesn't carry these.

Reading newsgroup articles

Now that you've subscribed to a "short list" of newsgroups, it's time to enter a group and start readying the articles. Begin on the Your USENET Newsgroup List window and select a group. Click on the Go to Newsgroup button, and you'll see a list of articles for that group, sorted by subject (see fig. 12.4).

Fig. 12.4

Examining a list of articles in the **news.announce. newusers** newsgroup.

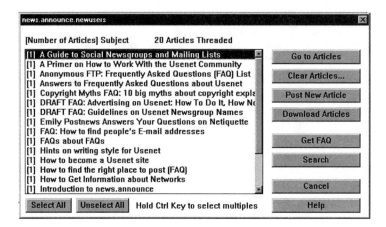

TIP

You can select the age of articles you want to read by changing the date in the View Articles Since box. The default date is today's date.

Reading an article is as easy as selecting the subject in the list, and then clicking on the Go to Articles button. You'll see an article window, like that shown on the next page. Just scroll through the article to read the whole thing.

 Plain English, please!

A **thread** is a group of newsgroup articles on the same subject. The thread starts when someone replies to an original article, and then someone replies to that, and on and on.

TIP

If you get tired of reading annoying articles from the same people day in and day out, you can create a personal Ignore List. Messages from anyone on this list will be automatically filtered out of your listing of available newsgroup articles! Just click on the Ignore button when reading an article from someone you want to ignore, and that person is automatically added to your Ignore List!

Q&A *The newsreader says there are articles in a certain newsgroup, but when I go to read them, it tells me that there aren't any new articles. How can I read older articles?*

It's as simple as changing the date in the View Articles Since box in the Your USENET Newsgroup List window. Set the date for a day or two prior to the current date and you should be able to read a larger list of articles.

Replying to newsgroup articles

Responding to an article is as easy as clicking on the Respond button. You'll be asked if you want to respond publicly (via a public reply in the newsgroup or via a "new note"—a newsgroup article with a new header) or privately via e-mail (to the article author or to all participants in the thread). Choose your preferred method, and click OK. You'll be presented with an empty Post window—the only thing filled in will be the Subject line.

Since it's proper newsgroup etiquette to "quote" the article to which you're replying, click on the Quote button. You'll be presented with a Quote Original window, with the text from the original message listed—complete with right brackets in front of each line. (It looks like this: `>This is a quote`.) These brackets tell readers that this text is "quoted" from the previous article, which helps remind them about what you're responding to. Highlight the text you want to quote (it's bad form to quote really long passages), and then click the Copy button. You're returned to your Post window. Position your cursor in the reply box, and click on the Paste button—your "quoted" text is automatically inserted in your reply message.

Now you can type in your new text. When you're done, your screen should look like the one in figure 12.5. Click on the Post button to send the message.

Understanding the article window

It's important to understand a typical article window. From this window you can read an article, print it, save it to disk, respond to it, or move to another article or thread.

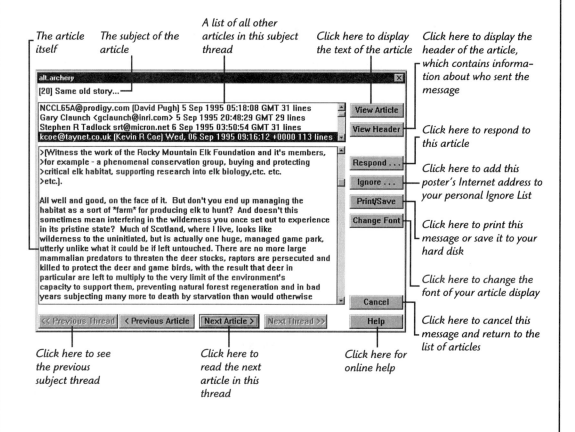

The article itself

The subject of the article

A list of all other articles in this subject thread

Click here to display the text of the article

Click here to display the header of the article, which contains information about who sent the message

Click here to respond to this article

Click here to add this poster's Internet address to your personal Ignore List

Click here to print this message or save it to your hard disk

Click here to change the font of your article display

Click here to cancel this message and return to the list of articles

Click here to see the previous subject thread

Click here to read the next article in this thread

Click here for online help

Fig. 12.5
Replying to a
newsgroup article—
note the quote from
the original article.

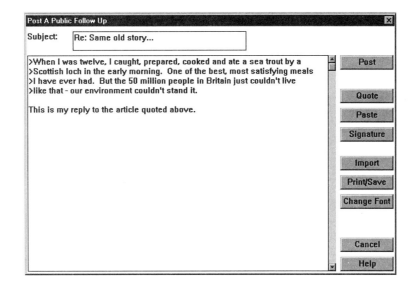

Composing your own newsgroup articles

If you want to create your own original article, click on the Post New Article
button in the newsgroup article list window. You're warned that "you are
about to send this text to thousands of computers and potentially millions
of people around the world...are you sure you want to do this?" (Prodigy is
trying to be a responsible Internet citizen!) Click Continue, and you'll see the
Post A New Article screen. Fill in the Subject, and start typing your message.
When you're done, click on the Post button to send the article.

Turning newsgroup articles into pretty pictures

Some newsgroups specialize in posting articles that contain pictures. Many of
these groups are in the **alt.binaries** groups, such as **alt.binaries.clip-art.**

CAUTION **Remember, USENET is part of the Internet—and is therefore**
completely uncensored. You will be wise to supervise your children's
access here.

Since USENET can't transmit graphics files directly, these pictures are **encoded** so that they appear as ASCII text. If you look at one, it looks like pages and pages of gibberish. But when this gibberish is **decoded**, you get a picture in GIF or JPEG format that you can view on your computer monitor.

To decode these pictures, you need a special utility, which you can find in Prodigy's Utilities Download section (Jump:**utilities download**). Search for the utility described as "Converts binary files to ASCII for e-mail—Windows." This file is named **WNCODE.EXE**. Download this file and install it on your PC.

Before you decode one of these pictures, you first have to download it to your PC. This is done by selecting the article (or articles—some pictures take up several articles) from the article list and clicking on the Download Articles button. You can then use WNCODE to decode the encoded files and view all those Internet pictures!

Adding your signature to articles

At the bottom of most newsgroup articles is a "signature" from the message sender. This signature (just a few lines of text) generally gives the sender's name and Internet address, and sometimes a pithy saying of some sort.

You can create your own newsgroup signature to display at the bottom of all articles you post. Just click on the Options button in the Your USENET Newsgroup List window. You'll be presented with the default signature created for you by Prodigy—essentially your real name and Prodigy e-mail address. To change this signature, just type new text in the box. Click the OK button when you're done.

To add this signature to any article, just click on the Signature button. Your signature will automatically be added to the bottom of the current article.

13

Cruising the World Wide Web

● **In this chapter:**

- ● **What is the World Wide Web?**

- ● **What is a Web page?**

- ● **Use Prodigy's own Web browser to view Web pages**

- ● **What can I find on the World Wide Web?**

- ● **What is an interest group?**

- ● **What are some good Web sites to visit?**

With its ability to hyperlink graphics, sound, and video from all over the world, the Web is the coolest place to be in cyberspace . . . . ⊙

f Prodigy is an electronic version of a small town, then, like real small towns, it isn't alone in the world. Just as the main road in most small towns connects to a big interstate highway (which in turn connects to many other small towns across the country), Prodigy is connected to the rest of the online world via the electronic highway called the Internet. And the biggest, brightest, and most exciting cities along the route of this online superhighway are part of what is called the **World Wide Web**.

The World Wide Web—part of the Internet, but different

The World Wide Web, like USENET, is just a part of the thing we call the Internet. In particular, the Web is the part of the Net where tens of thousands of computer sites display sophisticated documents called **Web pages**. These pages—which actually look like pages from a book or magazine—contain **hyperlinks** to other documents that let you jump to related information with the click of a mouse button.

Hyperlinking sounds like something overly technical, but it's really quite simple. It's just the ability to click on a highlighted word or graphic and be automatically transported to a related document somewhere else on the Web. It's kind of like browsing through an encyclopedia. You see, when I read an article in an encyclopedia, I stumble across a reference to a related article, which references another article... and, before I know it, I have all 24 volumes of the encyclopedia open in front of me. It's the same way with hyperlinking on the Web—you click from one document to a related document to a related document, and pretty soon you have no idea where you started!

So what's on the Web? Lots and lots and lots of things. You'll find Web sites run by corporations trying to sell you something, universities trying to educate you, and individual users just out to have fun. You can find Web pages devoted to TV shows, art galleries, magazines, scientific facts, and beer. (Yes, there are *several* "beer pages" on the Web!) Like the rest of the Net, the variety is seemingly endless.

Reading a Web page

Information on the Web is displayed in pages. A Web page can contain text, graphics, audio clips, video clips, and hyperlinks.

Below is a sample page from the Web, viewed with Prodigy's Web browser. Each piece of under-lined text is a separate hyperlink. When you position your cursor over one of these hyperlinks and click the mouse button, your screen changes to display the linked document.

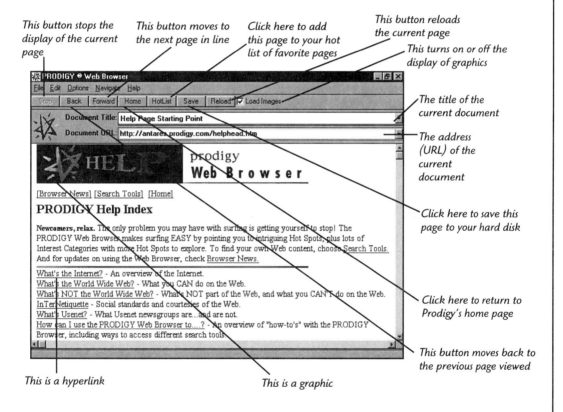

This button stops the display of the current page

This button moves to the next page in line

Click here to add this page to your hot list of favorite pages

This button reloads the current page

This turns on or off the display of graphics

The title of the current document

The address (URL) of the current document

Click here to save this page to your hard disk

Click here to return to Prodigy's home page

This button moves back to the previous page viewed

This is a hyperlink

This is a graphic

Using Prodigy's Web browser

You view Web pages with a **Web browser**. A browser is a software program that lets you display Web pages on your computer. When your browser goes to a Web page, it downloads the contents of that page to your computer's memory; depending on the size and complexity of the page, it can take from several seconds to several minutes to fully display the page.

 TIP **You can speed up the display of Web pages by turning off the** Load Images option on Prodigy's Web browser. This causes Web pages to display in text mode only, without graphics. While this speeds up the display, the trade-off is that you don't see any of the pretty pictures.

Web browsers have only been around for a couple of years. The breakthrough browser was **Mosaic**, developed at the National Center for Supercomputing Applications (NCSA) at the University of Illinois. Today there are dozens of browsers available, with names like Netscape and InternetWorks. All of these browsers work pretty much the same way, and all do a good job of displaying Web pages.

Launching Prodigy's Web browser

Since you're on Prodigy, you get to use Prodigy's Web browser. You access this browser from Prodigy's World Wide Web page (Jump:**www**). When you click on the Browse the Web button, the browser is launched.

 TIP **Prodigy's Web browser is a program that works more or less** independently from the normal Prodigy interface, which means you won't be able to use standard Prodigy commands when you're using the browser.

When the Web browser launches, the first page you see is Prodigy's home page (see fig. 13.1). From here you can hyperlink to any site listed on this page, or jump directly to a specific page.

 Plain English, please!

A **home page** is the opening page at any given Web site.

To close the Web browser and return to Prodigy, just pull down the File menu and select Exit. The browser will close, and you'll be back on Prodigy proper.

Fig. 13.1
Launching the Web browser and viewing Prodigy's home page.

Displaying other Web pages

Jumping to a hyperlinked page is easy. Just position your cursor over the blue underlined text (your cursor will change shape to a hand with pointing finger) and click the left mouse button.

To jump to a specific, non-linked page, you need to know the page's address, or **URL**. (URL stands for **uniform resource locator**, and it's how Web browsers locate specific Web pages.) Just enter the page's URL in the Document URL box at the top of the screen, and then press Enter.

TIP   **Almost all URLs for Web pages start with *http://*, followed by a** site address. The **http** (which stands for **h**yper**t**ext **t**ransfer **p**rotocol) tells the browser that you're going to be reading a Web page, as opposed to some other type of document. As you'll learn in chapter 15, "Downloading Files with FTP and Gopher," you can also use the browser to access FTP (**ftp://**) and Gopher (**gopher://**) documents.

It takes a little time to actually go to a new page and have it display on your PC. In fact, you'll see the page display in parts—text first, then graphics. (And the graphics display in low resolution first, and then "fill in" in higher resolution.) If you think a page is taking too long to load, just click on the Stop button and the display will halt where it's at. If you want to restart the display, just click on the Reload button.

You can move back and forth between previously displayed pages with the Back and Forward buttons. You can even mark the current page as part of a hot list of popular sites by clicking on the HotList button and then clicking on the Add to Hot List button.

 Plain English, please!

> A **hot list** is a list of Web sites that you compile. This list is stored with Prodigy's Web browser; you can go to any of these sites at any time by opening the hot list and clicking on them. 🙴

The hot list is a great way to store your favorite sites and then jump directly to the site you want. When you click on the HotList button, your list of favorite sites is displayed, as shown in figure 13.2. Just select the site you want to jump to and click on the Go button. (You can even create multiple hot lists with the Create List button; you can then select the list you want with the Select List list.)

Fig. 13.2
A hot list of favorite sites stored in Prodigy's Web browser.

Hot Lists	☒

Hot List

Select List: Main List ▾   Create List...
Delete List

Prodigy Home Page
Signup Results
Macmillan USA Information SuperLibrary (tm)
Prodigy Interest Groups
CDnow!
whats-new.html
Microsoft Corporation World-Wide-Web Server

Go
Close
Move Up
Move Down
Remove
Edit...
Help

Current Page

Title: Prodigy Home Page
URL: http://antares.prodigy.com/welcome.htm

Add to Hot List...

TIP **Use the Global History feature of Prodigy's Web browser to return** to pages you viewed previously during this session. Just pull down the Navigate menu and select Global History to display a list of all the pages you've recently visited. You can select any of these pages and click on the Go button to return to that page. You must have the Enable Global History box checked to use this feature.

 TIP **Because Prodigy caches the most popular Web pages on its own** Web server, you may not be viewing the most up-to-date version of any given page. If you think the page needs updated, click on the Reload button; this will load the latest version of the page directly from the original site.

 Q&A ***Why is the Web browser slower at some times and on some sites?***

There are two things that slow down Prodigy's Web browser:

1 Big, complex Web pages take longer to load than smaller, simpler pages. So if a Web page is overly long—or has a lot of graphic images— it will make it seem like your browser is slowing down. To speed up the display of complex pages, turn off the Load Images option at the top of the browser; this will let you display Web pages without those complex graphics that slow things down.

2 Since a World Wide Web site is just computer, when too many people access the same site at the same time, the computer at that site gets overworked. This causes all users connected at that site to experience slowdowns. If this gets too annoying, try accessing that site at a different time of day.

Q&A *Why can't I access a certain Web page?*

There are three main reasons why the Web browser won't connect to a Web page:

1 You may have entered the wrong URL. URLs are notoriously particular—and often quite complex. Make sure you entered the right combination of slashes and periods, and capitalized everything properly—URLs *are* case-sensitive! And don't assume that the all hyperlinks in all Web pages are correct; some hyperlinks are either old or just plain wrong!

2 It's quite likely that the site containing that particular Web page is too busy. You see, a Web page is stored on a computer, pretty much like your own PC. When that computer gets too many people using it at one time, it slows down and then ultimately won't let anybody new sign on until one of the current users signs off. Some popular Web pages are just about impossible to access during busy times of the day.

3 Of course, it's also possible that any particular page has moved or closed down. The Web is in constant change, which means pages change or go away with some frequency.

Mixing Prodigy and the Web: Prodigy's interest groups

Prodigy has introduced a novel new feature that organizes all available resources on a given topic—Web sites, USENET newsgroups, Prodigy Chat rooms, and Prodigy bulletin boards—in a single place. That place is called an **interest group**, and it resides on the Web.

Prodigy has created dozens and dozens of these interest groups. You access the list of interest groups at the following Web page: **http://antares.prodigy.com/mainpcoi.htm**. There are interest groups for all sorts of topics—from Alternative Medicine to Wrestling.

There are lots of Web sites listed, but there are also links to newsgroups, bulletin boards, and Chat rooms. When you click on a Web link, you obviously go directly to that Web page. But when you click on a newsgroup link, Prodigy's newsreader is automatically launched and you're taken to that newsgroup. Similarly, when you click on a Chat room link, you're taken back to Prodigy and dropped in that Chat room. (Same with Prodigy bulletin boards.)

Q&A ***Why aren't all the graphics on a page visible?***

Some Web pages use a version of HTML (the language used to create Web pages) that is not compatible with Prodigy's Web browser. Also, some types of graphics cannot be read by Prodigy's Web browser. In both cases, there's really nothing wrong with either the Web page or the Web browser; they're just not talking to each other as well as they should. Sometimes, though, the graphics just don't load right; try clicking the Reload button to view the entire page from scratch.

TIP   **Web pages are in constant development. It's likely that any page** I describe in this book will have changed somewhat by the time you get there!

Taking a quick tour of the Web

Okay, you now know a little bit about the Web and about Prodigy's Web browser, and you're itching to start browsing the Web. While the best way to learn about the Web is via clicking around yourself, I'll give you a quick tour of some representative sights to get you going!

Let's start by launching Prodigy's Web browser, which automatically loads Prodigy's home page. Scroll down to the Interest Categories section and click on the Arts & Entertainment hyperlink.

Prodigy's Arts & Entertainment page (shown in fig. 13.3) is now displayed. This page is still part of Prodigy's Web server, so it loads pretty quick. Let's begin our trek outside Prodigy-land and click on the Mr. Showbiz hyperlink.

Now you see the Mr. Showbiz page. This is one of the best entertainment pages on the Web (discussed in more detail in chapter 26, "Keeping Yourself Entertained"). As you can see in figure 13.4, there are lots of other links (underlined and in color) on this page; clicking on any one of these links will take you someplace else either on the Mr. Showbiz site or elsewhere on the Web.

Fig. 13.3
Prodigy's Arts &
Entertainment page—
click on Mr. Showbiz.

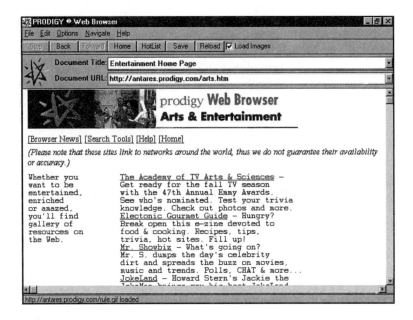

Fig. 13.4
The Mr. Showbiz
home page.

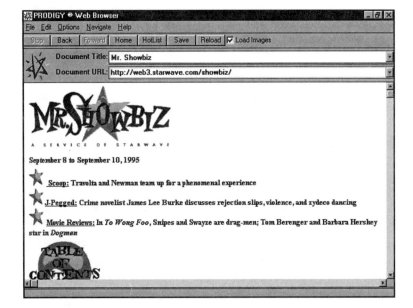

Now let's go to another page—but directly, by typing in the page's URL. Enter the following URL in the Document URL box at the top of the browser, and then press Enter:

http://voyager.paramount.com/VoyagerMenu.html

CAUTION It's important that you type this URL *exactly* as written— complete with upper- and lowercase letters as shown. (URLs are notoriously case-sensitive.)

This takes you to the home page for *Star Trek Voyager*, as shown in figure 13.5.

TIP Some pages display images that are hyperlinked to other pages. You know you're looking at one of these **image maps** when you pass your cursor over an image and it changes into the pointing hand shape. Just click on the appropriate spot on the image to follow the hyperlink.

Fig. 13.5
The *Star Trek Voyager* home page—click on any section of the PADD to get more information.

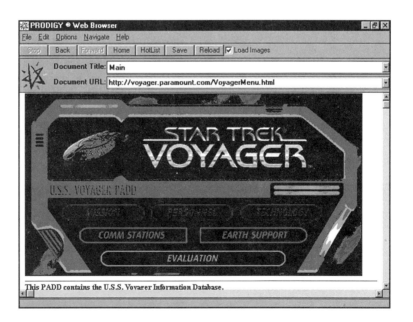

That should get you started on your Web cruising. To help you along, however, I've assembled a list of great "starter pages," which is next up in this chapter. In addition, chapters 16 through 31 cover all sorts of specific interests, and include lists of the best Web sites for each interest category.

Q&A *Sometimes when I click on an audio or movie file, nothing happens. What am I doing wrong?*

To view graphics or movie files—or to listen to audio files—the Web browser needs to have specific utility programs called **viewers** installed. Prodigy's Web browser includes built-in viewers for AU and WAV audio files, along with GIF and JPEG images. If you try to access something in a different format, the Web browser asks if you want to save the file on disk for viewing at a later time and with a separate program.

You may encounter this problem when you try to view a movie file in MPEG, AVI, or Quicktime format. Unfortunately, support for these standards is not included with Prodigy's Web browser, but you can download separate viewers that can be "plugged into" the browser.

To set up Prodigy's Web browser to work with these types of external viewers, pull down the Options menu, and select Advanced Options, and then select Viewer Setup. Select the Type of viewer (or add a new type), and then add the external Viewer to the list. Click OK when finished.

You can find more information on how to set up viewers by going to the following Prodigy Web page: **http://antares.prodigy.com/ viewmain.htm**.

Miller's list of the best Web starter pages

The following table lists Web pages that are great places to start at when you're cruising the Web. These pages all have one or more of the following attributes:

- Links to lots of other Web sites

- A great search engine to help you search the Web for the resources you want

- "Supersite" status—that is, they have tons of information and lots of subsidiary sites within the main site

Table 13.1 Miller's Short List of Web Starter Pages

Web site	URL	Description
Around the World in 80 Clicks	http://www.coolsite.com/arworld.html	A "clickable map" of the world—click anywhere to see sites in that area
Big Eye	http://emporium.turnpike.net/E/emailclub/goodurls.htm	A list of five-star Web sites
College and University Home Pages	http://www.mit.edu:8001/people/cdemello/univ.html	Some of the best Web sites are at universities; use this list to cruise the academic Web
Cool Site of the Day	http://www.infi.net/cool.html	Each day a new site is featured; browsing this site's archives reveals the very best sites on the Web—recommended
CUSI (Configurable Unified Search Index)	http://www.eecs.nwu.edu/susi/cusi.html	A site that lets you search the Web in multiple ways.
EINet Galaxy	http://www.einet.net/	A great supersite, with superb search tools
ESPNet SportsZone	http://espnet.sportszone.com/	A supersite for sports-related information; one of the best sites on the Web, period—recommended
Global Network Navigator	http://www.gnn.com/gnn/GNNhome.html	GNN is the granddaddy of "supersites"—just a ton of useful information all in one place
Lycos	http://lycos.cs.cmu.edu/	Perhaps the best search engine on the Web—recommended
Macmillan Information SuperLibrary	http://www.mcp.com/mcp/	Home of Que and other computer book publishers
Metaverse	http://www.metaverse.com/index.html	A supersite for music and counterculture resources
Microsoft	http://www.microsoft.com/	If you're using Windows, you should visit this site
Mother-of-all BBS	http://www.cs.colorado.edu/homes/mcbryan/public_html/bb/summary.html	A monster list of Web locations

continues

Table 13.1   Continued

Web site	URL	Description
Mr. Showbiz	http://web3.starwave.com/showbiz/	A supersite for entertainment-related resources
New Riders' Official World Wide Web Yellow Pages	http://www.mcp.com/nrp/wwwyp/	Part of the Macmillan SuperLibrary, lists of one of the best searchable Web sites available
Newbie's Guides to the Net	http://ug.cs.dal.ca:3400/franklin.html	Some great guides—and lists of hot spots—for new Net users
Onramp Access	http://onr.com/	A great place for new users to start
Point Communications Top Web Sites	http://www.pointcom.com/gifs/topsites/overall.html	One firm's list of the best of the Web
Prodigy	http://www.prodigy.com/welcome1.htm	Prodigy's home on the Web
Prodigy's List of W3 Search Engines	http://www.astranet.com/websearch.html	A great collection of Web-based search engines
Scout Report	http://rs.internic.net/scout_report-index.html	A weekly list of newly announced Internet resources, assembled by InterNIC and the InfoScout
Starting Point	http://www.stpt.com/	Just what it says—a great starting point for Web exploration, with lists of sites arranged by categories
Time Warner Pathfinder	http://www.pathfinder.com/	A terrific site, containing all sorts of Time Warner properties, with magazines (*Time, Life, Entertainment Weekly, People, Money, SportsIllustrated, Vibe, Fortune*, etc.), Time Warner books, Warner Bros. movies, *Encyclopedia Britannica* Online, HBO, and lots of other stuff; perhaps the best site on the Web—*recommended*
URouLette	http://kuhttp.cc.ukans.edu/cwis/organizations/kucia/uroulette/uroulette.html	Click to this site and get randomly spun to a different site somewhere on the Web
Useless WWW Pages	http://www.primus.com/staff/paulp/useless.html	The worst of the Web

Web site	URL	Description
WebCrawler	**http://webcrawler.com**	A nice search engine operated by a competitor of Prodigy's, America Online
What's New Page	**http://www.gnn.com/gnn/wn/ whats-new.html**	A Web standby, a daily listing of new Web sites—recommended
WWW Virtual Library	**http://www.w3.org/hypertext/ DataSources/bySubject/Overview.html**	The granddaddy of all Web lists
Yahoo	**http://www.yahoo.com/**	The name is a little wacky, but this site has superb lists and a good search engine—recommended

Tips for finding things on the Web

Aside from the listings in this chapter (and elsewhere in this book), let me give you some tips that will make it easier for you to find things on the Web.

- *Use Prodigy's Home page and Search Tools page.* These two pages are great resources for popular Web sites. You can't go wrong here.

- *Look for sites with their own lists of sites.* Many sites contain huge lists of other cool sites. Among these are the NCSA What's New Page (**http://www.ncsa.uiuc.edu/SDG/Software/Mosaic/Docs/whats-new.html**), the GNN Best of the Net page (**http://www.dec.com/gnn/wic/best.toc.html**), The WWW Virtual Library (**http://info.cern.ch/hypertext/DataSources/bySubject/Overview.html**), and New Riders' Official WWW Yellow Pages (**http://www.mcp.com/nrp/wwwyp/**). A complete list of FTP sites (see chapter 18) is maintained at the University of Illinois (**http://hoohoo.ncsa.uiuc.edu:80/ftp-interface.html**).

- *Look for sites that contain good search engines.* There are lots of these sites. Among the best are Lycos (**http://lycos.cs.cmu.edu/**), Yahoo (**http://www.yahoo.com**), EINet Galaxy (**http://www.einet.net/**), CUSI (**http://www.eecs.nwu.edu/susi/cusi.html**), and the World Wide Web Worm (**http://www.cs.colorado.edu/home/mcbryan/**

WWWW.html). If you want to search through FTP and Gopher sites, you can use a search engine called Archie; one of the best Archie services is at Rutgers University (**http://www-ns.rutgers.edu/htbin/archie**).

- *Think of the logical URL first.* If you're looking for a Web site for IBM, try **http://www.ibm.com** (**www** because it's a Web site, **ibm** because it's IBM, and **com** because it's a *commercial* site).

- *Buy a book.* There are lots of books that list lots of sites. I recommend a book from one of Que's sister companies called *The Official New Riders' World Wide Web Yellow Pages* (the book version of New Riders' terrific Web site). You'll find *thousands* of listings, all sorted by subject.

14

Creating Your Own Web Pages

● **In this chapter:**

- What is a Web page made of?

- What is HTML?

- What is Prodigy's Web Page Creator?

- How do you create a personal Web page?

- What kind of Web pages can you create?

- Prodigy lets you edit and organize your Web pages

- How can you find Web pages from other Prodigy members?

- What kind of help is there for creating Web pages?

Use Prodigy's Web Page Creator to establish your own Web Presence—without learning HTML code! . . . . ➤

Now that you've seen a few Web pages, wouldn't you like to create your own personal page on the Web? Well, in this chapter I tell you how you can create your own Web pages—with Prodigy's Web Page Creator!

How a Web page is created

A Web page is nothing more than a document, kind of like a word processing document—with some special additions. These additions are **codes** that tell your Web browser how to display different types of text. These codes are embedded in the document, so you can't see them—they're only visible to your Web browser.

The codes used to create Web pages are part of what is called **HTML**— **H**yper**T**ext **M**arkup **L**anguage. This is the special "programming" language read by all Web browsers. Documents created with HTML can have all the fancy features you find on Web pages—different font sizes, hyperlinks to other Web pages, and even graphics, sound, and video.

If you were to see a Web page with the codes visible, they'd look like words and letters enclosed within angle brackets, surrounding your normal text. Figure 14.1 shows the code behind a sample Web page—all text within angle brackets are HTML codes.

Fig. 14.1
A sample of HTML code—all the codes are within <angle brackets>.

```
<img src="/pwp.gif" alt="Personal Web Pages" width=580 height=100>
<h1>
Product News
</h1><P>
<A HREF = "#Bug">Bug Report</A><P>
<a href="credits.htm">Credits</a>

<ul>
<li><b>Photos</b>: Don't just tell us about your cat or your kids—
show us! You'll be able to upload JPEG and GIF photo files, and link
to them from your Web pages.<P>
```

Kind of confusing, isn't it? It's actually simpler than it looks. For example, the code **<h1>** is used to turn specified type into a headline. The code **<b>** is used to boldface text.

To create a Web page, then, you have to learn what codes result in what effects. In short, you need to learn how to code in HTML, and that sounds terribly complicated.

Unless, of course, that coding can be done *automatically.* Which is just what Prodigy has done with a new service called **Web Page Creator**—which lets you create your own personal Web pages *without needing to learn HTML coding!*

Using Web Page Creator

With Web Page Creator you can create your own personal Web pages—no HTML codes required! All you have to do is enter some basic information, and Web Page Creator figures out the best way to represent that on a Web page. In essence, it automatically translates your document into HTML code, and then places your personal page out on the Web.

The way Web Page Creator works is that you enter your text into some predefined forms. Web Page Creator codes your text according to where it is in the form. The result is a slick-looking Web page, and you didn't have to enter a single code or set of angle brackets!

Prodigy has several different types of forms available; each form creates a different type of Web page. Just pick the form that suits your purposes, click a few buttons, and you're ready to create your own personal Web page!

Creating your first Web page

Because Web Page Creator is actually out on the World Wide Web, let's start by firing up Prodigy's Web Browser (Jump:**www**). Once you're on the Web, jump to **http://pages.prodigy.com/** to access the home page for Web Page Creator.

You come to this page whenever you want to do anything with your Web pages—whether it's creating your first page, adding a new page, editing an existing page, or even searching the Web for personal pages from other Prodigy members. For now, however, click on Create Your First Personal Web Page.

The page shown in figure 14.2 is where it starts. Essentially, you have to provide Prodigy with a little bit of personal information before you can create your first Web page. You're asked for the following information:

Fig. 14.2
Filling in some personal information.

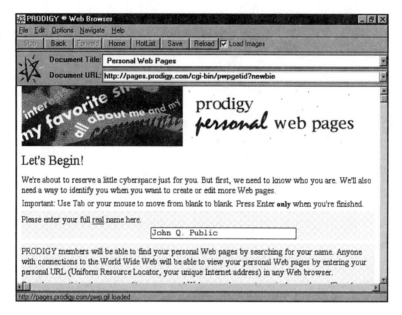

• Your full name (this should be your *real* name, not your Prodigy ID or nickname!)

• An ID number for your Web page—this will become part of your URL (Web page address)

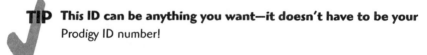

TIP This ID can be anything you want—it doesn't have to be your Prodigy ID number!

• A secret password, so no one else can edit or delete your personal pages

• Your state (Prodigy sorts all its personal Web pages by state)

• Your Prodigy ID

• Your Internet e-mail address (if you have a different e-mail address from your normal Prodigy address)

When you're done entering this information, click the Continue button.

Q&A *I received a message that I didn't fill in a particular blank. What do I do now?*

Prodigy won't let you proceed until all the required blanks are filled in. You're returned to the initial screen—with all the blanks empty. You have to start from scratch and fill in *all* the blanks!

Now you see the HTML Scratchpad™ page (see fig. 14.3). Scratchpad™ is the main part of Web Page Creator—it lets you enter your information and then determines what kind of HTML coding to apply.

Fig. 14.3
The Basic Web page template.

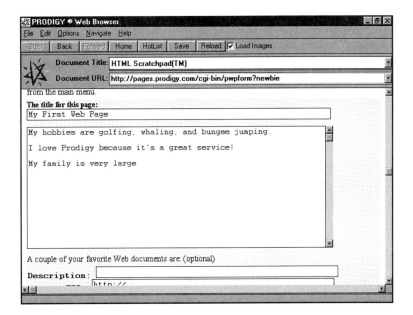

This initial HTML Scratchpad™ page presents you with a template for a Basic Web page. With this template you can create a serviceable initial Web page— nothing too fancy, but enough to get you up and running.

Begin by scrolling down to the first text box and adding a title. This title can be anything, of any length—for my first page, I entered **Miller's Personal Web Page on Prodigy**.

TIP **To see an example of what a personal Prodigy Web page looks** like, go to my personal Prodigy page at **http://pages.prodigy.com/IN/ jese31a/index.html**.

Now move to the next text box (the big, scrolling one). You'll find that Prodigy has already entered some text to get you started—"My hobbies are...," "I love Prodigy because...," and "My family is..." If you're like me, you'll want to ignore these suggestions. Simply highlight this text and hit your Delete key.

Now you can start entering your own text in this big text box. You can enter anything you want, up to a reasonable length—Prodigy automatically scrolls the text down if you go past 15 lines. Also—don't worry about hitting the Enter key at the end of a line; Prodigy automatically wraps the text for you. You will need to enter a blank line between paragraphs, however, or Prodigy will start to run all your text together.

TIP **If you know HTML, you can enter HTML codes within the** Scratchpad™ boxes for additional user-controlled formatting.

The next blanks are for creating hyperlinks to other Web pages. For example, if your business has its own Web address, you'd want to enter its name in the Description box and its URL (Web address) in the URL address.

TIP **Most Web URLs start with http://—which is why Prodigy has** already entered this text for you.

You don't have to enter anything in these boxes. If you leave them blank, Prodigy will ignore them.

Now you get to create a name for this page. Use something simple (like the ID number you gave earlier); Prodigy will append the correct file extension (.html) for you.

When you're done, click the Submit button. Prodigy then compiles the underlying code, creates an HTML document, and places it on the Web— all automatically!

You're then dropped to a final page which displays the URL for your newly created page. Click on Take a Peek to look at your new personal Web page. Figures 14.4 and 14.5 show a completed form and the resulting page.

Fig. 14.4
When you enter this code...

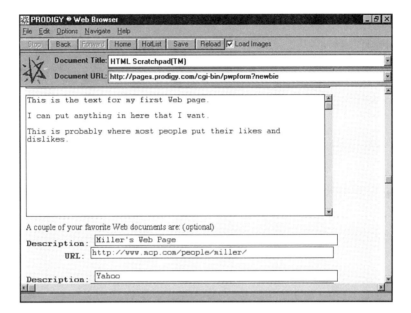

Fig. 14.5
...it creates this Web page!

Q&A *What if I don't like the page I created—can I change it?*

Yes, you can. Go back to the Web Page Creator home page and click on Edit an Existing Web Page. Enter your ID and password, and when your Web page template appears, edit to your heart's content!

Creating other types of Web pages

After you've created this Basic Web page, you can create additional Web pages using different templates. To do this, return to the home page for Web Page Creator (**http://pages.prodigy.com/**) and click on Add a New Personal Web Page.

When you see the Welcome Back! screen, you'll need to enter the User ID and Password you used when you created your first Web page. Then choose the appropriate state and click the Continue button.

CAUTION Remember, this ID is NOT your Prodigy ID—it's the ID you gave when you created your personal Web page.

Q&A *The Welcome Back! screen didn't recognize my User ID (or Password). What do I do now?*

First, make sure you entered the right User ID. If you entered your normal Prodigy ID, that's your mistake. (Unless, of course, you used your Prodigy ID for your Web page ID!) Also, make sure you enter both your User ID and Password in all lowercase letters; this section is "case sensitive," meaning you can confuse it by mixing uppercase and lowercase letters.

Select the kind of page you want to create, and click the Create Page button. Prodigy will then take you to the template you selected.

Highlight the best of the Web with a Top Ten List page

In this template you get to list—and link to—up to ten different Web pages. To do this, you need to know the page's URL (Web address) and a little bit about the page. Simply enter a page title, a URL, and a brief description for each page, and then click the Submit button.

Get down to business with a Business Card page

This template creates a very professional-looking page, which you can use to display your business information. Fill in the following blanks:

- Your title

- What you *really* do at work (a brief description)

- Your company name

- Your company address, including city, state, ZIP code, and country

- Your business e-mail address

- Your company fax and phone numbers

- The type of business you're in (or if you're self-employed)

- The Web address of your company (for a hotlink)

- The Web address of your company logo (if it exists)

You can leave any of these blanks empty, if you so choose. Just click the Submit button to finalize this page.

Get social with an Out on the Town page

This template lets you tell your fellow Internauts all about your hometown— kind of like your own personal "best of" list. Just fill in the following blanks:

- The name of your hometown, and what state it's in

- Your favorite restaurant

- The nearest all-night diner

- The best coffee in town

- Your favorite bar

- Your favorite club

- The best places to hike or bike outdoors

- The best museum in town

In addition, you can create up to three addition "best of" entries. For each of these entries you can also enter some free form text to describe what you like (or don't like, for that matter) about the establishment. Feel free to use your imagination here; pretend you're a critic doing an in-depth review!

You can leave any of these blanks empty, if you so choose. Just click the Submit button to finalize this page.

Do your own thing with a Free Form page

This is the page for those of you who already know how to code in HTML. Essentially, you're presented with a blank box, in which you can enter your own HTML-coded page. If you don't know HTML coding, Prodigy presents you with some basic codes; however, I'd advise skipping this one unless you're already an HTML pro.

 TIP **Go to Prodigy's Image Library (http://pages.prodigy.com/Art/)** to find images you can insert in your personal Web pages! This page also explains how to insert the appropriate HTML code into your pages to display each image.

Tie all your pages together with an Index page

This page lets you create a master page—an index, if you like—to all your other Prodigy personal Web pages. Simply create some intro text for this index page, and then enter the title, file name, and description of all your other Web pages. (You can enter up to 7 pages in each index.) After you select whether you want to include your e-mail address, click the Submit button.

Editing and organizing your Web pages

After you've created one or more Web pages, you may want to change your page—or rearrange the order in which your pages appear on the Web. To do either of these maintenance activities, go to the Web Page Creator home page (**http://pages.prodigy.com/**).

To edit an existing Web page, click on Edit an Existing Web Page. On the Welcome Back! page you need to enter your Web page User ID, your Password, and your State. When you click the Continue button, you're presented with a list of your existing Web pages. Select the page you want to edit, and click the Continue button.

You're now taken to the template for the selected page. Make any changes you want, and then click the Submit button. Your Web page will be automatically updated and returned to the Web.

If you want to manage multiple Web pages, click on Manage your Web Page Directory. After completing the Welcome Back! page, you're presented with the following list of options:

- **Set New Front Page**. This lets you determine which Web page users will see first.

- **Delete a Web Page.** This lets you delete one or more of your personal Web pages.

- **Rename a Web Page.** This lets you assign a new name to any of your Web pages.

- **List disk space used.** This tells you how much space you've used up—on Prodigy's computer—with your Web pages. Prodigy lets you use up to 500K; if you try to use more than that, Prodigy won't let you create any new pages.

- **Delete all your Web Pages and/or Account.** This lets you erase all your pages at one fell swoop.

Use these options to manage your Prodigy Web pages. Of course, if you just have a single page, you probably won't need to access these options.

Browsing Web pages from other Prodigy members

Now that you've created your own personal pages, you might be interested to see what kinds of pages your fellow Prodigy members have created. To do this, you want to browse through all of Prodigy's personal Web pages.

Start at the Web Page Creator home page (**http://pages.prodigy.com/**).
When you select View Other Members' Personal Web Pages, you're presented
with a Search screen. This screen allows you to search for:

- People in a specific state

- People whose name begin with a specific letter (and, optionally, who
  also live in a specific state)

- People with a specific name (or parts of a name)

When you click the appropriate Search button, Prodigy presents you with a
list of personal Web pages that meet your criteria. Click on the name you
want to view that particular page.

That was easy, wasn't it? Prodigy's personal Web pages are a great way to
find other Prodigy members—and find out about them!

Q&A *How come when I select a person's page, I got this
strange screen that says it's an Index?*

Sometimes when a member deletes his or her Web page, Prodigy doesn't
get it removed from the main list in a prompt manner. So when you click
on the link to that page, there's no page there to go to. Instead, you're
presented with a brief view of the guts of Prodigy's computer—to be precise,
the contents (empty) of the directory where the Web page in question *used
to reside*. Ignore this, and hit the Back button on Prodigy's Web browser to
return to the previous screen. (Note: If you click on Parent Directory, you'll
just be taken to the next highest directory on Prodigy's computer.)

An HTML primer

If you're interested in learning more about HTML, there are lots of places to turn. There is a raft of online help available—much of it from Prodigy, and most of it right on the Web itself!

- **Beginner's Guide to URLs (http:// www.ncsa.uiuc.edu/demoweb/url- primer.html)**, a guide to Web addresses from the folks at NCSA—where the first Web browser was created

- **Composing Good HTML (http:// www.willamette.edu/html- composition/strict-html.html)**, a solid guide to HTML from a graduate student at Carnegie Mellon University

- **Crash Course on Writing Documents for the Web (http://www.ziff.com/ ~eamonn/crash_course.html)**, a good guide to Web page creation from the folks at *PC Week Labs*

- **Do's and Don'ts of Web Style (http:// millkern.com/do-dont.html)**, some handy pointers for novice Web page designers

- **Elements of HTML Style (http:// bookweb.cwis.uci.edu:8042/Staff/ StyleGuide.html)**, a takeoff on Strunk & White's *Elements of Style*, applied to Web pages

- **HTML Scratchpad™ Quick Reference (http://pages.prodigy.com/ pwpquickref.html)**, with handy information on how to create HTML code with

Prodigy's Web Page Creator—without having to write the code yourself!

- **HTML Tutorial (http:// pages.prodigy.com/ pwphtmlhelp.html)**, a short online introduction to HTML from Prodigy

- **Macmillan's HTML Workshop (http:// www.mcp.com/general/workshop/)**, a great guide to HTML from the folks who publish Que books

- **Personal Web Page Guidelines (http://pages.prodigy.com/ pwpguidelines.html)**, where you can find out what Prodigy does and doesn't allow on their Web pages

- **Personal Web Page Product News (http://pages.prodigy.com/ pwpnews.html)**, where you can learn about the latest features—and discover the latest bugs—in Prodigy's Web Page Creator

- **Personal Web Pages FAQ (http:// pages.prodigy.com/pwpfaq.html)**, a list of "frequently asked questions" about creating Prodigy personal Web pages

- **Prodigy Internet Support Bulletin Board (Jump:internet support)**, with several sections devoted to Prodigy's personal Web pages

- **prodigy.web.author.tools** newsgroup (Jump:**newsgroups**), which discusses Prodigy's Web Page Creator software

- **prodigy.web.pages** newsgroup (Jump:**newsgroups**), with general discussions about Prodigy's personal Web pages

If this isn't enough, I recommend a few good books on the subject: Que's *Special Edition Using HTML* and Sams.net's *Teach Yourself Web Publishing with HTML*. Both of these are fine books that lead you from Web page basics to advanced HTML coding.

15

Downloading Files with FTP and Gopher

● **In this chapter:**

- ● **Why would I want to download files?**

- ● **How do I find the files I want?**

- ● **How do I use FTP to download files?**

- ● **How can Gopher help me find a specific file?**

With FTP and Gopher, you can find all the information you need—and download it to your personal computer. . . . . . ➤

One of the key attractions of the Internet is the sheer volume of information stored out there—*somewhere*. To find this information—and to download it to your computer—you need to master two file retrieval mechanisms, called FTP and Gopher. Fortunately, you can use Prodigy's Web browser to do both of these activities.

How information is stored on the Net

Information is key to staying on top of things. You have a lot of information stored on your personal computer. That information—all of it—is stored in a series of computer files. You have hundreds, maybe even *thousands*, of these files on your hard disk. You have word processing files, and spreadsheet files, and database files, and graphics files. Every type of information you use is stored in some sort of file.

Information on the Internet is stored the same way—in files. So if you want to locate specific information—whether you're looking for tax advice, a legal brief, a travel guide, or a picture of the hottest supermodel—you need to look for the right file.

Because the Internet is nothing more than a collection of hundreds of thousands of separate computers, that one file you're looking for could be on *any* of those computers. That file could be on a computer connected to the Prodigy network, or on a computer at a university in Hong Kong. You don't know *where* it is, all you know is that you need it.

Given the size of the Internet, then, how do you find the file you're looking for? And how do you download it to your computer after you find it?

Two important file tools: FTP and Gopher

Prodigy offers two ways to find and download files from the Internet: FTP and Gopher. Each does a similar job, but in different ways.

FTP (which stands for **f**ile **t**ransfer **p**rotocol) is probably the quickest way to download files. You tell it which file you want (the exact file name and extension) and where that file is (the precise computer site and directory on that computer), and FTP automatically downloads the file to your PC.

With **Gopher**, on the other hand, you don't need to know the exact file name. All you have to do is connect to a specific computer site on the Net, and then use Gopher to search all the files on that site in a very organized fashion.

So, when should you use FTP and when should you use Gopher?

- If you know an exact file name and location, use **FTP**.

- If you know which site contains the file you need, but you don't know the name of the file, use **Gopher**.

Using the Prodigy Web browser for FTP and Gopher

If you had a separate Internet connection via an Internet service provider, you'd probably want to use separate FTP and Gopher software. With Prodigy's Internet service, however, you use the same tool for both FTP and Gopher—and that tool is Prodigy's Web browser.

You get to Prodigy's Web browser (Jump:**www**) by clicking on the Communications button on Prodigy's Highlight screen, and then clicking on the Internet Forum button, and then clicking on the World Wide Web button. You now see the main World Wide Web screen.

You're probably tempted to click on the FTP/Gopher button to launch the browser, but this only gives you some introductory information about FTP and Gopher. Instead, click on the Browse the Web to launch the browser.

Basic browser use was discussed back in chapter 13; turn back if you need to brush up on your skills. Otherwise, read on and I'll show you how to use the browser for FTP and Gopher searches.

A typical FTP session

Using the browser for FTP is as simple as typing in the proper URL. When you want to go to an FTP site, you have to start the URL with **ftp://**, followed by the address of the site.

For example, let's say you want to go to Macmillan Computer Publishing's FTP site. (MCP is the parent company of Que, the publisher of this book.)

This site's address is **ftp.mcp.com**, so you enter the following URL in the Document URL field:

ftp://ftp.mcp.com

When you press Enter, the browser automatically goes to this site and loads the first level of the FTP directory, as shown in figure 15.1.

Fig. 15.1
MCP's FTP site.

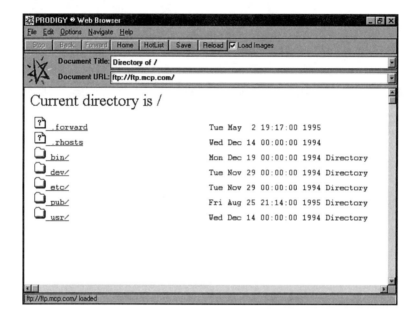

Let's say you're looking for a file with the file name pkunzip.exe, and it's located in the /pub/que/net-cd subdirectory. From the top level directory shown in figure 15.1, you need to first click on the pub directory, and when the contents of that directory are displayed, click on the que directory, and when the contents of that directory are displayed, click on the net-cd directory.

 TIP **You can avoid all this clicking to move from directory to directory** by simply typing the entire directory path as part of the URL. In this example, you'd enter **ftp://ftp.mcp.com/pub/que/net-cd/**.

When the contents of that directory are displayed, click on the pkunzip.exe file. You'll get a message that says There is no viewer available for this item. Do you want to retrieve it anyway? Answer Yes, and you'll see another message—this one stating No viewer is available for this object type. Do you want to save this object to disk? Answer Yes again, and you'll be prompted for a file name and directory (on your hard disk) for this file. Give the file a name and a directory, click OK, and the file will be downloaded to your computer.

 TIP **Most sites have an "Up one level" link, which you can click on to** return to a higher level in the directory tree.

Some types of files—like text files—will automatically display when you click on them in the browser. If this happens, just click on the browser's Save button to save the file to your hard disk.

 TIP **Most directories have a "readme" file that you can click on to get** more information about the contents of that directory.

As you can see, this is fairly straightforward when you know the file name and the directory it's located in. If you don't know this information, however, you can click around all day at an FTP site and never get anything accomplished. It's times like this that you need Prodigy's other file tool—Gopher.

 TIP **A complete list of FTP sites is maintained at the University of** Illinois (**http://hoohoo.ncsa.uiuc.edu:80/ftp-interface.html**).

A typical Gopher session

Using Prodigy's Web browser for a Gopher search is a lot like using it for FTP. After you launch the browser, all you have to do is enter the proper URL for the Gopher site you want to access. Make sure you start the URL with **gopher://**, followed by the address of the site.

Let's search the Gopher server at the University of Illinois for some information about computer file compression. The address for this server is **gopher.uiuc.edu**, so you enter the following URL in the Document URL field:

gopher://gopher.uiuc.edu

When you press Enter, the browser automatically accesses the top level of UIUC's Gopher directory. As you can see in figure 15.2, this Gopher directory is a lot more user-friendly than the FTP directory we looked at earlier. You see that the University has arranged its files in several very logical *folders*; you click on the folder to see what's inside.

Because we're interested in computer information, click on the Computer Documentation, Software, and Information folder. When the contents of this folder are displayed, scroll down the list and click on **Frequently Asked Questions on the Network**.

Fig. 15.2

The top level of the Gopher server at the University of Illinois—click on any folder to see what's inside.

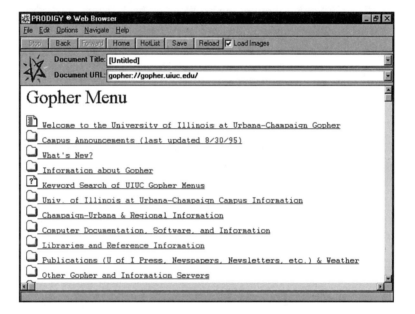

66 Plain English, please!

Frequently asked questions lists (also known as **FAQs**) are files on many Internet sites that answer common questions for new users. FAQs are great places to find essential information about a topic. **99**

When the contents of this file are displayed, you see even more folders for different topics. But if you scroll down a little, you see a file (note how the icon looks different from the folder icon) titled File Compression. Click on this to display the file on your screen.

Because this is a text file, it's automatically displayed on-screen. (If this were another type of file, you'd be prompted for downloading information at this point.) If you want to download this text file to your PC, just click on the Web browser's Save button. You'll be prompted for a file name and directory for the file; click OK to begin the downloading.

As you can see, using Gopher to find information you're only vaguely familiar with is fairly easy—a lot easier, in fact, than trying to use FTP for the same chore. Of course, if you did know the file's name and location, FTP is actually a lot *faster* than Gopher in just downloading a single file. The key is to use the right tool at the right time—and you'll be able to find and retrieve files to your heart's content!

For a listing of popular FTP and Gopher sites, see chapter 23, "Keeping Computer Literate."

 TIP **If you want to search through FTP and Gopher sites, you can use** a search engine called Archie; one of the best Archie services is at Rutgers University (**http://www-ns.rutgers.edu/htbin/archie**).

Protect against deadly viruses

Anytime you download an executable program file from any other computer, you run the risk of also downloading a computer virus. **Viruses** are programs that attach to other programs—*not* to graphics files or documents, by the way—and do damage to your computer system when you run the infected file. Viruses are real, and they're really dangerous to the health of your computer system.

Whereas commercial online services like Prodigy scan all the files for viruses they make available for downloading, this isn't the case with files you download from the Internet. Because the Internet isn't really run by any one entity, there are no guarantees about the safety of any file you find anywhere on the Net.

Now, if you're downloading files from a major Net site—like a big U.S. university or major

corporation—you're probably okay, since these organizations tend to police the files put on their servers. But if you're downloading from a site you've never been to—or heard of—before, who knows where those files have been?

The best protection is prevention. Practice "safe computing" and use an antivirus program to scan for viruses on all files you download from the Net. Microsoft Anti-Virus or Norton Antivirus are both good programs, and they work. (Note that Windows 95 doesn't come with any built-in antivirus program; you'll need to purchase a third-party program if you're a Windows 95 user.)

When it comes to the safety of your computer system, it pays to be a little bit paranoid.

Part IV: Using Prodigy for News, Weather, and Sports

16

Reading the Daily News

● **In this chapter:**

- **What kind of news does Prodigy offer?**

- **How can I browse today's headlines?**

- **Prodigy is your Associated Press connection**

- **Where can I find more in-depth news analysis?**

- **Viewing news photographs on Prodigy**

- **What news sources are available on the Internet?**

Whether you want in-depth reporting or just the headlines,
Prodigy has the right news for you. . . . . **>**

f Prodigy is like an electronic small town, complete with shops and clubs, then you'd expect to find a street-corner newsstand somewhere on Main Street. Indeed, Prodigy offers a selection of news via its own online newsstand, all at the click of a button.

All the news that's fit to view

Prodigy is designed to fulfill all your online needs; one of those needs is the need for news. In fact, Prodigy takes news so seriously that it generally puts the day's leading story right on its Highlights page. (If you want to read this lead story, just click on its associated button.)

Prodigy offers a wide variety of news services to suit your individual news needs. With Prodigy you can do everything from skimming today's headlines to perusing in-depth news analysis. In fact, you can even *talk about the news* with other Prodigy users!

It's easy to get to Prodigy's news services. Just click the News/Weather hyperlink on the Highlights page, or Jump:**news**. Figure 16.1 shows you Prodigy's main news screen. (Note that Prodigy's News screen also includes weather information, which I talk about in the next chapter.)

Fig. 16.1
Prodigy's main News screen.

Prodigy's headline news

If all you want to do is read the headlines, you don't have to go any further than Prodigy's main News screen (Jump:**news**); important stories are head-lined right on this main page.

All you have to do to read a story is click on the headline in the headline list. The story then appears in a scrolling window below the headline list. (Note that the time and date the story was filed appears at the top of the story.)

Get briefed on the major news—quickly

Quick News (Jump:**quick news**) is a feature provided by Associated Press, separate from the AP Online section discussed later in this chapter. With Quick News you get kind of a "news wire" approach to the news—that is, you read one long multiple-page article that contains several brief news stories. It is compiled from stories on the Associated Press news wire by the staff of AP Online.

AP updates Quick News hourly, so you always have a half dozen or so of the hour's hottest stories. In fact, you can also read briefs of the hottest Sports and Business news by clicking on the Quick Sports and Quick Business buttons.

 TIP **If you're looking for news about a specific topic, use Prodigy's** Search function. Make sure you're in the Prodigy News section (anywhere will do), and then pull down the <u>S</u>earch menu and select either <u>Q</u>uick Search or <u>P</u>ower Search. Enter the word(s) you're looking for, and begin your search.

Get the complete world view from Associated Press

Headline news and Quick News are fine if you just want to skim the top of the news, but what if you want to see what's happening beyond page one?

When you want to see the *whole* newspaper—not just the front page—you can turn to **AP Online** (Jump:**ap online**). This service, compiled by the folks at Associated Press, brings you news articles in a variety of categories.

TIP   **In addition to AP News, you can find several complete online** newspapers on Prodigy. Just Jump:**newspapers** to select from a variety of regional newspapers online. See chapter 19, "Browsing Online Newspapers and Magazines," for more information.

Get an in-depth perspective on the news

If you like your news in large, satisfying pieces—rather than short, bite-sized chunks—then **News Perspective** is for you. This is the part of Prodigy news where you can sit down and absorb all the details behind the headlines, kind of like the *New York Times* of online news.

To access these longer stories, just Jump:**news perspective**. You'll see a listing of articles; most of these articles are several screens long, providing ample space for in-depth coverage of the issue at hand.

TIP   **To print out a copy of the news story you're currently reading,** select File, Print from Prodigy's pull-down menu. In some cases you'll be asked whether you want to print the current PAGE, the complete STORY, or to CANCEL. If asked, select your option; if not, select OK to print a copy of the information you selected.

More news than you'll know what to do with

If you're looking for more than just the regular news, Prodigy has a variety of specialty news services. By that I mean entertainment news, business news, people news, health news, etc.—news that goes beyond today's headlines.

You can find a lot of this other news by clicking on the More News button from the main News screen. On any given day you'll find news grouped under categories like Business News, Health/Science News, Lotteries, People News, and Political Profile. Under any given category you'll find a ton of light news articles, photos, polls, and other "softer" news.

See it happen with news photos

Many news stories on Prodigy are accompanied by one or more news photos. (This is the case when you see a Photo button appear on the same screen as a news article.)

For your viewing pleasure, Prodigy lists all news photos in their own separate section. Just click on the Photos button from the main News screen (or Jump:**photos**), and you'll see a listing of current news photos. (At the bottom of the list is a button for an Index of Past News Photos; click here to see photos from days previous.)

 TIP **Photos sometimes take a long time to display on your computer.** If you want to stop a photo from displaying, just click on the close button in the upper-left corner of the photo window.

If you want to save a photo in a file on your PC, you have to take what Prodigy calls a snapshot. It's a six-step process that goes like this:

1 Display the photo you want to save.

2 Pull down the Edit menu and select Snapshot.

3 When the Snapshot dialog box appears, elect to take a snapshot of the Area Only and click OK. (If you select Whole Screen, you'll get all the text that goes with the photo, too.)

4 Your cursor will change shape from the normal arrow to a cross. Position your cursor at the top left corner of the photo, and then click and hold the left mouse button while you drag the cursor to the bottom right corner of the photo. You'll see a box appear around the area you've selected, and when the box is correct, you can release the mouse button.

5 When the next dialog box appears (also called Snapshot), choose to send the snapshot to File and click OK. (You can also choose to print the snapshot, but—as Prodigy warns—this can take a long time, and might not look too hot.)

6 When the Save As dialog box appears, give the file a name (ending with the extension .BMP) and select the directory to save the file in. Click OK when you're done, and you've saved the photo to a bitmap file on your hard disk!

TIP **You can also view up-to-date political cartoons with Prodigy's** NewsToons (Jump:**newstoons**). This displays a screen with today's current cartoons; click on the associated button to view a specific cartoon.

Talk about the news with other users

If reading the news isn't enough, you can use Prodigy's News bulletin board to talk about the news with other users. When you Jump:**news bb**, you're taken to the News bulletin board. On any given day you'll find hundreds of notes on dozens of topics. Pick the topic(s) you like, and get ready to rant and rave away!

(See chapter 7 for more details on using Prodigy bulletin boards.)

TIP **Click on the Polls button (or Jump:polls) to partake in—and view** the results of—popular opinion polls.

TIP **In addition to these news services, Prodigy also offers the PR** Newswire (jump:**pr newswire**), which lets you view up to 90 days worth of press releases on over 40 different industries and subjects.

Finding news on the Internet

If the news available on Prodigy isn't enough for you, you can venture out onto the Internet for even more news headlines and stories.

Reading news-related newsgroups

There are hundreds of USENET newsgroups (Jump:**usenet**) devoted to news. The best of these are from ClariNet, a semi-official organization that posts news articles to the Internet. Look for any newsgroup that starts **clari.***, such as **clari.biz.economy** (business and economic news) or **clari.news.europe** (European news). You can even find ClariNet news on a state-by-state basis (**clari.local.*** groups)!

Getting your news from the Web

The World Wide Web offers several news services that rival anything you find on Prodigy itself. Just start up Prodigy's Web browser (Jump:**www**) and tour these interesting sites:

- **ClariNet** (**http://www.clarinet.com/**), a Web page that lets you access all the news in the ClariNet newsgroups

- **Commercial News Services on the Internet** (**http://www.jou.ufl.edu/commres/webjou.htm**), a large listing of major news services on the Web—a good place to start looking for news-oriented sites

- **Newspaper Association of America** (**http://www.infi.net./naa/**), includes a massive listing of Internet-based newspapers

- **The Electronic Newsstand** (**http://www.enews.com/**), a site with articles from—and links to—a variety of major newspapers and magazines

- **TimesFax** (**http://nytimesfax.com/**), an eight-page news digest from *The New York Times* (registration required)

- **Trib.com** (**http://www.trib.com/**), one of the best online newspapers—includes up-to-the-minute Associated Press news

- **USA Today Online** (**http://www.usatoday.com/**), an online version of the popular news daily

- **Yahoo's News Index** (**http://www.yahoo.com/News/**), perhaps the best place to start when you're looking for news on the Web—this page lists hundreds of online news sources by type of news

 TIP Some of these are commercial Web sites that may require payment for full access.

In addition to these sites, don't forget to check out Prodigy's News Web browser page (**http://antares.prodigy.com/news.htm**) for more news-related sites, newsgroups, and Chat rooms.

 TIP   **Jump:newsstand to see a list of electronic newspapers and** magazines available on Prodigy and the Internet.

17

Forecasting Today's Weather

● **In this chapter:**

● **What weather services does Prodigy offer?**

● **View the nation's weather from Prodigy's national weather map**

● **How do I get my local weather forecast?**

● **Create your own personal travel weather forecast**

● **Is Prodigy always the best source for weather information?**

● **What weather resources are available on the Internet?**

Don't be stuck out in the rain—stay warm and dry with the latest maps and forecasts from Prodigy's online weather service . . . . ▶

You're getting ready to go out for the afternoon, and you don't know whether to wear a light jacket, a raincoat, or just a sweater. You need the latest weather forecast, but it's hours until the next TV newscast—and the forecast in your morning paper is notoriously unreliable. What to do? Turn to Prodigy for your up-to-the-minute weather needs!

How to get the latest weather info on Prodigy

There's no way, in my opinion, that an online weather service can replace those colorful TV weather people who "swoop" over their weather maps, introduce you to the winner of the local Miss Pumpkin Rind contest, and stand outside in the pouring rain *just to prove* that it really *is* raining in your fair city. Even without the presence of an electronic Willard Scott, however, Prodigy does offer a nice selection of fairly reliable and current weather forecasts that you might find useful.

To get to Prodigy's Weather services, Jump:**weather**. You'll see the list of weather services shown in figure 17.1.

Fig. 17.1
Choose from this list of Prodigy's weather services.

As you can see, you have the option of viewing weather maps, the specific forecast for any major U.S. city, weather info for a complete region, or forecasts for major international cities. Clicking on any option takes you to that specific weather information.

Reading the big map

You're familiar with the big national weather maps you see on TV, the kind the weatherperson stands in front of while pointing at big symbols representing high pressure systems and cold fronts and the like. Prodigy actually offers *three* of these types of maps for your viewing pleasure!

When you select the US Weather Map option from Prodigy's Weather list (Jump:**weather maps**), you're shown a map that represents tomorrow's forecast weather, nationwide. You can use this map to get an idea of what kind of weather to expect across the nation.

As you can see in figure 17.2, this map shows forecast temperatures, areas of rain and snow, sunshine and cloudiness, etc. It's just like the weather maps you see on TV, and it's prepared by the Accu-Weather service (the same service used by many local TV weather teams).

Fig. 17.2
Get the big picture forecast from Prodigy's national weather maps.

When you click on the next page button on Prodigy's tool bar, the map changes to a "scientific" forecast. This map shows cold fronts, warm fronts, the flow of the jet stream, areas of low and high barometric pressure, and even the *levels* of barometric pressure.

TIP   **If you know your way around the meteorological world, you can** figure out how to predict weather by observing the movement of weather fronts and areas of high and low pressure.

Finally, you can view a forecast map for the day after tomorrow by clicking on the next page button a second time.

Getting your local forecast

Okay, the national map is interesting, but it doesn't tell you if it's going to rain where you are today. For that, you need to access Prodigy's forecast for your specific city.

Prodigy lists weather forecasts for more than 200 separate localities. To get the forecast for your city, just select US City Forecasts from the Weather menu (Jump:**us city**). You'll see a listing of cities, in alphabetical order. You can use the next page button to move through the entire list, or type the first few letters of your city name and then press Enter to move (in the list) directly to your city.

When your city's name is selected, just click on its button and Prodigy will display the current forecast. The forecast is updated hourly, and includes temperature, current conditions, sunrise/sunset times, and the forecast for the remainder of the day.

TIP   **You can access the forecast for an entire region by clicking on the** Map button on the local forecast screen, or by choosing a particular region from the Weather menu. The first screen you'll see is tomorrow's forecast map; use the next page button to view daily forecasts for the region.

Q&A   *Why isn't my city listed?*

There may be several reasons for this. First, if you select City Index from one of the regional map screens, you'll only see the cities included in that region; if you click on the Weather button and select US City Forecasts you'll see the entire list of U.S. cities. Second, Prodigy only lists the major cities in the U.S.; you may live in a smaller city or town that isn't included in the list. If this is the case, select the nearest city to your location.

Finding a forecast for another city

If you're getting ready to travel, you may find it useful to look up the weather in your destination city. Depending on where you're going, you look up non-local weather in the following ways:

- If you're visiting a specific U.S. city, go to the Weather menu, select US City Forecasts (Jump:**us city**), and search for the city's name.

- If you're visiting a general area in the U.S., go to the Weather menu and select the region you'll be visiting.

- If you're visiting a Canadian city, Jump:**canada weather** and select the city or region from the list.

- If you're visiting any other foreign city, go to the weather menu, select Int'l Weather (Jump:**internat'l weather**), and select the city or region from the list.

 TIP **The forecasts for foreign cities are often not as detailed as those** for U.S. cities.

Finding weather info on the Internet

If Prodigy doesn't offer enough weather information for you, check out these sites on the World Wide Web (Jump:**www**) for some amazingly comprehensive weather forecasts and maps:

- **The Daily Planet (http://wx3.atmos.uiuc.edu/)**, a weather service from UIUC's Department of Atmospheric Sciences

- **The Weather Channel (http://www.infi.net/weather/)**, the online version of the popular cable channel, complete with up-to-date forecasts and maps, as well as educational material—this is, without a doubt, the premiere weather-related site on the Web

- **WXP Weather Processor (http://thunder.atms.purdue.edu/)**, a solid Web-based weather resource, based at Purdue University

- **Yahoo's Meteorology List** (**http://www.yahoo.com/Science/ Earth_Sciences/Meteorology/**), a complete list of over a hundred different weather-related Web sites

Frankly, I'd give these Web-based weather sites an edge over Prodigy's normal weather service. They're all a bit more comprehensive than what you can get on Prodigy—and easily accessible via Prodigy's Web browser!

18

Reporting the Latest Sports

● In this chapter:

- **Where can I find the latest scores and sports news?**

- **Get the "inside scoop" on the current sports scene**

- **Create your own personalized sports report**

- **How can Prodigy help me with my Rotisserie sports teams?**

- **Online sports you can play**

- **What online sports services are available on the Internet?**

Prodigy and ESPN come together to offer one of the most complete sources of sports scores and reporting available anywhere! . . . . ●>

I f you're a sports fan, you want a reliable source for all your sports information. You want the latest scores, info on upcoming games, and some in-depth analysis of what's actually going on in your favorite sport. Well, you can find all that—and more—on Prodigy!

Catch all the sports on Prodigy

Prodigy does a great job reporting the latest sports news because it relies on ESPN (that's right, the cable sports people) and the Associated Press to provide most of its sports services. The sports reporting on Prodigy is of a particularly high quality, going well beyond the box office stats to give you a complete picture of the complex world of sports.

When you Jump:**sports** you see Prodigy's main Sports screen (see fig. 18.1). This screen contains both major stories and access to all the other sports services on Prodigy.

Fig. 18.1
Prodigy's main Sports screen.

Read the latest sports news

Prodigy offers a variety of sports-related news. Check out the following services:

- **AP Online Sports** (Jump:**ap sports**), the official sports line from Associated Press.

- **International Sports** (Jump: **international sports**), ESPN news on International sporting events.

- **Quick Sports** (Jump:**quick sports**) SportsTicker's "newswire" approach to major sporting news; a half-dozen or so stories are included in one long, scrolling article.

- **Sports News** (Jump:**sports news**) ESPN's full sports report.

- **Sports Perspective** (Jump:**sports perspective**), for in-depth sports analysis.

Of these options, I tend to prefer Sports News. This section lists the major headlines, and serves as a gateway to even more news stories.

 TIP   For in-depth football analysis, Jump:football talk.

Get the scores and the schedules

Prodigy also provides sports scores and team schedules. When you Jump:**scores**, you see a list of various college and professional sports. Pick the sport you're interested in, and Prodigy presents a screen full of up-to-the-minute scores. When you click on the button next to the score, you get a detailed report from the game.

To see a list of scheduled games and events, Jump:**sports schedule**. You see a list of schedules for college and professional basketball, baseball, football, golf, and tennis. Click on the sport you're interested in, and ESPNet displays a schedule of upcoming games, complete with times and team records.

 Q&A   *Is there any way to jump directly to a score for a specific team?*

Yes, if you know exactly what to type. Prodigy includes JumpWords for many major professional sports teams. For example, you can Jump directly to New York Knicks scores with Jump:**knicks**. Note, however, that not all teams or sports are listed—and this service is for pro teams only, not college teams.

Get the inside scoop

If you want to go behind the headlines, ESPNet offers Inside Info. When you click on the ESPN Inside Info button on the main Sports screen (Jump:**espn inside**), you're taken to the Inside Info screen. From here you can read the stories behind the headlines by clicking on the appropriate hypertext links.

TIP **For more inside info, follow the latest business transactions and** trades in the world of sports. Just click on the Transactions button on the main Sports screen, or Jump:**sports transactions**.

Follow your favorite sport

You know, all the various sports options available on Prodigy can get a little overwhelming. If you tend to follow only a single sport, you might prefer to get all the info on that sport in one place, with a single button click.

Fortunately, Prodigy can handle that.

When you're on Prodigy's main Sports screen, click on the More About Sports hyperlink. When the dialog box appears, click on the Features button to see a list of sports; click on the sport you're interested in.

TIP **You can find excellent football info through Prodigy's online** version of the Dallas Morning News' Pro Football Report (Jump:**dmn**). See chapter 19, "Browsing Online Newspapers and Magazines," for more information.

Since I tend to follow basketball and auto racing exclusively, I find this option quicker than sorting through all the other sports reports available on Prodigy.

Create your own personalized sports report

What if you don't want to mess with all these different sports reports and options—what if you just want info on your favorite teams, nothing more, nothing less?

Prodigy's Sports Track service is designed just for you. **Sports Track** gives you info on your favorite teams—without wading through all the other sports drek available. Just click on the Sports Track button on the main Sports screen, or Jump:**sports track.**

With Sports Track you can choose to track up to 24 teams from the following sports, depending on the season:

- NBA
- NFL
- Major League Baseball
- NHL
- College football
- College basketball

Figure 18.2 shows you what a typical Sports Track screen looks like. Basically, all you see are the scores for the teams you've selected; click on the button by the score to see details from the game.

To add or delete teams to or from your list, click on the Personalize button. When the next screen appears, click the Add button to add new teams. If you want to delete a team, click on the team's button and then click the Delete button. When you're done with your list, click the Save button and return to the main Sports Track menu.

 TIP   *Sports Track tracks a team's scores **and** schedule.*

Fig. 18.2
The main Sports Track screen shows you the scores for your favorite teams. Click the Personalize button to add or delete teams from your personal list.

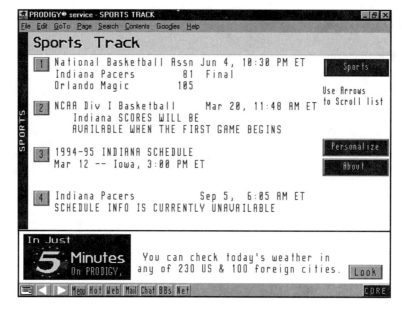

I think Sports Track is great. It lets me follow my favorite teams with a minimum of fuss and muss.

Coach your private Rotisserie team with Player Track

If you're into Rotisserie football or baseball, you'll love Prodigy's Player Track service. **Player Track** lets you keep a personal stat pool of players; you can easily add, drop, or trade players, and Player Track will do all the work for you.

You get to Player Track (Jump:**player**) by clicking on the Player Track button on the main Sports screen. Once you're on the Player Track screen, you need to click on the right button for your current sport—Baseball Track or Football Track. You can view your current player roster by clicking on the Player Track button.

For complete instructions on using Player Track, click on the How To button.

To add a new player, click on the Edit button, and then on the Add button. Select the conference and position you're interested in, and Player Track gives you a list of available players. Click on the player you want, and it is automatically added to your online team.

To delete a player, just highlight the player's name on your list by clicking on the small gray box next to the player's name. Click on the Edit button, then on Delete; this automatically deletes the player from your list.

You need to define the date range for the stats in your Player Track. To do this, click on Customize and then Track Period. You can choose either Cumulative for the entire season thus far, or Weekly tracking.

 TIP If you want to work with the data in your Player Track in your own word processor or spreadsheet program, you can download your player list to a file on your computer. Click on the Download button to save your stats as a text file somewhere on your hard disk.

This ends up being a little bit of work, but after you have it set up it's the best way I've found to keep track of all the players on your Rotisserie teams.

Talk about sports with other fans

Prodigy offers several sports bulletin boards where you can exchange online messages with other fans. When you click on the Sports BBs button on the main Sports screen, you see the list of available BBs:

- **Auto Racing BB** (Jump:**auto racing bb**) for coverage of all types of racing

- **Baseball BB** (Jump:**baseball bb**) for baseball fans

- **NFL BB** (Jump:**nfl bb**) for NFL fan action

- **Sports BB** (Jump:**sports bb**) for general sports talk

- **Sports Play BB** (Jump:**sports play**) for talk about participatory sports

- **Trading Cards BB** (Jump:**trading cards**) for talk about sports cards

TIP **As I write this section, Prodigy is adding new BBs for Football,** Basketball, and Hockey. Watch the Highlights screen for announcements about these and other new sports-oriented BBs!

I talk about Prodigy's bulletin boards in more detail in chapter 9.

Sports on the Internet

While it's tough to beat Prodigy's ESPNet sports coverage, there are a few Sports-related newsgroups and Web sites you might want to visit.

In terms of newsgroups (Jump:**usenet**), check out those newsgroups in the **alt.sports.*** area. There are dozens of groups here—including groups for most professional baseball and basketball teams! There are also a lot of sports groups in the **rec.sport.*** area (mainly devoted to recreational sports), and in the **clari.sports.*** groups.

On the Web (Jump:**www**), look for these sites:

- **ClariNet (http://www.clarinet.com/)**, a Web page that lets you access all the news in the ClariNet newsgroups

- **ESPNet SportsZone (http://espnet.sportszone.com/)**, absolutely the most comprehensive, most in-depth, and just plain *best* sports site on the Web, put together by the same folks who do most of Prodigy's sports services (see fig. 22.6)

- **Fox World Sports (http://www.foxnetwork.com/sports/ index.html)**, the online home for sports from the Fox network

- **Grandstand Sports Services (http://www.gstand.com/)**, one of the newer all-purpose sports sites

- **Guide to the 1996 Olympic Games (http:// www.atlanta.olympic.org/)**, the official online introduction to the upcoming Olympics in Atlanta

- **NandO X Sports Server (http://www2.nando.net/SportServer/)**, with tons of online sports scores and stories

- **NBC Sports Online** (**http://www.nbc.com/sports/index.html**), the online home for NBC Sports

- **SportsLine** (**http://www.sportsline.com/**), a good all-purpose sports site

- **SportsWorld** (**http://sportsworld.line.com/**), real-time sports scores and information

- **t@p online sports** (**http://www.taponline.com/tap/sports.html**), more online sports scores and stories

- **World Wide Web of Sports** (**http://www.tns.lcs.mit.edu/cgi-bin/ sports/**), a list of links to other sports-related sites

- **Yahoo Sports Listing** (**http://www.yahoo.com/text/Recreation/ Sports/**), a great master list of hundreds of sports-related Web sites

Of course, you also want to check out Prodigy's Sports Interest Group on the Web, at **http://antares.prodigy.com/in10coi.htm#spor**. This page links to Web pages that cover specific sports, from auto racing to wrestling. Each of these sports-specific pages feature dozens of links to resources for their respective sports.

Prodigy also has a separate Sports Web browser page at **http:// antares.prodigy.com/sports.htm**. Between all these pages—and the two main ESPNet resources—Prodigy has you covered, sports-wise!

19
Browsing Online Newspapers and Magazines

● In this chapter:

- What is an online publication like?

- What online newspapers and maga-zines does Prodigy offer?

- Which online publications are right for me?

- What kinds of online newspapers and magazines can you find on the Internet?

Forget ink-stained fingers when you read your favorite news-papers and magazines online with Prodigy . . . . ➤

n the last three chapters I told you about Prodigy's various news, weather, and sports services. If you combine these three types of services, you get something that more or less resembles an online newspaper or magazine—only it's a little disjointed and uncoordinated and is probably missing some important stuff. Wouldn't it be nice to have a real, honest-to-goodness newspaper or magazine online, without having to bounce around a half-dozen different Prodigy services?

Prodigy puts the printed page on your PC

Well folks, I'm one step ahead of you on this one. Prodigy offers a variety of newspapers and magazines in electronic form that you can read right on your computer screen. This way you can get your news *immediately*, without having to wait on normal delivery. Some of these online periodicals also offer additional features over and above their print cousins, such as more in-depth analysis or the ability to provide instant feedback.

So, what is an online publication like? First off, it's not *entirely* like a regular newspaper or magazine. For example, it doesn't include every article or photograph you find in the full-text version. For that matter, the articles are in no certain order; it's entirely *nonlinear*. And, of course, you have to read it on your screen, not in your hands.

To me, reading an online periodical is kind of like the *highlights* of a normal newspaper or magazine. You get the top stories and the top photographs, and you can read them in any order you want. And, in many cases, you get to read them *before* they hit the newsstands or your mailbox.

 TIP **You can also use e-mail to easily post letters-to-the-editor for** most major newspapers and magazines. This provides very rapid response to the publications, and these e-mail letters quite often get published in the print versions of the periodicals.

Prodigy is adding new online publications every month. As I write this, the following online newspapers and magazines are available:

Table 19.1   Prodigy's Online newspapers and magazines

Publication	JumpWord
Access Atlanta (Journal-Constitution)	**access atlanta**
Advertising Age Online	**ad age online**
American Heritage	**american heritage**
Consumer Reports	**consumer reports**
Dallas Morning News' Pro Football Report	**dmn**
Kiplinger's Personal Finance Magazine	**kiplinger**
Los Angeles Times TimesLink	**timeslink**
Mac Home Journal	**mac home**
Multimedia World	**multimedia world**
On Wisconsin (Milwaukee Journal Sentinel)	**on wisconsin**
Newsday Direct	**newsday**
Newsweek Interactive	**newsweek**
PC World Online	**pcworld**
Playbill Online	**playbill**
Sports Illustrated for Kids	**si kids**
Tampa Bay Online	**tampa bay online**

You can find an up-to-date list of online publications available both on Prodigy and on the Internet by clicking on the Newsstand hyperlink on the main highlights page. Alternately, you can Jump:**newsstand**.

Notice that several of these online publications are *not* part of Prodigy's free services. That is, some of them cost you money to read. I'll point these out to you in the sections that follow.

TIP **You can print many of the articles in these online publications by** clicking on the Print button in Prodigy's tool bar. You may be asked whether you want to print the current page or the entire article; choose the method you want, and print away! (In many cases only the text of the article is printed; most online periodicals won't allow you to print their graphics.)

Delivering an online newspaper

Prodigy offers several different online newspapers. All are pretty neat and end up being quite different from their print versions. (All, except Newsday Direct, also cost money—$4.95/month per paper, on average, which is cheaper than reading the printed versions!)

Q&A *When I type a JumpWord from some online publications I can't get to the service I want. What am I doing wrong?*

All of these online newspapers are separate (but related) services from Prodigy. As such, when you type a JumpWord from within these services, you can only jump to services *within the publication*. To jump back to Prodigy, make sure you click the Prodigy button in the JumpWord dialog box—*not* the normal OK button!

Put Georgia on your mind with Access Atlanta

Access Atlanta (Jump:**access atlanta**) is an online version of the *Atlanta Journal-Constitution*. It was the first newspaper in the world to present an online edition.

Learn to love L.A. with *Los Angeles Times'* TimesLink

For residents of Southern California, the *Los Angeles Times* is often the newspaper of note. TimesLink (Jump:**timeslink**) is the electronic version of the *Times*, offering just about everything you get in the regular paper, along with a little bit more.

East Coast news with Newsday Direct

If you like your news with a New York flavor, Newsday Direct (Jump:**newsday**) is for you. In addition to the normal national news stories, you'll find all the local news, weather, and sports. (In fact, this is *the* spot for Knicks, Rangers, Yankees, and Mets fans.) You'll even find borough-by-borough reports, and all of Newsday's normal columnists. While it's not as classy as the *New York Times*, it is a little bit of New York online. Newsday Direct is also one of the few *free* online newspapers on Prodigy—which makes it one heck of a deal!

 TIP **When you first subscribe to Newsday Online, you can choose** between a New York or a New Jersey front page!

Electronic news from the Sunshine State: Tampa Bay Online

I've already talked about online newspapers for residents of California, Georgia, and New York. Well, this is another one, this time for people living in the Tampa Bay area.

Tampa Bay Online (Jump:**tampa bay online**) is an electronic version of the *Tampa Tribune,* and features most everything from the regular newspaper. Included are local news, sports, and weather; a Baylife section for area goings-on; and an online version of the classified ads.

Pick the pros with the *Dallas Morning News'* Pro Football Report

There's one source of pro football news talked about the world over—the Pro Football Report from the *Dallas Morning News.* Now that report is online, so you can get your pigskin predictions via your computer screen.

The online version of the Football Report (Jump:**dmn**) includes both general pro ball stories and reports specific to the Dallas Cowboys. As such, it's an invaluable service for any pro football fan.

On Wisconsin—Prodigy's newest online newspaper

Prodigy's latest addition to their lineup of online newspapers is the online version of the *Milwaukee Journal Sentinel*, called On Wisconsin (Jump:**on wisconsin**). Like the other online newspapers, On Wisconsin offers all the basic parts of a regular newspaper, plus numerous extras—including several regional specialty papers. See figure 19.1 to see what a state-of-the-art online newspaper looks like.

Fig. 19.1
Prodigy's newest online newspaper—On Wisconsin.

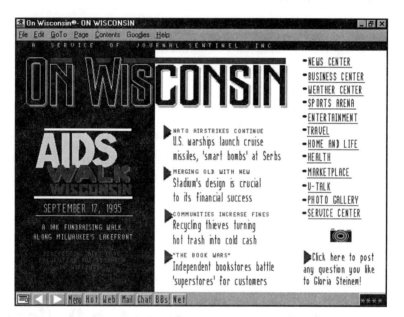

Flip through the pages of an online magazine

In addition to these electronic newspapers, Prodigy also offers a variety of online magazines. The quality and content of these vary wildly; you probably ought to evaluate each one separately to see whether or not you like it.

My favorite online magazine: Newsweek Interactive

Why do I like Newsweek Interactive (Jump:**newsweek**) so much? Maybe it's because it pretty much has the whole magazine (except for most of the photos) online. Maybe it's because it *looks so good* on-screen (complete with the full cover on the main screen, as shown in fig. 19.2). Maybe it's because I can read it online on Sunday evening, several days before I get my real copy in my office. Maybe it's because it has a few online extras not found in the hard copy version. Or maybe it's just because I'm a big fan of *Newsweek* anyway because of its superior coverage of computers and other technology.

Fig. 19.2

The best online magazine of them all, Newsweek Interactive.

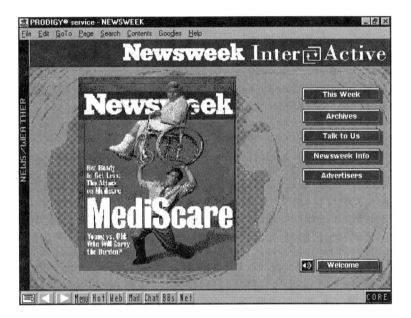

Whatever the case, I urge you to check this one out. I think Newsweek Interactive represents what all online magazines ought to be.

Get your media news electronically with Advertising Age Online

With Advertising Age Online (Jump:**ad age online**), advertising professionals can get their industry news right from their computer screen, in most cases *before* the normal version hits their desks. Since this is an industry magazine, however, it is a little pricey. (I wouldn't advise subscribing to this one unless you're pretty serious about the advertising industry!)

CAUTION **Advertising Age Online is *not* a free service. Your first two hours a month are at no charge, but after that it costs $4.80/*hour*. (That's right, almost a fin an hour!)**

Rate your goods online with *Consumer Reports*

Consumer Reports is a long-respected magazine that rates various consumer products. (It's a great way to determine the relative merits of two competing products—is the lowest price always the best deal?)

Consumer Reports' online version (Jump:**consumer reports**) includes most of the current and past reports from the magazine. It's actually a little easier to look them up in electronic form than it is to rifle through back issues in your basement (or in the library)!

Invest like the best with *Kiplinger's Personal Finance Magazine*

Kiplinger's Personal Finance Magazine is a great source for investing and financial planning advice. The online version (Jump:**kiplinger**) presents many of the most important articles from the magazine, past and present, as well as additional information useful for the personal investor.

A great online magazine for computer users: PC World Online

Prodigy's newest online magazine is an electronic version of *PC World*. PC World Online (Jump:**pcworld**) offers a new look for Prodigy's online magazines, with lots of hypertext links, like what you find on the World Wide Web.

In fact, most of PC World Online is actually out on the Web! When you click on the Home Page button, Prodigy automatically launches its Web browser and connects to PC World's Web site (see fig. 19.3). Clicking on the other buttons takes you to PC World's Prodigy-based bulletin board and Chat room, launches Prodigy's newsreader so you can read PC World-related USENET newsgroups, and even lets you subscribe to the printed version of *PC World*, right online.

This blending of Prodigy and Internet services is something you're going to be seeing more of. PC World Online is a good place to catch a glimpse of this interrelated future!

Fig. 19.3
PC World Online really isn't on Prodigy—it's at PC World's Web site!

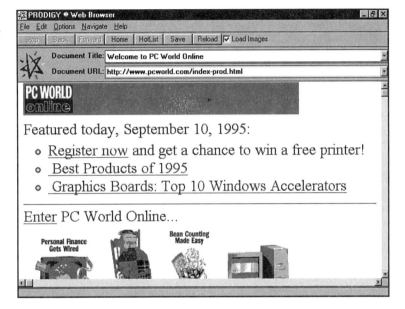

For the Apple core and more: Mac Home Journal Online

The online version of the *Mac Home Journal* is a really good resource for all of Prodigy's Macintosh users. It features all the major articles from the magazine, as well as back issues and a bulletin board. If you're a Mac user, you'll like this one.

Get your entertainment tonight with Playbill Online

Playbill is the famous New York magazine dedicated to live theatre. Now with Playbill Online (Jump:**playbill**) you don't have to go to Broadway to read about your favorite plays and musicals.

Playbill Online covers live theatre around the world, with dedicated sections for Broadway, Off-Broadway, London, Regional theater, and National Tours. There's even a bulletin board to discuss your favorite plays with other aficionados!

Online fun for young sports: *Sports Illustrated for Kids*

The online version of *Sports Illustrated for Kids* (Jump:**si kids**) has many of the features from the regular magazine, as well as some special Prodigy-only sections. In particular, take a look at the Ask the Athlete and Pro & Con Debate sections, exclusive to this online version.

If your kids are online and into sports, steer them to SI for Kids—you won't go wrong!

Finding newspapers and magazines on the Internet

The World Wide Web is a great medium for online magazines. It's graphical, hyperlinked (to related articles or services), and capable of being constantly updated.

Because of this, there are a ton of online magazines on the Web. Here's just a short list of magazine-related resources on the Web.

- **Electronic Newsstand (http://www.enews.com/)**, a great resource to dozens of online magazines and newspapers

- **Enterzone (http://enterzone.berkeley.edu/enterzone.html)**, an online magazine available *only* on the Web!

- **MecklerWeb (http://www.mecklerweb.com/)**, home of *InternetWorld* and *VRWorld* magazines

- **Mother Jones (http://www.mojones.com/)**, an online version of the controversial magazine of exposés and politics

- **Netsurfer Communications (http://www.netsurf.com/)**, a company that produces a series of what they call "E-Zines" on the Net

- **Newspaper Association of America** (**http://www.infi.net/naa/**), a massive listing of all online newspapers

- **Popular Mechanics** (**http://popularmechanics.com/**), where you can enter their online magazine called *PM Zone*

- **TechWeb** (**http://techweb.mcp.com/**), the online home of various CMP publications, including *Communications Week, Computer Reseller News, Computer Retail Week, Electronic Buyers' News, Electronic Engineering Times, HomePC, Informatiques Magazine, InformationWeek, Interactive Age, NetGuide, Network Computing, OEM Magazine, VAR Business*, and *Windows Magazine*

- **Time Warner Pathfinder** (**http://www.pathfinder.com/pathfinder/ welcome.html**), the "megasite" with links to various online Time Warner magazines, including *Time, Life, Money, Fortune, Sports Illustrated, Entertainment Weekly*, and *People*

- **ZD Net** (**http://www.ziff.com:8009/**), home of *PC Week, PC/ Computing, Computer Shopper, MacUser, MacWeek, Computer Life, Interactive Week, Computer Gaming World*, and *Windows Sources* magazines

Between Prodigy's newspaper and magazine resources and those on the Web, you have a lot of online reading to do!

TIP *Living Digital* **is a Web-based electronic magazine that covers a** variety of computer and technical-related topics. To get there, start up Prodigy's Web browser (Jump:**www**) and go to **http:// antares.prodigy.com/web/livedigi/ldhome.htm**.

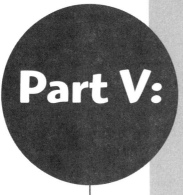

Part V: Using Prodigy for Work

20

Retrieving Financial Information

● In this chapter:

● **What financial services does Prodigy offer?**

● **Track the portfolio performance**

● **Where can I find business news on Prodigy?**

● **Find out more about a specific company**

● **Is online investing for me?**

● **What financial resources are available on the Internet?**

Whether you just dabble in the stock market or make your living from it, Prodigy has a wide variety of financial services to cover all your investment needs . . . . ❯

Do you own any stocks? Do you follow the stock market on a daily basis? Do you read your newspaper's financial pages occasionally—or religiously?

If you answered yes to any of these questions, you're in for a treat. Prodigy offers a wide variety of financial services designed to give you the financial news you need—whether you're an occasional investor or a stock market pro.

About Prodigy's financial services

Prodigy's financial services run the gamut from simple retrieval of stock quotes to complete online investing. In fact, Prodigy's range of financial services is so broad that I can't cover all of them in-depth in this chapter; I'll simply try to point out the *best* services for various types of investors.

Let's start by examining the types of financial services offered by Prodigy. Table 20.1 lays it out for you.

Table 20.1   A sampling of Prodigy's financial services

Type of service	Service name	JumpWord
Stocks/investments	Quote Check	quote check
	Quote Track	quote track
	Stock at a Glance	stock at a glance
	Tradeline Performance History	price history
	Economic Indicators	economic
Business news	Quick Business News	quick business
	Headline Business News	business news
	CNBC Market News	cnbc
	Wall Street Edge	wall street
	Julian Block on Taxes	block on taxes
	Brendan Boyd's Money List	money list
	Brendan Boyd's Investment Digest	investment digest
	Robert Heady on Banking	heady on banking
Financial research	Company News	company news
	Company Reports	company reports
	Strategic Investor	strategic investor
	Stock Hunter	stock hunter
	Mutual Fund Analyst	mutual fund analyst

Type of service	Service name	JumpWord
Online trading	PC Financial Network	**pcfn**
	Bull & Bear	**bull & bear**
	Dreyfus Investment Center	**dreyfus**
	Fidelity Online Investment Center	**fidelity**
	The Kaufman Fund	**kaufman**
	Scudder	**scudder**
	Wells Fargo Online	**stagecoach**
Bulletin boards	Money Talk	**money talk**
	Your Business	**your business**

You can access most of these services by clicking on the Business/Finance hyperlink on Prodigy's Highlights screen. This takes you to the screen shown in figure 20.1, where you can read today's business news highlights or move to any of the other sections shown at the right of the screen.

Fig. 20.1
Prodigy's main Business/Finance screen—the best place to start for financial information.

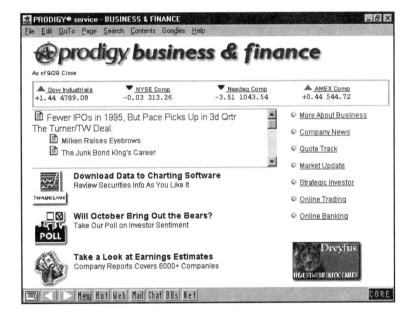

As you'll find once you get into this, many of Prodigy's business/financial services are interrelated. For example, while you're checking on today's performance of your favorite stock, you can click on a button to see a chart of the stock's performance over time, to see a news brief about that company, or to download a copy of the company's most recent company report—without having to type a JumpWord to go to that particular service.

TIP **While you *can* type a JumpWord to go directly to a specific** service, if you're only interested about a single stock, the automatic linking of services pertaining to that stock is a lot easier than retyping the stock symbol and starting from scratch every time you jump around.

You'll also find that many of these services are available at a charge above and beyond your normal Prodigy usage rates. I'll try to mention current pricing as I go along, but always check your on-screen messages for the most up-to-date pricing information.

TIP **If you don't know a bear from a bull, check out Prodigy's** Investor's Glossary (Jump:**investor's glossary**), an online dictionary of finance and investment terms.

Keeping track with stock quotes and charts

Retrieving stock quotes is a must for most investors. You want to find out how a particular stock or group of stocks is doing. Is your stock up or down? Did the market rise or fall today? What's the trend of your stock portfolio?

Prodigy offers several services that provide you with this information.

Seeing stock performance at a glance

Prodigy's newest stock service is called Stock at a Glance (Jump:**stock at a glance**), and it offers—not surprisingly—a single-screen glance at any stock. As you can see in figure 20.2, you get the latest stock price, its performance over the past week, a brief report on company financials, and the latest headline news about the company. You can click on any of the buttons to see more detailed information.

Fig. 20.2
All most people want
to know—Stock at a
Glance report.

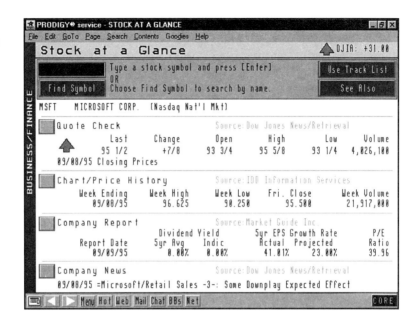

Retrieving stock quotes

If you just want to retrieve a simple stock quote, use Prodigy's Quote Check
service (Jump:**quote check**). Quote Check shows you the latest price of a
given stock, along with the day's high and low prices and trading volume. In
addition, you can quickly access the following services for the selected stock:

- Get a summary of the latest news about the company by clicking on the
  Company News button.

- View a copy of the latest company report by clicking on the Report
  button.

- Display a chart of the stock's historical performance by clicking on the
  Chart button.

To look up a quote, all you have to do is type the stock symbol in the box in
the upper-right corner and then press Enter. If you don't know the symbol for
a particular stock, click on the Find Symbol button and Prodigy will help you
find it.

TIP **You can print a copy of the current quote by selecting File, Print** from Prodigy's pull-down menu. You can also download a copy of this quote to your hard disk by clicking on the Download button. (You have the choice of downloading the data in TXT, WKS, comma-delimited, or Quicken formats—in case you want to work with the data in another program, such as 1-2-3 or Quicken.)

If you want to track the performance of your entire portfolio, use Prodigy's Quote Track service (Jump:**quote track**). This service lets you enter a variety of stocks, the number of shares you own, and what you paid—and then tracks them over time.

Looking at long-term trends

To evaluate the performance of a stock long-term, it helps to view the stock's pricing data in chart form. To do this, use the Tradeline Performance History service (Jump:**price history**).

It's easy to view the performance of a specific stock with Tradeline. Just click on the View a Chart button, and you'll be prompted for the stock's symbol (or the name of a mutual fund). Type the symbol in the box and press Enter; Tradeline will display a chart with pricing for a twelve-month period (including daily highs and lows), and trading volume for the stock on a weekly basis.

CAUTION **It costs 50 cents to view a Tradeline chart. (The fee is 25 cents if** you're a member of the Strategic Investor service [Jump:**strategic investor**]).

In addition to viewing charts for specific stocks, you can use Tradeline to display a list of top performing stocks in various categories. (Just click on the Top Performers button to see the list of categories.) When the list of stocks is displayed, click on any stock to see its Trendline chart.

TIP **You can't print any of these charts, but you can download the** data behind the chart. When you click on the Download Data button, you're prompted to download various views of this data—for a fee, ranging up to $5 per report.

Getting smarter with Prodigy's business and financial news

Prodigy offers a wide variety of business and financial news services. Whether you want brief headlines or detailed analysis, there should be something there to suit your needs!

If all you want is the important headlines, Jump:**business news** to get Prodigy's Headline Business News. You'll see a half dozen or so of the day's most important headlines; click on the number button by the headline to read the entire story. (You can also use this screen to jump to more detailed International Business News, Company News, and other financial news services.)

On the other hand, if you want to read a quick "news wire" of the most important stories, Jump:**quick business.** This presents you with a single article, containing a dozen or so news briefs in paragraph form from the Associated Press.

Finally, take a look at Wall Street Edge (Jump:**wall street**). This is a unique online digest, published every business day, with news from the best financial newsletters, hotlines, and 900-number advisory services. Each online issue of Wall Street Edge will set you back $1.95, or you can subscribe for $19.95 per month.

 TIP   **If you'd like a personalized news report, including news only on** those topics you select, check out the Heads Up service (Jump:**heads up**). This service lets you select up to ten different topics you want covered, for $29.95/month, and then sends you a customized news report via Prodigy on a daily basis.

Doing financial research online

If you want to make smart investments, you need to do some research before you invest. Prodigy offers several different financial research services; I'll tell you a little about the best of the bunch.

Read the latest news about specific companies

The Dow Jones News/Retrieval Service has created a huge database of stories about companies and industries. You can find out a lot about a specific company or industry by pulling articles from this database.

To access the Company News service, Jump:**company news**. Now enter the symbol for the company you're interested in (or go through a slightly longer search by clicking on one of the category buttons—Company Name, Industry News, Market News, or news from the *Wall Street Journal* and Barron's), enter a date range for applicable stories, and press Enter. Company News then presents all the stories for that company or category in the specified date range, one at a time on your screen. You can print or download any or all of these stories or choose to begin a new search.

View a detailed company report

Even more important than recent news about a particular company is financial information about that company. Prodigy supplies this information via its Company Reports service.

After you Jump:**company reports**, you're presented with the main Company Reports screen. From this screen there are various ways to look up the company you're looking for:

- Enter the company's stock symbol (or look it up if you don't know it)
- Use Stock Hunter (discussed in a few paragraphs) to list a group of stocks that meet a specific criteria
- Look for companies based on industry, dividend yield, five-year EPS growth, or P/E ratio
- Use stocks listed on your Quote Track list (discussed earlier in this chapter)

After you narrow your choices down to a single company, press Enter and select either a Quick Report (1-5 pages) or a Full Report (up to 12 pages). You can choose to print or download the report or just read it on your screen.

CAUTION   **These reports are NOT free! Regular Prodigy members will pay** $1.95 for each Quick Report, and $3.95 for each Full Report. If you're a Strategic Investor subscriber, your first 50 reports in any given week are free; after that, you pay $2.95 for each additional Full Report. (And that, my friends, is one of the primary reasons to subscribe to the Strategic Investor service!)

In most cases the Quick Report is adequate, and in some cases it's all that's available. A Quick Report is actually a subset of a Full Report, which generally includes full income statements for the selected company.

Pick your stocks with Stock Hunter

If you need help in deciding where to invest, check out Prodigy's Stock Hunter service (Jump:**stock hunter**). Stock Hunter analyzes the recent performance of a broad range of stocks to find those that meet the criteria you select.

After you select your criteria, you are presented with a list of stocks. When you select a stock from this list, you can view that stock's Company Report, described earlier in this chapter.

CAUTION   **Stock Hunter is a part of the Strategic Investor service** (Jump:**strategic investor**), which offers a fairly broad range of professional investment services for $14.95 a month. If you don't subscribe to Strategic Investor, you can access Stock Hunter for $1.95 per day.

TIP   **Prodigy offers a similar service to help you pick the right mutual fund for your portfolio. Jump:**mutual fund analyst** takes you to the Mutual Fund Analyst, which costs you $5.95 per day—or it's free if you're a Strategic Investor subscriber.

Going all the way with Prodigy: Online investing

So far we've done just about everything you can do, financial-wise, short of buying and selling stocks. Well, believe it or not, you can actually use Prodigy to make your investments online!

The PC Financial Network (Jump:**pcfn**) is a complete online brokerage service that you use with your own personal computer. A service of the Pershing Division of Donaldson, Lufkin & Jenrette Securities Corporation, the PC Financial Network executes more than one million trades a year. Numerous services are offered, including the trading and purchasing of stocks, options, money market funds, mutual funds, CDs and bonds, and IRAs. Commissions vary as to the type of account you open and the volume of the transaction.

In addition to handling your financial transactions, the PC Financial Network offers members additional online financial information. You can view details on your trading history, as well as the performance of your portfolio.

You open an account by clicking on the Open Account Now button. You can apply online or request a brochure and form to apply by return mail.

 TIP   You can trade war stories with other online investors in Prodigy's Money Talk bulletin board (Jump:**money talk**).

Is online investing for you?

With all the wealth of financial information available on Prodigy, should you take the plunge and become an online investor?

Let's look at the pros and cons:

- **Pros:** It's fairly inexpensive, and it's easy to do. And you can get a lot—really, just *tons*—of good financial information via Prodigy's numerous financial services.

- **Cons:** You don't get any professional investment advice online—which means you're on your own, bunky. And, whether you're a new or an experienced investor, you probably need more advice than what you can get online.

My advice is to use Prodigy's financial services—all the stock quotes, trends, news articles, and reports—to help you make your financial decisions. But, unless you're an experienced but casual investor—and totally comfortable with your own decisions—you probably want to go to a traditional brokerage firm for your actual financial transactions.

In other words, go it on your own with the PC Financial Network at your own risk!

Finding financial info on the Internet

There aren't that many USENET newsgroups (Jump:**usenet**) devoted to financial/investment topics. The groups to try are the **misc.invest.*** groups, the **clari.biz.finance.*** groups, and the **clari.biz.invest** group.

The best place to look for financial information and services, however, is on the World Wide Web. So start up Prodigy's Web browser (Jump:**www**) and take a look at these financial-oriented Web sites:

- **American Stock Exchange (http://www.amex.com/)**, contains information on and news about all listed companies

- **Canada Net Pages (http://www.visions.com/)**, the most comprehensive resource for Canadian business and financial data

- **Experimental Stock Market Charts (http://www.ai.mit.edu/stocks/graphs.html)**, price and volume performance charts on 400 major stocks

- **Financial Information Link Library (http://www.mbnet.ca:80/~russell/)**, a list of links to financial sites around the world, grouped by country

- **FinanCenter (http://www.financenter.com/resources/)**, an online personal finance resource center that helps you evaluate borrowing and investing options and includes glossaries, statistics, concise how-to reports, and advice from professional loan counselors. A recommended site

- *Financial Times* **(http://www.usa.ft.com/** in the U.S., or **http://www.ft.com/** in the U.K.), an online version of the venerable British newspaper, including news summaries and lots of financial information

- **Hoover's Online (http://www.hoovers.com/)**, a great source for company-specific information

- **LEXIS-NEXIS (http://www.lexis-nexis.com/)**, one of the premier sources for corporate information

- **Mortgage Strategies (http://www.ais.net:80/netmall/mortgage/mortgage.html)**, an online report on how to save on your mortgage interest

- **NETworth (http://networth.galt.com/)**, from GALT Technologies, Inc., with in-depth information on over 5,000 mutual funds

- **New York Stock Exchange (http://www.cob.ohio-state.edu/dept/fin/nyse.html)**, a third-party resource to the NYSE, including a TAQ database that lists all trades and quotes

- **PC Quote (http://ds9.spacecom.com/Participants/pcquote/)**, real-time securities quotations and news

- **Quote.Com (http://www.quote.com/)**, providing financial market data, such as current quotes on stocks, commodity futures, mutual funds, and bonds—as well as business news, market analysis, and commentary

- **Security APL Quote Server (http://pawws.secapl.com/cgi-bin/qs)**, from the PAWWS Financial Network, providing a variety of online quotes, charts, and financial information

- **Wall Street Direct (http://www.cts.com/~wallst/)**, an online financial "superstore"

- ***Wall Street Journal* on the Web (http://www.wsj.com/)**, with lots of WSJ offerings, including the continually-updated Money & Investing Update

- **Wall Street Net. (http://www.netresource.com/wsn/)**, a site designed primarily for issuers and investment banks, nonetheless includes a lot of information on issues relating to corporate debt and equity financings

That enough for you? If not, don't forget to check out Prodigy's Investing and Finance Resources Interest Group on the Web, at **http://antares.prodigy. com/invsting.htm**. Here you'll find a lot of links to stock and investing resources across the Net and on Prodigy proper.

Doing Business on Prodigy

● **In this chapter:**

● **How can Prodigy help me run my small business?**

● **Where can I find essential business forms and documents?**

● **Does Prodigy offer good business advice?**

● **Can I use Prodigy to talk to other business people like me?**

● **Are there any small business resources available on the Internet?**

Use Prodigy to help you grow your small business into a large one. . . . . **>**

Prodigy was designed primarily as an online service for home PC users. But many home users also run small businesses from their home. To serve the needs of these small and home businesses, Prodigy has added a wealth of useful services—which I tell you about in this chapter!

Let Prodigy help you with your small business needs

Most of the Prodigy services of interest to small businesspeople can be found by using Jump:**prodigy for business**. The main Prodigy for Business screen, shown in figure 21.1, provides access to services that help you:

Fig. 21.1
Prodigy for Business: The starting point for your small business needs.

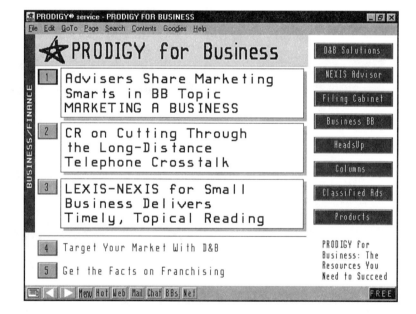

- Research and market your business with **D&B Solutions**
- Obtain useful information from the **NEXIS Advisor**
- Download essential reports and forms from the **Filing Cabinet**
- Create a customized news report with **HeadsUp**

- Get good advice from business experts in online business **Columns**

- Place and respond to classified ads via Prodigy **Classified Ads**

- Talk to other businesspeople in the **Business BB**

Market to other businesses with D&B Solutions

If your business involves marketing to other businesses, it's essential for you to uncover information about your potential business customers. (At the very least you need their addresses and phone numbers!) One of the best ways to get detailed information about specific companies is through **D&B Solutions** (Jump:**d&b**).

 Plain English, please!

Dun & Bradstreet is one of the world's largest companies providing financial information on large companies. D&B has been gathering information since 1841 and is respected the world over.

D&B Solutions is a part of the larger Dun & Bradstreet Information Services. Essentially, what you get is access to a large database of company information—on companies both public and private. D&B charges by the report; it's $2.50/each for your first 10 complete reports, and the per-report fee drops on larger quantities. (The smaller "contact" reports cost less—starting at 60 cents each.) In addition, you'll be charged 25 cents per minute if you don't order any reports.

When you find a company you're interested in, you can select to view either a Complete Report or a Contact Plus Report. A Complete Report is just that—a lot of business info, including revenues, number of employees, etc. A Contact Plus Report looks kind of like a Rolodex card, with just the company name, address, phone number, and name of the top executive. Contact Plus Reports are good for assembling sales leads; Complete Reports are better for determining the financial health and other details about a company.

To read your report, you'll need to start up some sort of text editor and load the file. Windows WordPad, Notepad, or Write work fine, but any word processor will do. (You'll just need to make sure your word processor knows it's opening a text file with a TXT extension.)

Q&A   ***Why can't I find the company report on my hard disk?***

It's probably there. Unless you specified otherwise, D&B Solutions saved the file in your PRODIGY directory. The file name is probably of the format **dunsXXYY.txt**, where **XX** is the month and **YY** is the day. For example, if you downloaded a report on March 5th, the file is probably in your PRODIGY directory under the file name **duns0305.txt**.

Look in the Filing Cabinet for business essentials

When you're ready to pursue a new business opportunity, it's time to Jump:**filing** to Prodigy's Filing Cabinet. The Filing Cabinet contains two "drawers":

- **Biz Opp Reports**, a database of reports about various new business opportunities

- **Business Forms**, a database of essential business forms

Both of these services cost you money: Biz Opp Reports run anywhere from $3 to $15, and the price for Business Forms varies depending on the length of the form.

Grow your business with the Small Business Advisor

Sometimes you just don't know what to do. You're in a pickle and could use some expert advice on how to proceed. Where do you turn?

Well, one place to turn is Prodigy's **Small Business Advisor** service (Jump:**nexis**), provided by LEXIS-NEXIS Research Services. This service gives you practical advice and information that will help you run a better business.

The Small Business Advisor is an online database that provides you with more than 1,000 articles on items of interest to you and other small businesspeople. Articles are chosen from the LEXIS-NEXIS staff from publications like *Commerce Business Daily, Business Wire, Computerworld, Marketing News, Inc. Magazine,* the *Harvard Business Review,* and numerous newspapers across the nation.

Articles are saved as text files (with TXT extensions) on your hard disk. Use a text editor (like Windows Write) or word processor to view articles.

TIP **To see a preview of any article before you officially download,** click on the Preview button. This way you can determine whether or not the article is worthwhile before you have to pay for it.

Q&A *I lost my Prodigy connection during the download of an article. Do I have to pay for the article again to complete the download?*

No, if your download was interrupted, it wasn't your fault—and you don't have to pay for it. The next time you return to the Small Business Advisor, you will be prompted to continue downloading where you left off, at no additional charge.

Share your experiences with other businesspeople on the Business bulletin board

When all is said and done, however, some of the best advice you'll get is from people just like you—other Prodigy members running their own small businesses. To communicate with your fellow entrepreneurs, check out the Business/Home Office bulletin board (Jump:**business bb**).

This bulletin board features a wealth of topics of interest to independent businesspeople. On a recent visit I found a list of topics that included Business from Home, Managing a Business, Marketing a Business, Accounting/Finance/Taxes, Healthcare/Insurance, DTP/Secretarial Services, Network Marketing, and International Business. Suffice to say, this is one bulletin board you want to frequent—for the good of your business!

Finding business help on the Internet

If you want to leave the confines of Prodigy and venture off onto the Internet, you can find quite a bit more useful business information.

Business-oriented newsgroups

After you access Prodigy's newsgroup newsreader (Jump:**usenet**), the first place to look for business-oriented information is in the **biz.*** newsgroups. These groups (like **biz.comp.services**) focus on business issues—and some of them are even "sponsored" by various businesses.

There are also a few business-related groups in the **alt.business.*** section, and you can find lots of business news in the **clari.biz.*** groups.

Web sites for small businesses

Some of the most interesting business-related stuff (as usual) is out on the World Wide Web. Jump:**www** to enter the Web and start browsing for business info.

For straight business news and information, or if you're interested in putting your small business on the Internet, check out these sites:

- **AdMarket** (**http://www.AdMarket.com/**), where you can find advertising and marketing information

- **Business Information Resources** (**http://sashimi.wwa.com/~notime/eotw/business_info.html**), a good list of business resources on the Net

- **Business Resource Center** (**http://www.kciLink.com/brc/**), dedicated to helping businesses get useful information to help them grow

- **CookWare ClubWeb** (**http://www.iquest.net/cw/**), a put-you-on-the-Web firm that prides itself on providing "one-stop-shopping for all your World Wide Web needs"

- **Creative Edge** (**http://www.halcyon.com/midnight/**), an online newsletter for growing companies, large and small

- **Cross Ink** (**http://www.cts.com/browse/crossink/**), another firm specializing in setting up your business up on the Web

- **Dun & Bradstreet Information Services** (**http://www.dbisna. com/**), for all-around business information and advice

- **Entrepreneurs on the Web** (**http://sashimi.wwa.com/~notime/ eotw/EOTW.html**), a place where entrepreneurs and small businesspeople can find useful information and resources—and offer their goods and services to businesspeople

- **Free Range Media** (**http://www.freerange.com/**), a firm specializing in setting up Web servers and Web sites for other businesses. (They helped set up the Que/Macmillan Information SuperLibrary site.)

- **Home Business Solutions** (**http://netmar.com:80/mall/shops/ solution/**), with resources and tips for running a home-based business

- **IndustryNet** (**http://www.Industry.Net/**), an "online marketplace" for business resources and tools

- **Internet Advertising Corporation** (**http://www.iaco.com/**), one of several ad firms specializing in Internet-based advertising

- **Internet Business Center** (**http://www.tig.com/IBC/index.html**), with lots of information about conducting business on the Internet

- **Open Market** (**http://www.openmarket.com/**), providing business solutions, products, and services for Net-based businesses, and a comprehensive list of commercial sites on the Internet

- **SBA Online** (**http://www.sbaonline.sba.gov/**), the Small Business Administration's online presence, with lots and lots of resources (government and otherwise) for small businesses—including starting a business, financing a business, and expanding a business

- **Target Call Center** (**http://www.isisnet.com/target_call_center/**), providing professional telereception and telemarketing services for businesses

- **The Company Corporation** (**http://incorporate.com/tcc/ home.html**), where you can incorporate your business online

- **Webvertising** (TM) (**http://www.sccsi.com/welcome.html**), another Web-based advertising agency

- **Yahoo's Business Listings** (**http://www.yahoo.com/Business/**), probably the best place to start looking for business-related Web sites— a giant list of all business sites on the Web

And don't forget Prodigy's Small Business/Entrepreneurship Interest Group on the Web, at **http://antares.prodigy.com/smallbus.htm.** This page lists tons of Prodigy bulletin boards and Chat rooms, USENET newsgroups, WWW sites, and online magazines of interest to small business owners worldwide.

Between all these Web sites and the services available on Prodigy proper, you should be able to find the help you need to keep your small business running in tip-top shape!

22

Making Online Travel Plans

● **In this chapter:**

- **What kinds of travel services does Prodigy offer?**

- **How do I obtain the latest travel news?**

- **Using travel guides to help plan your trip**

- **Making airline and hotel reservations**

- **How to find even more travel information on the Internet**

*Prodigy is your one-stop online travel agency—offering
everything from travel planning to airline reservations. . . .*

Prodigy makes a darned fine travel agency. Just as a good travel agent prepares you for all aspects of a trip, so does Prodigy. From trip planning to city guides to important travel tips to actual airline and hotel reservations, Prodigy does it for you. The only thing missing are those gorgeous travel posters hanging on the wall of a real travel agency—you'll have to supply your own!

Planning the perfect trip with Prodigy

Prodigy offers just about everything you need to plan the perfect trip. You get to Prodigy's travel section (Jump:**travel**) by clicking on the Travel hyperlink on Prodigy's Highlights screen (see fig. 22.1). From this screen you can access all of Prodigy's travel services—including the Travel bulletin board.

Fig. 22.1
Prodigy's main Travel screen.

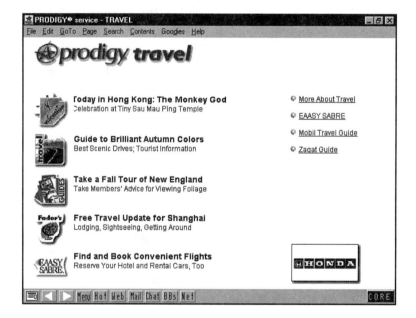

Before you go on your next trip, I recommend the following check list:

- Read up on your destination via Prodigy's City Guides (Jump:**city guide**), Regional Guides, or the Mobil Travel Guide (Jump:**mobil guide**)

- Check with fellow travelers in the Travel bulletin board (Jump:**travel bb**) to see if they have any tips for your trip

- Check the Travel Talk (Jump:**travel talk**) and Travel News (Jump:**travel news**) sections for any news or advisories regarding your destination

- Check the weather (Jump:**weather**) in your destination city

- Use EAASY SABRE (Jump:**eaasy sabre**) to make your hotel, rental car, and airline reservations

Prodigy: Your online travel guide

Every smart traveler wants to learn more about their destination—preferably *before* they get there. That way you know what kind of clothes to pack, what sort of restaurants to expect, what kinds of attractions to visit, and so on. To help the smart traveler, Prodigy offers several different types of online travel guides.

Make any city your own with Prodigy's City Guides

If you're traveling to a major U.S. city, you should check out Prodigy's City Guides (Jump:**city guide**). Prodigy has guides for Atlanta, Boston, Chicago, Dallas, Los Angeles, Miami, New York City, Philadelphia, San Francisco, and Washington, D.C.

The City Guides are comprised of information compiled from surveys of your fellow Prodigy members. The surveys (created in 1992-1993) asked members to list their favorite places to go in and around each city. The results were then written up and augmented by nationally syndicated travel journalists Elizabeth Harryman and Paul Lasley.

Wander America with Regional Guides

What if your destination city doesn't have a Prodigy City Guide? Well, the next step is to look for a Prodigy Regional Guide.

Prodigy has online guides for the following regions:

- Caribbean (Jump:**caribbean guide**)

- Florida (Jump:**florida guide**)

- Hawaii (Jump:**hawaii guide**)

- New England (Jump:**new england guide**)

The information in each of these guides is tailored to the specific region. For example, the Caribbean guide lists information about the most popular islands in the region; the Florida guide has information on spring baseball training spots, diving spots, and golfing spots. Like Prodigy's City Guides, these Regional Guides are compiled from surveys completed by your fellow Prodigy members.

Use the all-in-one Travel Guide from Mobil

Okay, you've looked through both the City Guides and the Regional Guides, and you're obviously going someplace different—and not listed. Where can you turn for travel planning advice?

Prodigy offers a very good online version of the popular Mobil Travel Guides (Jump:**mobil guide**). This guide is a premier source of information for both business and vacation travelers and includes restaurant, lodging, and other information on more than 3,300 cities and recreation areas.

Other guides to make your travel easier

Prodigy also offers a variety of specialized guides to help you better plan your next trip. Table 22.1 lists these guides:

Table 22.1 Prodigy's other travel guides

Guide	Description	JumpWord
AAA of Southern California	So. California-specific travel info	**aaa**
City of Merced	A forum for the city known as the "Gateway to Yosemite"	**merced**
The Flyer's Edge	A guide to airline frequent-flyer programs	**flyers edge**
National Parks of the American West	A guide to the West's main National Parks —including Redwood, Yellowstone, and the Grand Canyon	**national parks**
Ski Guide	A guide to major ski resorts.	**ski guide**
The Zagat Restaurant Survey	The premier guide to restaurants in 25 major U.S. cities	**zagat**

Getting there, with reservations

Now that you've planned for your trip, it's time to finalize things and make your reservations. Since Prodigy is your complete online travel agency, it's no surprise to find that you can use Prodigy to make your own airline, hotel, and rental car reservations.

Prodigy's reservations are through a service called EAASY SABRE (Jump:**eaasy sabre**). EAASY SABRE is the reservations service run by American Airlines (hence the two a's in EAASY). It lets you make your own airline, rental car, and hotel reservations—and have tickets delivered overnight via the related EAASY/QuikTix service.

CAUTION **If you have trouble jumping to this service, make sure you typed** the JumpWord correctly. It's **eaasy** (with two a's) **sabre** (with the r before the e).

Before you can use EAASY SABRE, you have to be an EAASY SABRE member. The first time you enter the EAASY SABRE area you'll be taken through the enrollment process. Enrollment is free, and you'll be assigned an EAASY SABRE number and password. Remember your password for future visits to EAASY SABRE; Prodigy automatically inserts your number for you.

Q&A **I can't remember my EAASY SABRE password. Do I have to reenroll?**

You can if you want to (EAASY SABRE doesn't prohibit multiple memberships). However, you're probably better off calling EAASY SABRE support at 1-800-331-2690 during normal working hours to get it sorted out.

TIP **The information you entered when you enrolled in EAASY SABRE** is registered as your travel profile. To change any of this information—like your address or credit card number—select Travel Profile Review from the main EAASY SABRE menu.

After you've entered your password, you're taken to the EAASY SABRE main menu. Select EASY SABRE RESERVATIONS MENU to proceed. This is where you check availability and make your reservations.

Making a flight reservation is a rather long, but not terribly complicated process. Just follow these steps:

1 From the Reservations menu, select Flight Reservations.

2 When the Flight Request screen appears (shown in fig. 22.2), enter the following information: Month and Date of the first leg of your flight; the earliest Time you want to leave (you can also leave this blank); where you're leaving From; where you're traveling To (your destination city); and the number of tickets you'll need. If you have an airline or connecting city preference, enter that information, as well (although it's okay to leave these blank). Leave everything else blank and click OK.

TIP **If you don't know the proper code for an airline or city, click on** CODES to see a list of appropriate codes.

3 EAASY SABRE will display a list of available flights, as shown in figure 22.3. Click on a flight to display more information.

4 When the flight detail screen appears (see fig. 22.3), select the desired fare (if you can figure out all those confusing fare codes!).

5 You're asked what travel profile to use. In most cases you should use your regular profile.

6 If you have a frequent flyer number, enter it on the next screen. If not, press Enter to continue.

Fig. 22.2
Enter flight details on the Flight Request screen.

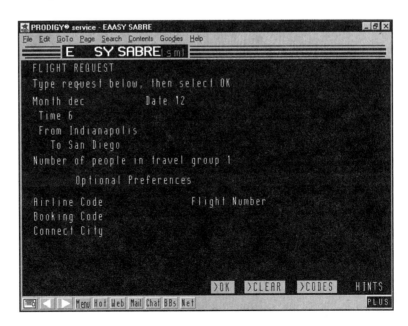

Fig. 22.3

The list of available flights.

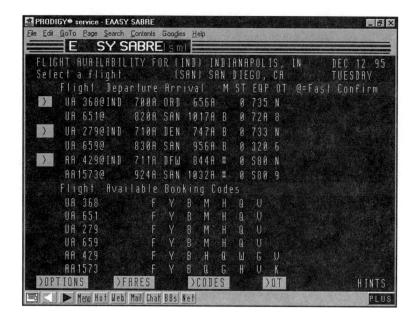

7 A confirmation screen appears. Either confirm or cancel your reservation.

8 The Continue/Complete Request screen appears. If you want to complete a round-trip reservation or add rental car or hotel reservations, do so from this screen. If your reservations are complete, select the Request is complete option.

9 If you elected to use Bargain Finder in step number 4, it now goes to work locating the lowest possible fare for your flight. You'll be presented with a list of options (lowest fare, no advance purchase, no penalty, etc.), with associated fares. Select the fare that meets your requirements.

10 A new screen appears, listing the current cost of your total trip. Select the Continue option to proceed.

11 After another interim screen, you'll be shown a detailed review of your current itinerary. From here you can add additional items, cancel your reservations, or mark it all as correct to proceed.

12 You'll now be whisked to the QuikTix screen. Use this screen to purchase your tickets online (and get them delivered the next day).

Well, that was a little involved, but certainly worth it. If you want to make hotel or rental car reservations, the procedure is fairly similar—just make sure you select either Car Reservations or Hotel Reservations from the Reservations menu.

TIP **You can check flight availability without making reservations by** selecting the Flight Schedules option. You can also check the actual arrival and departure times for any flight (assuming you know the flight number) by selecting the Departure/Arrival Status option.

Q&A *Help! I just wanted to check availability and EAASY SABRE is going ahead and booking my reservations! How do I get out of this?*

Not to worry. There are numerous stages in the process where you can cancel your reservations, up to and including the actual QuikTix purchasing process. If you miss *all* of these cancellation points, just give the EAASY SABRE help desk a call at 1-800-331-2690 to cancel your reservations by phone.

Taking Prodigy on the road

All the information in this chapter simply gets you to where you want to go. Once you get there, remember to take Prodigy along on your laptop computer. You can use Prodigy from anywhere in the United States—all you need to do is find the local dialing number for wherever you're at.

The best time to find Prodigy phone numbers is before you leave. While you're dialing from home, Jump:**phones** and select the Accessing the PRODIGY Service When You Travel option. Read the instructions and then select Find Your Best PRODIGY Access Phone Number. Enter the 3-digit area code for your destination city, and *write it down* or print it out. When done, press CANCEL—do not actually change the number at this time!

CAUTION **Again—do *not* change your access number at this time! You still** need to log on from your local number until you actually leave on your trip!

TIP   **If you don't know the area code of your destination city, look it** up in the Mobil Travel Guide (Jump:**mobil guide**).

Once you've arrived at your destination, you can change your dialing number. Before you log on, select SETUP on the sign-on screen. (If you normally use Autologon, do not use it when you want to alter your setup.) Enter your new phone number when prompted—and be sure to include the correct network code (either Q or Y) in the space provided.

Properly configured, you should have no problems using Prodigy when you're on the road. In fact, it's great for checking local weather conditions— and using the Mobil and Zagat guides for local attractions and restaurants!

Finding travel information on the Internet

Prodigy probably has all the travel information and services you need—but it's still worth checking the Internet to see if there's anything of interest there.

To begin with, there are several newsgroups (Jump:**usenet**) devoted to travel issues, including **rec.travel**, **rec.travel.air**, **rec.travel.asia**, **rec.travel.cruises**, **rec.travel.europe**, **rec.travel.marketplace**, and **rec.travel.usa-canada**. Use these to connect with other travelers with your specific interests.

Once you get on the World Wide Web (Jump:**www**), there are many Web sites of interest to anyone planning a trip. Check out the following sites:

- **AccomoDATA U.K.** (**http://www.cityscape.co.uk/users/eb19/ index.html**), a site that lets you make direct bookings with hotels, bed and breakfasts, and cottages in England, Wales, Scotland, and Ireland

- **Air Traveler's Handbook** (**http://www.cs.cmu.edu/afs/cs.cmu.edu/ user/mkant/Public/Travel/airfare.html**), a great site for air travelers, with basic info and links to lots of other air travel resources on the Net

- **Beautiful Cultural European Home Pages** (**http://s700.uminho.pt/ cult-europ.html**), with links to many European travel sites

- **City.Net** (**http://www.city.net/**), a comprehensive guide to cities around the world—lots and lots and *lots* of hotlinks!

- **GNN Travel Resource Center** (**http://gnn.com/meta/travel/ index.html**), one of the Web's premier travel-related sites

- **Subway Navigator** (**http://metro.jussieu.fr:10001/bin/cities/ english**), a unique site that displays routes in subway systems in cities around the world

- **TravelData Guide to Bed & Breakfast Inns** (**http:// www.ultranet.com/biz/inns/**), listing thousands of bed and breakfast inns across America

- **TravelSphere** (**http://www.kcom.com/travel/main.htm**), a guide to travel-related resources across the Web

- **USA CityLink Project** (**http://www.NeoSoft.com:80/citylink/**), a listing of Web pages for selected U.S. cities and states

- **Virtual Tourist II** (**http://wings.buffalo.edu/world/vt2/**), a map-based interface to City.Net—highly recommended!

- **Xerox PARC Map Viewer** (**http://pubweb.parc.xerox.com/map**), a really cool site that lets you create your own maps by "zeroing in" on the region you're interested in

And let's not forget Prodigy's Travel interest group on the Web, at **http:// antares.prodigy.com/in11coi.htm#trav**. This main travel page links to three other pages (Adventure Traveler, Air Travel Unlimited, and Travel Pleasures/Values), each of which has dozens of links to travel resources on Prodigy and across the Internet.

Prodigy also has a Travel Web Browser page at **http://antares.prodigy.com/ travel.htm**. This page lists a half-dozen additional travel-related sites on the Web.

Gee whiz—with all this travel information available, why would you want to stay home?

23

Keeping Computer Literate

● **In this chapter:**

- **Learn more about computers from Prodigy**

- **Buy the right software with help from Prodigy**

- **How can I get the latest computer-industry news?**

- **Finding answers to computer questions—online**

- **Free software available on Prodigy**

- **How can I use the Internet to find computer software?**

Prodigy is a great place to meet other computer users and find computer-related information. . . . . ❯

Because Prodigy is a service explicitly designed for computer users, it comes as no surprise that it's a good place to meet other computer users—and find lots of computer-related information. In fact, you can rely on Prodigy to service pretty much all your computer needs, from technical support to how-to advice, from computer-industry news to add-on utility software.

Stay on the leading edge with Computer News

Prodigy offers a veritable plethora (I've always wanted to use that phrase!) of computer-related news and information. In fact, the major technology news stories of the day are right on the main Computers screen (Jump:**computers**), shown in figure 23.1. Just click on the icons to read the news behind the headlines.

Fig. 23.1
Prodigy's main
Computers screen.

Most of the main news stories are actually out on the World Wide Web as part of Prodigy's Web-based computer magazine, *Living Digital.* When you click on the news icons you automatically launch Prodigy's Web browser, which goes directly to the *Living Digital* pages.

For more news—without having to venture onto the Web—check out these Prodigy-based computer news services:

- **PC News** (Jump:**pc news**), a half-dozen or so short daily computer-related news stories

- **PC Previews** (Jump:**pc previews**), John Edwards' regular daily columns previewing upcoming computer products

- **PC Trends** (Jump:**pc trends**), weekly columns from John Edwards (he's everywhere!) about trends in the PC industry; this is a good place for some rare hard data

- **Software Chart** (Jump:**software chart**), for listings of the best-selling software in various categories

Learn something from the computer experts

While you get Prodigy's computer news from one expert (John Edwards), there are other experts online, too. Prodigy offers the following online columns:

- **Larry Magid on PCs** (Jump:**magid**), three columns a week on new software products, from the renowned *Los Angeles Times* computer columnist

- **Steve Rosenthal on Macs** (Jump:**rosenthal**), two columns a week about Macintosh-related issues, from the respected author and computer columnist

- **Steve Rosenthal on Multimedia** (Jump:**multimedia**), two columns a week about multimedia software and hardware, from the same guy who writes the Mac column

Get help from other users on the computer bulletin boards

Prodigy offers numerous bulletin boards targeted to computer users. These are all good places to get computer-related questions answered and problems solved.

Among the most popular computer-related bulletin boards are:

Table 23.1   Computer-related bulletin boards

Bulletin Board	Description	JumpWord
AST BB	For users of AST-brand PCs	**ast bb**
COMPAQ BB	For users of COMPAQ-brand PCs	**compaq bb**
Computer BB	The big, main computer bulletin board for all computer users	**computer bb**
Gateway 2000 BB	For users of Gateway-brand PCs	**gateway bb**
Hardware Support BB	For any PC users with hardware-related problems; the following vendors have their own areas on this board: Acer America, Dell Computer, GVC, Leading Edge, Pionex, Quantex Microsystems, Reveal, and VTech	**hardware bb**
IBM Club BB	For users of IBM-brand PCs	**ibm club bb**
IBM OS/2 Club BB	For users of the IBM OS/2 operating system	**os/2 club bb**
Intuit Financial BB	For users of Intuit's Quicken and QuickBooks software	**intuit financial bb**
Intuit Tax BB	For users of Intuit's TurboTax and MacInTax software	**intuit tax bb**
Reveal BB	For users of Reveal's hardware products	**reveal bb**
Software Support BB	For PC users with software-related problems	**software support**
Westwood BB	For users of Westwood's PC games	**westwood bb**

Look before you make the software leap: Home Office Computing's Software Guide

Where do you go for advice if you're thinking of buying new software? You want to know if it's any good, if it will run on your machine, and if it's suitable for your tasks. Where can you find this information? On Prodigy, that's where.

Prodigy offers an online software guide from *Home Office Computing* magazine (Jump:**software guide**). This online guide provides reviews of major software products from 1988 to the present. You can search for software by title or by specified criteria, or you can list all titles or just new titles.

Keep your hardware and software up-and-running with online computer support

Okay, you're having some trouble with your computer system. Your hardware is on the fritz, or your software is acting buggy—or both. Where do you turn?

Well, if you have enough of your system left to get online, you can turn to Prodigy's Product Support area. Here is where you'll find official technical support from major hardware and software companies.

Jump:**computer support** to go directly to the Computer Support Center. From the main screen, click on the HW/SW Support button, and you'll see a list of categories.

Choose from one of the categories to list all appropriate products, or simply select Support by Name. When you choose this top option, you see a complete listing of computer-related companies present on Prodigy.

 CAUTION   **If the company you want isn't listed, you're out of luck...sorry!** (And some of the biggies—like Microsoft and Lotus—aren't listed. Shame on them!)

When you select a company, you're either taken to a special product support area or to the company's bulletin board. For example, Gateway 2000 sends you to their bulletin board, but AST Computer sends you to a special product support area they call AST On-Line, custom-tailored for PC user technical support.

A cheap way to get more software

You've probably heard your friends talking about how they found some neat new software program recently. Online. For free.

Well, you have access to all that free online software, too. When you Jump:**downloads** you see a list of places on Prodigy that offer things to download.

While the Internet is the best place to find lots of free software (see the section later in this chapter), you can find software for downloading right on Prodigy. Prodigy's software resource is called the Utility Downloads section (Jump:**utility**). When you click on the Library button, you're shown a long list of special utilities that you can use to enhance Prodigy's operation.

 CAUTION **Whenever you're downloading files, you should take precautions** to avoid contracting a computer virus. The best thing to do is run a commercial virus protection program, such as Norton Anti-Virus. Note, however, that Prodigy runs all of its files through four different virus scans, including scanning software by Symantec, McAfee, IBM, and Central Point. Only after passing all four scans is a new file made available for downloading.

Downloading one of these programs is a snap—just follow these simple steps:

1 Click on the button next to the file you want to download.

2 When the description screen appears, click on the Download button.

3 When the Download window appears, select the directory you want to hold the downloaded file, and then click on the BEGIN DOWNLOAD button.

4 The download begins; Prodigy notifies you when it is complete.

Magazines, files, and more: ZDNet on Prodigy

There is a whole other service linked to Prodigy that includes its own bulletin boards and file areas. That service is called ZDNet, and it's run by the same folks who bring you *PC Magazine, PC Week, MacWeek,* and *PC Computing* magazines. (I should also note that Macmillan Computer Publishing—the parent company of Que—also publishes books under the Ziff-Davis Press imprint.)

Jump:**ziffnet** to enter ZDNet. (It used to be called ZiffNet, and still uses that JumpWord.) ZDNet requires its own membership (which is the Enroll in ZDNet or Custom Choice option), or you can browse via the ZDNet Selections option.

ZDNet's membership fees are above and beyond the normal Prodigy fees. You'll pay $3.50 per month to download ZDNet software.

As you can see in the figure, ZDNet offers a variety of computer-related services. You'll find everything from product reviews to lots and lots of software files prime for downloading.

Is ZDNet worth it? Well, yes, but only if you download a *lot* of files. Otherwise, you can probably find what you need either on Prodigy or on the Internet.

But don't let me influence you unduly. Select the ZDNet Selections options, take a free twirl, and make up your own mind.

ZDNet's main screen.

Find more computer software on the Internet

While all the computer information on Prodigy is impressive, it's a drop in the bucket compared to the virtual sea of information available on what some people call the Information Superhighway—the Internet.

One of the key attractions of the Internet is the sheer volume of information stored out there—*somewhere*. To find this information—and to download it to your computer—you need to use Prodigy's Web browser (Jump:**www**). With the Web browser you can download files from Web sites (addresses starting with **http:**), FTP sites (addresses starting with **ftp:**), and Gopher sites (addresses starting with **gopher:**).

 TIP   **See chapter 15 for more information on using Prodigy's Web** browser to download files.

Here are some of the best sites for finding software on the Net:

- **Apple Computing (ftp://ftp.info.apple.com)**, the official site for downloading of Mac-related files

- **Center for Innovative Computing Applications (ftp://ftp.cica.indiana.edu)**, the site for Indiana University's Center for Innovative Computing Applications—a prime site for lots of Windows utilities and programs

- **Imperial College (ftp://ftp.doc.ic.ac.uk)**, a London-based site with lots of academic files, plus games and utilities

- **Indiana University (ftp://ftp.indiana.edu)**, the general site at my alma mater, Indiana University

- **InterNIC (ftp://ds.internic.net** or **gopher://gopher.internic.net)**, collections of important Internet-related documents and information

- **JUMBO Shareware Archive (http://www.jumbo.com/)**, one of the largest collections of shareware on the Web

- **Macmillan Computer Publishing** (**ftp://ftp.mcp.com** or **http://www.mcp.com/softlib/software.html**), the home site for Que and other computer book publishers; lots of utilities, program code, sample files, etc.

- **Microsoft** (**ftp://ftp.microsoft.com** or **http://www.microsoft.com**), official Microsoft software, utilities, drivers, and bug patches

- **MIT** (**ftp://rtfm.mit.edu**), the archives of all the Net's FAQs (frequently asked questions)

- **National Center for Supercomputing Applications** (**ftp://ftp.ncsa.uiuc.edu**), the official NCSA server at the University of Illinois—the home of Mosaic and many other Internet programs

- **National Science Foundation** (**gopher://gopher.nsf.gov**), a nice Government-based Gopher site

- **NEARnet** (**ftp://ftp.near.net**), NEARnet information, Internet Talk Radio, and Commerce Business Daily

- **Oak Archives** (**ftp://oak.oakland.edu** or **http://www.acs.oakland.edu/oak.html**), a *mirror site* that holds copies of software from other sites

- **Shase Virtual Shareware Library** (**http://www.fagg.uni-lj.si/SHASE/**), a large archive with more than 58,000 programs for all computer platforms

- **University of Birmingham** (**ftp://ftp.cs.bham.ac.uk**), one of the U.K.'s premiere sites—home of USENET newsgroup archives

- **University of Illinois at Urbana-Champaign** (**ftp://ftp.cso.uiuc.edu**), a general purpose site with lots of software

- **University of Minnesota** (**gopher://gopher.micro.umn.edu**), the first and foremost Gopher server on the Net

- **University of North Carolina** (**ftp://sunsite.unc.edu**), a major site for academic information

- **UUNet** (**ftp://ftp.uu.net**), the central distribution site for netnews traffic

- **Walnut Creek** (**ftp://ftp.cdrom.com**), lots of files from Walnut Creek's CD-ROM products

- **Washington University at St. Louis (ftp://wuarchive.wustl.edu)**, one of the largest FTP sites available on the Net

- **Windows Shareware Archive (http://coyote.csusm.edu/cwis/winworld/)**, a *huge* collection of Windows shareware at California State University San Marcos—the #1 place to start looking for files on the Web

- **Wiretap (ftp://wiretap.spies.com** or **gopher://wiretap.spies.com)**, an eclectic collection of controversial documents, from the government and elsewhere

66 *Plain English, please!*

A **mirror site** is an Internet site that "mirrors" the contents of another site. That means that both sites have the same contents. Mirror sites are used to reduce traffic to overused sites by spreading the traffic between multiple sites. 99

That's a lot of sites with a lot of software—and that's not all. Don't forget to go to Prodigy's Computers interest group on the Web, at **http://antares.prodigy.com/in4coi.htm#comp**. This page links to six other pages (Electronic Frontier Foundation Home Page, Information Highway, Internet Help, MIDI Computer Music, Virus Help, and Windows Help), which add up to hundreds of links to hot Internet and Prodigy computer-related resources.

Prodigy also has a special Computers/Technology page, with about a dozen more links to computer companies and magazines at the Web. Check it out at **http://antares.prodigy.com/comput.htm**.

Part VI: Using Prodigy at Home

24

Doing Your Banking Online

● **In this chapter:**

- **What types of banking can I do online?**

- **Is my bank online with Prodigy?**

- **How can I pay bills electronically if my bank isn't online?**

- **Is my bank on the World Wide Web?**

- **Should I use Prodigy's online banking?**

If your bank is online with Prodigy, you can do most of your banking right from your personal computer . . . . ▶

Online banking is just what is sounds like—the ability to do most of your banking tasks right from your personal computer. Think of it as an electronic version of your small-town bank; all you have to do is supply your account number and PIN, and you can do just about everything you do at the teller's window—transfer funds between accounts, look at account information, even make electronic bill payments.

What types of banking can you do online?

While it differs a little from bank to bank, most online banks let you perform the following tasks:

- Make electronic payments—as well as schedule your bank to make recurring payments automatically

- Access information about your accounts—including full monthly statements

- Transfer funds between accounts

- Send notes to your bank's customer service department

Here's what you *can't* do with an online bank:

- Make deposits

- Make withdrawals

- Talk to the cute teller at the third window

So if you need cash, you still need to hit the old cash machine.

Finding an online bank

Not every bank in America is online with Prodigy. And, of course, you can't do online banking unless your bank is online. (Note, however, that you can pay your bills electronically even if your bank isn't online—see the section on BillPay USA later in this chapter.)

To see if your bank is online, Jump:**bank** and check the list of Prodigy's online banks.

TIP **Online banking isn't free. Most banks charge from $5–$10/month** for accessing their services online.

Doing it online: A typical online banking session

To enter Prodigy's online banking area, Jump:**banking online**. You'll be presented with the option of going to your local bank or using Prodigy's BillPay feature (discussed later in this chapter). Click on Your Local Bank to select from a list of banks in your area.

TIP **You can also go directly to your bank by typing its JumpWord,** or select from a list of all U.S. banks online with Prodigy with Jump:**bank**.

I'm going to use my bank, NBD BankCorp, as an example. Note, however, that your online bank may not do things the same as mine—and you may not have the same types of accounts available as I do. So your session could look different from this.

When I first log on, I'm asked for account number from my bank card and my personal identification number (PIN), as shown in figure 24.1. I enter this information and then press Enter.

After I enter this information, I'm presented with a list of tasks. I choose a task from this list—in this case, Account Information. I'm now presented with a list of the types of information available. With NBD I can choose from info on my deposit or load accounts, info on a specific check, or I can choose to read my entire account statement online. I like this last option because I can actually see my monthly statement in progress, *before* I receive the hard copy version in the mail.

Fig. 24.1
To enter your online
bank, you need to
provide your account
number and PIN.

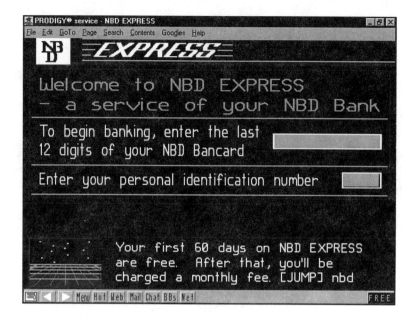

Of course, you can do all sorts of other banking tasks while you're online.
About the only things you can't do are make deposits or withdraw cash. I
guess that last one will have to wait until we get really high-quality color
printers on every desktop!

Pay your bills online with BillPay USA

How would you like to stop writing checks, and do all your bill-paying from
your computer? How would you like to schedule automatic payments in
advance, so you don't have to do anything but push a button to make the
payment? What if you want to do all this and your bank isn't online with
Prodigy?

Well, with Prodigy's BillPay feature, you can do all this, and more. BillPay
(Jump:**billpay**) lets you pay all your bills electronically, from your computer
keyboard—and your bank doesn't even have to be online!

BillPay USA is a service of CheckFree, one of the country's largest online
check bureaus. When you set up a BillPay account, you instruct BillPay to
debit your account and electronically pay the bills you select. (If, for some
reason, BillPay can't pay a specific bill electronically, it will write a hard copy
check to that payee and mail it for you.)

Before you "write" any electronic checks, however, you need to set up your personal account and a list of payee accounts. This is as simple as filling in the blanks with information from your bank account and all your monthly bills. BillPay sets up your individual account and creates a list of payees that you can select from when entering individual bills to pay.

Here's how an individual transaction works:

1 Jump:**billpay** to enter the BillPay area.

2 Select whom you want to pay from your list of accounts—or add a new account.

3 Enter the date you want the bill paid. (This lets you enter the info when you receive the bill, but schedule payments in advance of the actual due date.)

4 Enter the amount of the payment.

Using BillPay doesn't guarantee instant payment of your bills. It takes about five days for your payment to arrive after you enter it with BillPay. On the first day BillPay gathers all entered payments for processing. On Day 2 BillPay prints out hard-copy checks for those accounts that aren't linked electronically, and drops them in the mail. On Day 3 the funds for these checks are electronically withdrawn from your checking account. On Day 4 payments are sent to those accounts who are linked electronically with BillPay. And on Day 5 the account processes your payment.

Naturally, BillPay isn't free. It costs you $9.95/month for up to 30 monthly payments, with additional payments costing $3.50 for groups of ten. This is about half of what you pay for normal checks, envelopes, and stamps.

Banking on the Internet

In addition to the banks you find online with Prodigy, many banks are beginning to move to the Internet—specifically, the World Wide Web.

Use Prodigy's Web browser (Jump:**www**) to access Yahoo's list of banks (**http://www.yahoo.com/Business/Corporations/Financial_Services/ Banks/**). If your bank is online, chances are it's on this list.

Online banking—Is it for you?

Should you avail yourself of Prodigy's online banking features? Well, if you're comfortable with doing away with hard-copy checks—and you check your account diligently for mistakes—you're a perfect customer for an electronic payment service (either through your bank or with BillPay). Even if you don't want to pay your bills electronically, the ability to check your account information and transfer funds between accounts is pretty handy.

However, you have to balance all this against the cost. In my case, NBD charges me $6.50/month to do my banking online with Prodigy. Is it worth $6.50 to save a few trips to the corner bank? It is for me, since I tend to do my banking after normal banking hours. But if your bank is conveniently located and you keep normal hours, you may want to stick with doing things the old fashioned way.

It's your choice.

25

Making an Online Shopping Trip

● In this chapter:

- What is online shopping all about?

- What merchants and products are available online with Prodigy?

- How do I shop an online merchant?

- How do I find out more about the products I'm interested in?

- Shopping on the Internet

Shop from the convenience of your own PC with Prodigy's

online merchants . . . .

f Prodigy is like a small town, it's bound to have a lot of shops and stores lining its electronic streets. Well, Prodigy has over 100 different merchants online for your cybershopping convenience. All you need is your keyboard and your credit card, and you're ready to go!

Doing your shopping online

Why would you want to shop online? Well, the prime reason is probably convenience. You can browse on your own time—and at your own time. It's kind of like catalog shopping, except you can order directly from your PC and have the products delivered right to your door.

 TIP If you're not sure where to look for what, use Prodigy's Find a Gift service (Jump:**find a gift**). This service helps you determine which merchants to shop at based on what kind of gift you need.

Once you find the online merchant you want, all you have to do is browse through the merchandise they offer, select what you want, and then supply your shipping and credit card information. Within a matter of days your purchases will be delivered right to your front door.

Shopping in the Prodigy marketplace

Prodigy has a slew of online shopping services available. Most are accessed from the Prodigy Marketplace screen (Jump:**shopping**) shown in figure 25.1. This main screen lists some featured items, but the meat of the Marketplace appears when you click the More About Marketplace hyperlink.

When the More About Marketplace box appears, you can access the following areas:

- **Interact**, which takes you to shopping-related bulletin boards

- **Web Pages**, which lists major Web-based shopping sites

- **Newsgroups**, which presents a handful of marketplace-oriented USENET newsgroups

- **Catalogues**, which links you to all the catalogs you can order online from Prodigy

- **A-Z**, which lists all of Prodigy's online merchants, alphabetically

- **Categories**, which lists all of Prodigy's online merchants, by category

- **All Highlights**, which returns you to the Prodigy's main sections, as listed on the Highlights screen

Fig. 25.1
The Prodigy
Marketplace.

Jump:shopping specials to see the latest specials and deals from Prodigy's online merchants.

Don't forget to read the classified ads from your fellow Prodigy members—just Jump:**classifieds**.

Going shopping on the Internet

There are a large number of places to shop on the Internet; lots of companies think they'll make a fortune setting up "virtual shopping malls" on the Net. All these online retailers are on the World Wide Web, so fire up Prodigy's Web browser (Jump:**www**) and take a look at the sites that follow.

TIP   **Before you shop for major items, you may want to consult** *Consumer Reports'* online product reviews. When you Jump:**cr library** you're taken to a list of topics covered by *Consumer Reports* magazine since 1988.

CAUTION   **Transactions on the Internet aren't as "secure" as transactions on** the Prodigy service. Be careful about providing your credit card number to Internet-based merchants; you may be better off dialing their voice phone numbers to place your order.

- **Access Market Square (http://www.icw.com/)**, ranked as the #3 site for Net shopping (by *Interactive Age* magazine)

- **Branch Mall (http://branch.com:1080/)**, a massive listing of Internet retailers, selling everything from art to vacations

- **Commercial Services on the Net (http://www.directory.net/)**, Open Markets' searchable directory of commercial services, products, and information on the Net

- **EUROMALL (http://www.internet-eireann.ie/Euromall/)**, an online mall for European merchants

- **FTD-INTERNET (http://www.novator.com/FTD-Catalog/FTD-Internet.html)**, the place to order flowers via the Net

- **Grammercy Press (http://www.mci.com/gramercy/gramercy.html)**—I can't help it, I really like this site (from MCI); you can spend hours clicking around the various offices in this fictitious publishing company

- **Hall of Malls (http://nsns.com/MouseTracks/HallofMalls.html)**, a listing of dozens of online malls

- **Internet Mall (http://www.mecklerweb.com/imall/imall.htm)**, dozens of online retailers all in one place

- **Internet Shopping Network (http://www.internet.net/)**, ranked as the #1 place for Net shopping (by *Interactive Age* magazine)

- **MarketplaceMCI (http://www2.pcy.mci.net/marketplace/ index.html)**, MCI's shopping megasite, ranked as the #5 shopping site on the Web (by *Interactive Age* magazine)

- **Movie Madness Store Directory (http://www.openmarket.com/ stores/MovieMadness/store/StoreFront.html)**, a very large selection of movie and television-related merchandise

- **NetCity (http://www.netcity.com/)**, an "electronic metropolis" for Web-based commerce—includes a Farmer's Market, Auto Center, Convention Center, and Shopping Mall

- **Shopping IN (http://www.onramp.net/shopping_in/)**, ranked as the #2 place for Net shopping (by *Interactive Age* magazine)

- **Ticketmaster Online (http://www.ticketmaster.com/)**—order tickets to upcoming concerts, online!

- **VirtuMall (http://virtumall.com/)**, ranked as the #4 site for Net-based shopping (by *Interactive Age* magazine)

- **Yahoo's List of Products and Services (http://www.yahoo.com/ Business/Products_and_Services/)**, a comprehensive list of businesses on the Net

Prodigy also has a Web page devoted to shopping. Point Prodigy's Web browser to **http://antares.prodigy.com/shop.htm** for additional Web-based shopping resources.

So, with all these retailers literally at your fingertips, why leave your house to shop? Just make sure your mouse is working and your credit card is under the limit—then you can shop online until your fingertips are sore!

26

Keeping Yourself Entertained

● **In this chapter:**

- ● **Television and cable news**

- ● **Movie and video news**

- ● **Music news**

- ● **Theater news**

- ● **Book best-sellers**

- ● **Celebrity news and photos**

- ● **Entertainment news on the Internet**

Use Prodigy to keep up on the latest news from the entertain-
ment industry . . . . ⊳

f you're looking for news about your favorite TV show or your favorite celebrity, chances are you can find it on Prodigy. Prodigy's Entertainment services offer you news and information about all aspects of the entertainment industry—from the cheeziest sitcoms to Tony Award-winning plays.

Prodigy means entertainment

Prodigy offers more entertainment news than you'll find on an episode of *Entertainment Tonight* or in an issue of *People* magazine. All you have to do is click on the Entertainment hyperlink on Prodigy's Highlight screen (or Jump:**entertainment**), and you're taken to Prodigy's main Entertainment section (see fig. 26.1).

Fig. 26.1
The main Entertainment screen.

From this section you can access news about all the various parts of the entertainment industry, from television to movies to music to live theater.

Get the latest TV news and views

Prodigy's Television section (Jump:**tv**) is the place to find out what's happening on the small screen. You'll find the following TV-related services:

Table 26.1 Prodigy's TV-related services

Service	JumpWord	Description
Total TV Online	**total tv**	A national online guide to the coming week's TV listings.
Today's TV	**today's tv**	Total TV's listings for today.
Networks Online	**cable/tv networks**	Separate sections for major broadcast and cable networks, including AMC, Bravo, C-SPAN, Cartoon Network, CBS, CMT, CNBC, CNN, Comedy Central, Court TV, Discovery Channel, E!, Encore, ESPN, ESPN2, HBO, HLN, Jones Computer Network, Lifetime, Mind Extension University, Nickelodeon, Sci-Fi Channel, Showtime, TBS, The Disney Channel, The Family Channel, The Movie Channel, TLC, TNN, TNT, Turner Classic Movies, USA Network, and the WGN Superstation. (You can also jump directly to these network services.) Each service typically offers program listings, press releases, feature stories, and a way to provide feedback to the network.
TV News & Views	**tv news**	The latest news about the television and cable industries.
Nielsen TV Charts	**nielsen**	The latest Neilsen ratings of the most-watched TV shows.
Soaps	**soaps**	Separate sections for major network soap operas, including *All My Children, Another World, As the World Turns, The Bold and The Beautiful, Days of Our Lives, General Hospital, The Guiding Light, Loving, One Life to Live,* and *The Young and the Restless.* (You can also jump directly to these soap opera sections.) Each of these sections include a recap of recent episodes and gossip from the set.

Let's stop a minute. That table included no fewer than 65 different Prodigy sections. That's more than *sixty-five* sections devoted to television information! You can spend hours and hours browsing through Prodigy's TV info, and still have some parts left over. Sure beats the 15 minutes it takes to read *TV Guide*, doesn't it?

What's on the big screen—Prodigy and the movies

Prodigy's movie offerings aren't quite as extensive as its TV offerings—but again, there are more new TV and cable shows each year than there are new movies. Take a look at what Prodigy has to offer to movie and video fans.

Table 26.2 Prodigy's movie and video services

Service	JumpWord	Description
Current Films	**current films**	Reviews of current films by other Prodigy members (as part of the Reel Poll)
Movie Charts	**movie charts**	Current box-office performance of the top new films
Movie Guide	**movie guide**	Reviews of more than 15,000 films, from *Magill's Survey of Cinema*
New on Video	**new on video**	Info on the latest videotape releases
Action Video	**action video**	The latest action films released on video
Comedy Video	**comedy video**	The latest comedies released on video
Drama Video	**drama video**	The latest dramas released on video
Kid Video	**kid video**	The latest videotapes for the whole family
Special video	**special video**	The latest special interest and documentary videos
Video Charts	**video charts**	The top rental and sale videotapes across the country

Of this movie-related information, I find myself going back to a few key resources. I particularly like the information in Magill's Survey of Cinema (Jump:**movie guide**); it's extremely complete and goes back to the dawn of cinema. In addition, the New on Video section (Jump:**new on video**) capsulizes all the new release information in the other video sections.

Now playing: Playbill's theater coverage

If you're a fan of live theater, Prodigy's Playbill section (Jump:**theater**) is for you. Playbill is the renowned publication devoted to professional theater, and Prodigy's online version is rich with news and other information.

There's a lot of information in the Playbill section, including the major stories on the opening screen. Unlike most areas of Prodigy, you can't use JumpWords to go to the various subsections; you have to click on the appropriate button on the main Playbill screen. Table 26.3 details the available options:

Table 26.3 Playbill's theater information

Services	From Button...	Description
Broadway Shows (by Title)	Broadway	Current Broadway shows, listed alphabetically by title
Broadway Shows (by Style)	Broadway	Current Broadway shows, grouped by style (Comedy, Drama, Musical, Performance, or Shakespeare)
Theatre Map	Broadway	Maps of NY's theater district
At This Theatre	Broadway	A listing of NY's major theaters, and what's playing where
National Tours	National Tours	A list of major national touring companies and their upcoming schedules
Regional Shows (by Title)	Regional	A listing of major regional productions, alphabetical by title
Regional Shows (by Style)	Regional	A listing of major regional productions, grouped by style (Comedy, Drama, Musical, Performance, or Shakespeare)
Regional Shows (by City)	Regional	A listing of major regional products, sorted by city of performance
Off-Broadway Shows	Off-Broadway (by Title)	Current Off-Broadway shows, listed alphabetically by title
Off-Broadway Shows	Off-Broadway (by Style)	Current Off-Broadway shows, grouped by style (Comedy, Drama, Musical, Performance, or Shakespeare)
London-based Shows	London (by Title)	Current London shows, listed alphabetically by title
London-based Shows	London (by Style)	Current London shows, grouped by style (Comedy, Drama, Musical, Performance, or Shakespeare)

TIP **In addition to all this useful information, you can also check out** the Playbill bulletin board (Jump:**playbill bb**) and Chat sections. Both regularly feature guest actors and actresses from hit Broadway plays.

Go to the top of the charts with Prodigy's music coverage

While you can't really listen to albums through your computer (yet!), you can use Prodigy to gather information about your favorite musical artists. With Prodigy you can find out who has taken home the most Grammies and who's on top of the charts, as well as read reviews of recent albums.

Jump:**music** or click on the Music hyperlink on Prodigy's main Highlights page to access Prodigy's main Music page (shown in fig. 26.2). This page links to the best music information on the Prodigy service and out on the Internet.

Fig. 26.2
Jump:**music** to access Prodigy's music offerings.

And what music services are available on Prodigy?

Table 26.4 **Prodigy's music services**

Service	JumpWord	Description
Music Awards	**awards**	Grammies, American Music Awards, and other entertainment awards (including Oscars and Golden Globes)
Music Charts	**music charts**	The hottest tunes and artists of the week, in the following categories: Pop, Adult Contemporary, Modern Rock, Dance, Rap, R&B, Country, Jazz, Classical, European Singles, and Top Concerts
Music Reviews	**music reviews**	Reviews of albums released since 1992

Read about it online—Prodigy's book section

I could try to get all enthused about all the book information available on Prodigy. But the fact is, Prodigy just doesn't have that much book info available. (Maybe Prodigy figures you're too busy watching TV to do much book reading?)

Aside from the Arts BB (Jump:**arts bb**) and Books & Writing BB (Jump:**books bb**), the only other place for book lovers on Prodigy is the Book Charts section. When you Jump:**book charts** you're taken to a series of book best-seller lists compiled by *Publisher's Weekly* (the leading book industry trade magazine). There are best-seller lists for:

- Hardcover Fiction
- Hardcover Non-Fiction
- Mass Market Paperbacks
- Trade Paperbacks

All the famous people, all the famous news

Of course, the most fun part of following the entertainment industry is following the antics of your favorite celebrities. Who's up for the leading role in that big upcoming movie? Who's hot and who's not? Who's sleeping with whom?

Well, Prodigy doesn't get into that last bit, but it does have a regular section for celebrity news. When you Jump:**people** you see the People News screen.

Talk with celebrities on Prodigy's bulletin boards and Chat sections

Prodigy's bulletin boards and Chat sections offer you a way to interact with celebrities from a variety of fields—actors, sports stars, and other media luminaries.

To see who's visiting Prodigy this week, Jump:**guest**. You can even read transcripts from Chat sessions with previous guests!

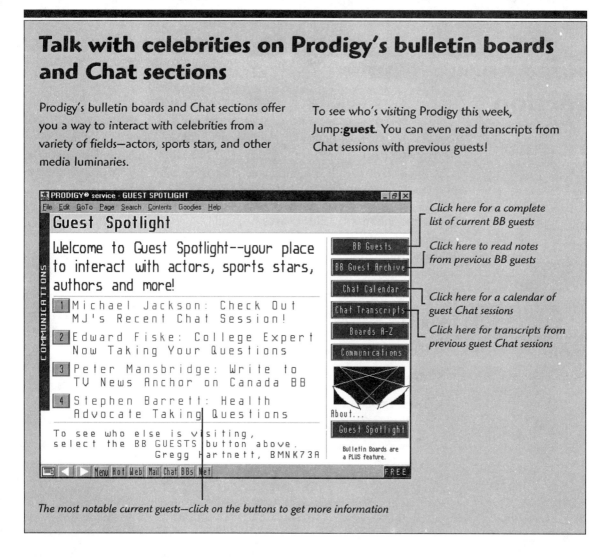

The most notable current guests—click on the buttons to get more information

This screen lists a half-dozen major celebrity news stories, and gives you access to the People Poll, Awards, and Celebrity Birthdays sections. News stories change daily, so this section should be a part of your daily Prodigy browsing.

The People Poll section (Jump:**people poll**) works just like the other Prodigy Polls. You respond to a series of questions about a specific topic, and then you can review the results of how your fellow Prodigy members voted.

The Birthdays section (click on the Birthdays button on the People News screen) lists those celebrities with birthdays over the past few days. Did you know, for example, that Shirley Jones turned 61 on March 31, 1995?

Finally, you can view the latest celebrity photos from the paparazzi when you Jump:**people photos**. You get the photo and a detailed caption, which you can save in a file on your hard disk. (See chapter 16 for more information on saving and printing Prodigy's pictures.)

Finding entertainment news on the Internet

As if Prodigy's entertainment offerings weren't enough, there's *even more* available when you venture off Prodigy onto the Internet! In fact, the number of entertainment offerings on the Net are a little staggering. Read on to find out more….

Entertaining newsgroups

There are probably more entertainment-oriented newsgroups than any other topic. The majority take the form of some sort of electronic fan club, and they're great places to meet die-hard fans of whatever TV show, movie, or rock group you're a fan of.

There are more newsgroups (Jump:**newsgroups**) available than I can list, but here are the best places to start looking:

- **alt.animation.***
- **alt.books.***
- **alt.comedy.***

- **alt.comics.***

- **alt.disney.***

- **alt.fan.*** (this is where most of the online fan clubs are)

- **alt.movies.***

- **alt.music.***

- **alt.radio.***

- **alt.rock-n-roll.***

- **alt.tv.***

- **rec.arts.***

- **rec.music.***

- **rec.radio.***

- **rec.video.***

In general, you'll find most of the entertainment-themed newsgroups under the **alt.*** and **rec.*** groupings. Good hunting!

Entertainment on the Web

There is a virtual overload of entertainment-related information on the World Wide Web. So start Prodigy's Web browser (Jump:**www**) and sample some of the best:

- **A Global Canvas** (**http://www.mcp.com/hayden/museum-book/ sites.html**), a list of fine arts sites, assembled by my coworkers at Hayden Books

- **Art Links on the World Wide Web** (**http:// amanda.physics.wisc.edu/outside.html**), links to a variety of art-related sites on the Web

- **Buena Vista MoviePlex** (**http://www.disney.com/**), the WWW home of the Walt Disney Company, and associated films and merchandise

- **Calvin and Hobbes Archive** (**http://www.eng.hawaii.edu/Contribs/ justin/Archive/Index.html**), a shrine to the popular comic strip

- **CBS Television: Eye on CBS (http://www.cbs.com/)**, the official CBS Web site

- **Cheezy 80s (http://web.mit.edu/user/t/o/tobye/www/cheezy80s.html)**, one of my favorite sites, dedicated to the worst music from the 1980s (from ABBA on!)

- **Country Connection (http://uptown.turnpike.net/C/country/)**, a massive listing of Web sites dedicated to various country and folk musicians

- **Elvis Home Page (http://sunsite.unc.edu/elvis/elvishom.html)**— and, no, he hasn't been seen on the Internet!

- ***Entertainment Weekly* (http://www.pathfinder.com/ew/Welcome.html)**, part of the Pathfinder site, a complete online version of the print magazine—plus movie reviews and bulletin boards!

- **Hollywood Online (http://www.hollywood.com/)**, a premiere source of online movie information and previews—loosely related to CompuServe's Hollywood Online service

- **Internet Movie Database (http://www.cm.cf.ac.uk/movies)**, which is just what it says—a huge online database of movie-related information

- **Internet Underground Music Archives (http://www.iuma.com/IUMA/index_graphic.html)**, a free music archive on the Web

- **Kaleidospace (http://amanda.physics.wisc.edu/outside.html)**, one of the premiere art sites on the Web

- **MCA/Universal Cyberwalk (http://www.mca.com/)**, a "supersite" for all of MCA and Universal's entertainment properties—includes a bonus site for Spencer Gifts!

- **Metaverse (http://www.metaverse.com/index.html)**, one of the coolest sites on the Web, with tons of music and alternative culture news

- **MovieWEB (http://movieweb.com/movie/movie.html)**, online previews of the hottest upcoming movies—as well as Top 25 Box Office lists

- **Mr. Showbiz (http://web3.starwave.com/showbiz/)**, a *must-see* site—one of the Web's very best entertainment sites, complete with reviews, previews, and all the TV/movie/entertainment info you can digest!

- **MTV (http://www.mtv.com/)**, the rockin' cable channel—and all its programs—online

- **MUSI-CAL (http://www.automatrix.com/concerts/)**, an online calendar database that lets you search for live music concerts by geographic area

- **NBC HTTV (http://www.nbc.com/)**, the official site for the NBC television network, including a special section for Jay Leno's *Tonight Show*

- **Paramount Pictures Online Studio (http://www.paramount.com/)**, for previews of new and upcoming Paramount movies—as well as Paramount TV shows, like *Star Trek*

- **Rock Web Interactive (http://www.rock.net/)**, one of the top music sites on the Web

- **Science Fiction Resource Guide (http://sundry.hsc.usc.edu/hazel/www/sfrg/sf-resource.guide.html)**, look here for a comprehensive list of science fiction on the Net

- **Sony Online (http://www.sony.com/)**, with lots of neat electronic goodies, Sony records, and Columbia Pictures information

- **Star Trek: WWW (http://www-iwi.unisg.ch/~sambucci/scifi/startrek/www.html)**, an unofficial—but very comprehensive—list of *Star Trek* resources on the Web

- **Star Wars Home Page (http://stwing.resnet.upenn.edu:8001/~jruspini/starwars.html)**, for all things *Star Wars*

- ***The Biz* (http://www.bizmag.com/)**, "the digizine for the entertainment industry," focusing on film, television, music, multimedia, and book and magazine publishing

- **Time Warner Pathfinder (http://www.pathfinder.com/pathfinder/Greet.html)**, a *must-see* "megasite" complete with all sorts of entertainment resources—including *Time* magazine, *People* magazine, *Sports Illustrated* magazine, and Warner Bros. records and movies.

- **United Media** (**http://unitedmedia.com/**), a master site for all sorts of syndicated comic strips—includes *The Dilbert Zone*, for Dilbert fans everywhere

- **VH1** (**http://here.viacom.com/vh1/index.html**), music first online with tons of music news, previews, and more

- **Web Site of Love** (**http://www.usgcc.odu.edu/˜ty/mst3k/ MST3K.html**), for fans of Comedy Central's *Mystery Science Theater 3000*

- **World Wide Web Virtual Literature Library** (**http:// sunsite.unc.edu/ibic/IBIC-homepage.html**), with links to a ton of Web-based literature

- **Yahoo's list of Entertainment sites** (**http://akebono.stanford.edu/ yahoo/Entertainment/**), perhaps the best list of entertainment-oriented sites on the Web

That's a *lot* of entertainment information—so where should you start? If I had to pick the *must-see* entertainment sites, I'd start with Time Warner Pathfinder and Mr. Showbiz. If you're looking for movie trivia or information, though, don't pass up the Internet Movie Database. And, before you turn off your computer, make sure you head to United Media's Dilbert Zone for your daily dose of Dilbert!

In addition, Prodigy has several of its own Web pages devoted to entertainment-oriented resources. Check out Prodigy's Arts & Entertainment Page (**http://antares.prodigy.com/arts.htm**) and the Entertainment interest group (**http://antares.prodigy.com/in7coi.htm#enter**)—the latter with links to other entertainment interest groups, including those focusing on Astrology, Books, Comedy, Contemporary Christian Music, Movies, Personal Connections, Science Fiction/Fantasy, Trivia, TV Online, and more!

27

Indulging Your Hobbies

● **In this chapter:**

- Science Fiction and Fantasy

- Collectibles

- Arts and Crafts

- Sex, Politics, and Religion

- Travel and Automotive

- Sports and Games

- Food and Drink

Share your interests with other hobbyists from all over the world with Prodigy bulletin boards . . . . >

Prodigy is the perfect place to exchange information with people who share your hobbies and special interests. In fact, that's why Prodigy bulletin boards were developed—to create a special place where members with the same interests could send and receive notes about their interests. This chapter examines a few of the BBs of particular interest to different kinds of hobbies.

Take off to other worlds: Science fiction and fantasy BBs

If you're a science fiction fan, there are lots of BBs you'll find interesting on Prodigy. Of these boards, the Science Fiction BB (Jump:**science fiction**) is far and away the best for general-interest fans of SF. However, if you're a died-in-the-wool Trekker, you'll want to split your time between the Science Fiction BB and the Star Trek BB (Jump:**star trek bb**).

The other boards are worth a look, but cater more to special interests, including:

- **Science Fiction BB** (Jump:**science fiction**). This is the obvious place to start, with sections on both screen sci-fi (*Star Wars, Dr. Who,* etc.) and print sci-fi (authors like Anne McCaffrey and Isaac Asimov). (See fig. 27.1.)

- **Sci-Fi Channel topic** on the TV Networks BB (Jump:**tv networks bb**). A lot of old sci-fi TV shows and movies show up on this cable network, and this is a good place to find discussion about those shows.

- **Star Trek BB** (Jump:**star trek bb**). *Star Trek* is too big a topic to hold within the Science Fiction BB—so it got its own board. You'll find discussions of all the movies and TV shows, as well as conventions, games, and trivia.

- **Myth & Fantasy BB** (Jump:**myth**). Fantasy is closely tied to science fiction, and some shows (like *Beauty and the Beast*) kind of bridge both worlds. SF fans should feel right at home on this board.

- **Sci-Fi Collectibles topic** on the Antiques/Collecting BB (Jump:**antiques**). If you're into collecting old SF stuff—books, toys, you name it—this is the board to be at.

- **Sci-Fi Games and Game Clubs topics** on the Games (Jump:**games bb**) and RPG (Jump:**rpg**) BBs. Lots of SF fans are also into role-playing games; take a look at these topics and several other fantasy game topics on Prodigy's two game-related boards.

Fig. 27.1
A note from an *X-Files* fan on the Science Fiction BB.

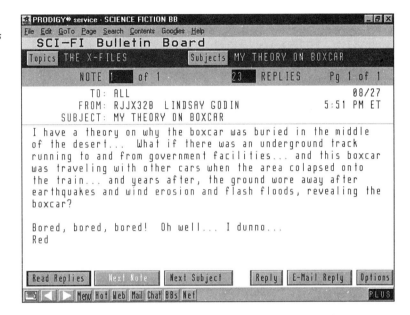

Collecting things for fun and money: Collectible BBs

A lot of science fiction fans like to collect SF memorabilia. But that's just a part of the range of items of value to collectors. Prodigy offers a variety of BBs for collectors; the two Collecting BBs have the most variety, but some of the other boards and topics are better for specific interests.

- **Collecting BBs** (Jump:**collecting 1** or **collecting 2**). Two BBs devoted to nothing but collecting topics. Collecting 1 covers antiques, autographs, books and magazines, china and pottery, clocks and watches, entertainment items, furniture, glass and crystal, jewelry and clothing, postcards, silver and metal, sports memorabilia, stamps, teddy bears, and toys and games. Collecting 2 covers action figures, Barbie, diecast and metal toys, cartoon memorabilia, fast food items, figures and miniatures, Hallmark items, limited editions, Pez, phonecards, plates, pogs, and sci-fi items.

- **Comics BB** (Jump:**comics**). There are several topics on this board of interest to collectors of comic books and comic book art.

- **Hobbies BB** (Jump:**hobbies bb**). While this BB tends to concentrate more on doing than on collecting, several topics (including the Model Making, Slot Cars, and Trains topics) tend to bridge the gap.

- **Memorabilia topic** on the Star Trek BB (Jump:**star trek bb**). If you're big into *Star Trek* collectibles, this is an even better source than the Antiques/Collecting BB.

- **Trading Cards BB** (Jump:**trading cards**). If you're into collectible cards—both sports and non-sports—check out this new BB.

- **Trading: Adult Cards topic** on the Lifestyles BB (Jump:**lifestyles**). Believe it or not, there are lots of *adult* trading cards out there—including those featuring Anna Nicole Smith, Betty Page, and models from *Penthouse* magazine. Definitely not for kids!

- **Wine, Beer and Spirts BB** (Jump:**wine**). If you're a wine collector, you need to call this board "home."

 TIP Jump:**collecting concourse** for a focal point for all of Prodigy's collecting-related services.

Make it yourself: Arts and crafts BBs

If you're into arts and crafts, Prodigy offers a variety of interesting BBs. The Crafts BB (Jump: **crafts**) is the number-one place to be, with the Arts and Crafts Pros topic on the Your Business BB (Jump:**your business**) an interesting second. The other boards are a tad weak, but worth checking out:

- **Crafts BB** (Jump:**crafts**). This is the main board for artisans and craftspeople. Topics range from beadwork and calligraphy to stained glass and woodworking.

- **Arts and Crafts Pros topic** on the Your Business BB (Jump:**your business**). Actually, quite a lively little area for discussions about various types of crafts.

- **Crafts topic** on the Marketplace BB (Jump:**marketplace**). Not a lot of traffic, but what there is involves buying or selling crafts or craft-making tools.

- **Hobbies BB** (Jump:**hobbies bb**). If you consider building your own model rocket or slot car a craft, you'll find things of interest on this board.

- **Arts BB** (Jump:**arts**). This board is mainly about the performing arts, but there are topics on Puppetry, Sculpture, and Architecture.

Something to argue about: Sex, politics, and religion BBs

Would you like a good argument? Well, skip the Monty Python topic and scoot over to one of these controversial BBs. After all, nobody agrees on sex, politics, or religion!

- **Lifestyles BB** (Jump:**lifestyles**). This is the main sex board, with topics ranging from men's issues to women's issues to various sexual and lifestyle issues.

- **Gay/Lesbian BB** (Jump:**gay**). This is a newer and slightly more radical board for homosexual discussion.

- **Politics topic** on the News BB (Jump:**news bb**). This is the main board for political discussion.

- **Politics topic** on the Teens BB (Jump:**teens bb**). Even teenagers have opinions about politics.

- **Politics/Separation topic** on the Canada BB (Jump:**canada bb**). Even those fiesty Canadians have their own political issues—in this case, the politics of separation.

- **Religion Concourse 1 and 2 BBs** (Jump:**religion 1** and Jump:**religion 2**). These are the two main religious BBs—the topic was so big it required two boards!

- **Religion topic** on the Newsweek BB (Jump:**newsweek bb**). *Newsweek* readers have their say on religious issues.

- **Religion topic** on the Teens BB (Jump:**teens bb**). It's those irascible teenagers again, this time arguing various religious issues.

- **Astrology & New Age BB** (Jump:**astrology**). Some folks say there's religion here, and the debates follow.

No favorites here. All these boards generate a lot of heat, and make for an interesting time.

Planes, trains, and automobiles: Travel and automotive BBs

Like to travel? Like to drive? Well, check out Prodigy's travel and auto-related boards when you're feeling a little wanderlust.

It's difficult to recommend one of these boards over the others—they cover such wildly varying topics. I can tell you, however, that travel and automotive buffs tend to be some of the most obsessed people I've met on Prodigy—which I think is a good attribute!

Here are the boards to check out:

- **Travel BB** (Jump:**travel bb**). The main travel board, with topics for all major destinations and types of travel.

- **Travel topic** on the Canada BB (Jump:**canada bb**). The place to go if you're going to Canada.

- **Travel topic** on the Seniors BB (Jump:**seniors**). Subjects of particular interest to senior travelers.

- **Travel topic** on the Careers BB (Jump:**careers bb**). Look here if you are, or are interested in becoming, a travel agent.

- **Automotive BB** (Jump:**automotive**). *The* forum for car buffs! Everything from new and used car info to auto racing, hot rod, and muscle car news.

- **Sports Play BB** (Jump:**sports play**). Topics of interest include bicycling, boating, and skydiving.

- **Auto Racing topic** on the Sports BB (Jump:**sports bb**). All the news about professional motorsports, from Formula One to IndyCar to NASCAR.

- **Aviation topic** on the Hobbies BB (Jump:**hobbies bb**). The meeting place for all do-it-yourself pilots.

It's not whether you win or lose: Sports and games BBs

Sports and games can be hobbies, or they can be a way of life. Whichever it is for you, check out Prodigy's list of sports and games BBs.

Which of these boards should you frequent? Well, if you like to *watch* sports, choose the Sports BB (Jump:**sports bb**). If you like to *play* sports, choose the Sports Play BB (Jump:**sports play**). And if you like to play *games*, choose the Games BB (Jump:**games bb**). Otherwise, browse the following list:

- **Sports BB** (Jump:**sports bb**). The main place for spectator sports fans. Whether you like basketball, baseball, football, or hockey, it's covered here.

- **Sports Play BB** (Jump:**sports play**). For fans of participatory sports, from SCUBA diving to skydiving.

- **NFL BB** (Jump:**nfl bb**). Topics for every NFL team.

- **Sports Illustrated for Kids BB** (Jump:**si for kids bb**). Sports for the small fry.

- **Auto Racing topic** on the Automotive BB (Jump:**automotive**). Where serious fans of Formula One, IndyCar, and NASCAR go to talk.

- **Trading Cards BB** (Jump:**trading cards**). Lots of talk about sports cards in this board.

- **Games BB** (Jump:**games bb**). Whether you're talking computer games, board games, or arcade games, you'll find it here.

- **Role Playing Games BB** (Jump:**rpg**). Specifically devoted to players of role playing games.

- **Video Games BB** (Jump:**video games bb**). From Atari and Nintendo to Sega and Sony PlayStation, this board covers it.

Eat, drink, and be merry: Food and drink BBs

After a long hard day indulging your hobbies, there's nothing better than a good meal and a stiff drink. If that sounds good to you, check out these boards:

- **Food BB** (Jump:**food bb**). The home for both gourmands and aspiring cooks. Topics range from breads to meat to vegetables.

- **Wine, Beer & Spirits BB** (Jump:**wine**). The place for wine and beer connoisseurs, with topics ranging from wine-making to breweries and pubs.

These two boards pretty much cover it. Go to the Food BB for good food discussions, and to the Wine, Beer & Spirits BB for a little after-dinner drink and merriment. Then head off to sleep, because if you visited all the boards I discussed in this chapter, it's well after midnight and you're probably pooped out!

Finding your hobby on the Internet

If you can't find a forum for your particular hobby on Prodigy, then venture out onto the Internet—the selection is even greater out there!

You probably want to start with hobbyist-related newsgroups (Jump:**newsgroups**). Start with these groups and areas:

- alt.sport.*
- rec.antiques
- rec.aquaria
- rec.arts.*
- rec.autos.*
- rec.bicyclcs.*
- rec.boats.*
- rec.collecting.*
- rec.crafts.*
- rec.games.*
- rec.gardens
- rec.guns
- rec.models.*
- rec.motorcycles.*
- rec.outdoors.*
- rec.pets.*
- rec.photo.*
- rec.radio.amateur.*
- rec.running

- rec.scouting

- rec.scuba

- rec.skate

- rec.skiing

- rec.skydiving

- rec.sport.*

- rec.toys.*

- rec.windsurfing

- rec.wordworking

Next, it's time to head to the World Wide Web (Jump:**www**) to see what hobbyist-related sites exist on the Web. Note that many of these sites are run by hobbyists themselves, not by big businesses—which means they update them on their own time, at their own expense. It also means that the sites are often a labor of love, and that makes them all that much better.

Try these sites on for size:

- **19th Hole (http://www.tr-riscs.panam.edu/golf/19thhole.html)**, a pretty good site for golfers at all levels

- **All Magic Guide (http://www.uelectric.com/allmagicguide.html)**, a guide to magic-related Web pages

- **American Horticultural Society (http://eMall.com/ahs/ahs.html)**, for gardeners everywhere

- **Autograph Collectors Database (http://cscmosaic.albany.edu/~ss4569/autograph.html)**, a good starting page for autograph hounds

- **Birding on the Web (http://compstat.wharton.upenn.edu:8001/~siler/birding.html)**, an index of birding-related Web sites

- **Cameron's Moto Page (http://www.dap.csiro.au/~cameron/moto/)**, with assorted motorcycle resources and links to other motorcycle sites

- **Collecting Resources (http://iquest.com/~tstevens/collecting/)**, a listing of Web-based resources for collectors of all shapes and sizes

- **Dive Destinations (http://www.atonet.com/dive/)**, an online magazine for divers

- **Fishing Page (http://www.geo.mtu.edu/~jsuchosk/fish/fishpage)**, devoted to everything there is to know about the fine art of fishing

- **GolfWeb (http://www.golfweb.com/)**, perhaps the best golf site on the Web

- **Great Outdoor Recreation Pages (http://www.gorp.com/)**, with tips for all sorts of outdoor activities, including hiking, biking, fishing, and climbing

- **Hang Gliding WWW Server (http://cougar.stanford.edu:7878/ HGMPSHomePage.html)**, with lots of information of use to serious hang gliders and paragliders—including lots of cool pictures

- **Hunter (http://www.wolfe.net/~hunter/)**, with all the hunting info you could ask for

- **Internet Textiles Server (http://palver.terminus.com/crafts/ index.html)**, a tremendous resource for crocheting, embroidery, knitting, lacemaking, quilting, rug hooking, sewing, spinning, weaving, and other crafts

- **Learn About Antiques (http://www.ic.mankato.mn.us/antiques/ Antiques.html)**, a good starter site for the antiques collector

- **National Model Railroad Association (http://www.mcs.net/ ~weyand/nmra/nmrahome.html)**, the official Web site for the largest organization devoted to model railroading

- **Philatelic Resources on the Web (http://www.execpc.com/ ~joeluft/resource.html)**, a listing of Web resources for stamp collectors everywhere

- **Plastic Princess Collector's Page (http:// deepthought.armory.com/~zenugirl/barbie.html)**, all about collecting Barbies and other fashion dolls

- **Radio Controlled Planes (http://www.epix.net/~loggins/ rc_page.html)**, a starter site for model plane enthusiasts

- **Real Beer Page (http://and.com/RealBeer/)**, one of several sites for brewmasters on the Web (see fig. 31.4)

- **Running Page (http://polar.pica.army.mil/people/drears/running/ running.html)**, a great index to the sport of running

- **Skiing the Web (http://www.middlebury.edu/~carruthe/ skipage.shtml)**, for skiers everywhere

- **Skydive! (http://www.cis.ufl.edu/skydive/)**, for when you get an urge to jump out of an airplane

- **Sport Virtual Library (http://www.atm.ch.cam.ac.uk/sports/ sports.html)**, a listing of dozens of Web-based recreational sports sites

- **World Wide Web Tennis Server (http://arganet.tenagra.com/ Racquet_Workshop/Tennis.html)**, the ultimate site for tennis players and fans

- **Yahoo List of Hobbies and Crafts Sites (http://www.yahoo.com/ Entertainment/Hobbies_and_Crafts/)**, the ultimate list of Web sites devoted to various hobbies and crafts

In addition, check out Prodigy's Pleasures and Pastimes Interest Group page (**http://antares.prodigy.com/in9coi.htm#plea**). This page includes links to other hobby-related interest groups, including beer, chocolate, collecting, crafts, fashion, motorcycles, trading cards, and more!

28

Family Interests on Prodigy

● In this chapter:

- **How can Prodigy help me with my family's health issues?**

- **Tracing the family tree with Prodigy**

- **What educational features are available on Prodigy?**

- **How can I make Prodigy safe for my kids?**

- **Online activities for kids**

- **What family-oriented resources are available on the Internet?**

Prodigy is the premiere online service for families and children . . . . ❯

P rodigy was designed with families in mind. You can set up separate IDs for each member of the family, and restrict access to parts of the service for younger family members. Heck, Prodigy even monitors bulletin boards to make sure nothing offensive appears. When you add in all the services Prodigy offers specifically for families, you have one great service for Mom, Dad, and all the kids!

Prodigy's family sections

Prodigy offers a variety of services of interest to all the members of your family—health and fitness, education, hobbies, kid's stuff, you name it, it's here.

The best place on Prodigy for families, however, is the Parenting BB (Jump:**parenting bb**). This is one of the friendliest places on Prodigy, and a place to find good advice on a variety of sensitive topics. Good people hang out on this board. Visit them and share in their experiences.

A bulletin board just for homeowners

When you Jump:**home & garden**, you're taken to the Home & Garden BB. This board is just for families and homeowners, and includes topics like Building and Repair, Interior Decorating, and Neighbor Relations. In addition, there are several gardening-related topics, from houseplants to landscaping.

Keeping your family fit and healthy

When you Jump:**health**, you get a list of various health-related services on Prodigy. Let's take a look at the most important sections on this list.

- **Health News** (Jump:**health news**). This takes you to AP Online's Health/Science news section. This section generally contains about 50 health and science-related stories.

- **Health Topics** (Jump:**health topics**). As shown in figure 28.1, this is an interesting little section filled with lots of little snippets of health and fitness information. When you click on any of the sections (like Wellness or Diseases) you get a list of articles related to that topic. In other words, this section is kind of a big database of older health news articles.

- **Consumer Reports** (Jump:**cr health**, **cr exercise**, or **cr diet & nutrition**). These sections contain reports from Consumer Reports that cover health and fitness related topics, dating from 1990 on.

- **Keeping Fit** (Jump:**keeping fit**). This section helps you determine your fitness level, and gives you lots of advice on how to keep fit.

- **Health BB** (Jump:**health bb**). Prodigy's Health bulletin board, with topics like Diet/Nutrition, Exercise, and Stress Management.

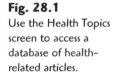

Fig. 28.1
Use the Health Topics screen to access a database of health-related articles.

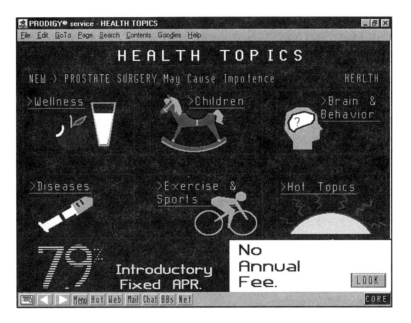

As much as I hate to admit it, I sometimes need to be reminded that I'm not in the best shape. I find the fitness test in the Keeping Fit section (Jump:**keeping fit**) a good reminder that I need to work on getting in shape.

Tracing your family tree

Genealogy is the science of determining your family lineage. Are you related to royalty, or are you a mutt? Use Prodigy's genealogy services to find out which.

If you Jump:**genealogy** you're taken to Prodigy's Genealogy section. This section helps you trace your ancestors and search for living relatives and friends. From this screen you can:

- Read Myra Vanderpool Gormley's weekly Genealogy column (Ms. Gormley is a certified genealogist and the author of the nationally syndicated "Shaking Your Family Tree" column)

- Browse through an archive of previous Genealogy columns

- Go to the Genealogy bulletin board (Jump:**genealogy bb**)

- Enter a genealogy-related Chat session

Learning to use Prodigy for education

Prodigy has a variety of educational resources of use to your family, including :

- **Education BB** (Jump:**education bb**). This is Prodigy's main educational board, with topics like Adult Education, Distance Learning, Gifted & Talented, and Home Schooling.

- **America Tomorrow Online Center** (Jump:**america tomorrow**), a unique gathering place for educators, administrators, and others interested in emerging trends in education and learning. See figure 28.2 for a list of topics. (This is a Plus feature, and will cost you $4.95 per month.)

- **Encyclopedia** (Jump:**encyclopedia**). This accesses Compton's Online Encyclopedia, Prodigy's Online Multimedia Encyclopedia.

- **Homework Helper** (Jump:**homework**). This accesses Prodigy's Homework Helper feature, which helps kids complete their homework with the help of a large reference database of important information.

Fig. 28.2
Where educators gather: The America Tomorrow Online Center.

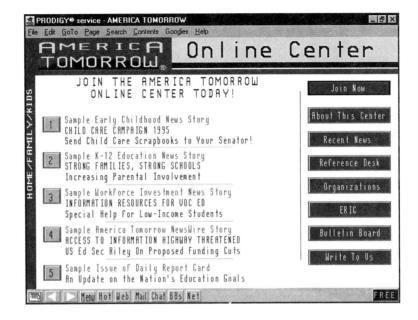

- **Mountain Challenge** (Jump:**mountain**). This section follows the exploits of 88-year old Norman Vaughan as he scales a 10,000-foot mountain in the Antarctic.

- **MayaQuest** (Jump:**maya**). This section follows the exploits of a team of cyclists on an expedition into the Mayan world of Central America.

- **National Geographic** (Jump:**national geographic**). A series of online quizzes and articles based on articles from *National Geographic* magazine. A great learning tool for kids.

- **NOVA** (Jump:**nova**). A series of neat online tours presented by the folks at Boston's station WGBH.

- **Schoolware** (Jump:**schoolware**). A list of best-selling educational software.

- **Science & Environment BB** (Jump:**science bb**). Prodigy's Science board, with topics like Archaeology, Chemistry, and Space Exploration.

- **Sesame Street** (Jump:**sesame**). An online play area for preschoolers, based on the famous Sesame Street characters.

- **Space Challenge** (Jump:**space**). Re-create a NASA space shuttle mission online—an exciting learning tool.

I've covered these areas somewhat lightly. But if you have kids—from pre-school to pre-teen—you should spend some time checking out these educational services. I'm particularly impressed by the Sesame Street and Space Challenge areas. There's really good stuff here, areas that definitely make your monthly Prodigy bill worthwhile.

Prodigy's kids' areas

There are two main areas on Prodigy for kids: Kids Zone (Jump:**kids**) and Teen Turf (Jump:**teens**).

Kids Zone is designed just for preteen children (see fig. 28.3). It includes links to Prodigy's online encyclopedia, Homework Helper, the Galaxy of Games, Prodigy's Sesame Street area, and other features of interest to young Prodigy members.

Fig. 28.3
Prodigy's Kids Zone.

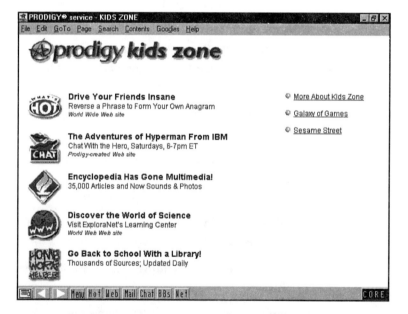

TIP   **Prodigy intends to add a directory of "safe and appropriate" Web** sites to Kids Zone, as well as a special Web browser that will block Web sites unsuitable for kids. Watch for these enhancements soon!

Teen Turf, on the other hand, is for older children (see fig. 28.4). While it includes some of the same links as Kids Zone (such as the online encyclopedia and Homework Helper), it also adds topics of interest to teenagers, such as sports and music areas.

Fig. 28.4
Teen Turf on Prodigy.

I'll discuss the individual areas for Prodigy kids in the balance of this chapter.

Talking the talk

Kids like to talk to each other—and they like Prodigy's kids-oriented bulletin boards. These BBs are a great way to learn social skills and enlarge your children's circle of friends.

When you click on the Kids Talk button on the Just Kids screen, you see the following list of kids-related BBs and services:

- **Ask Beth** (Jump:**beth**). This is an online parent/teen question and answer column. You can send questions to Beth, and she'll answer them online. ("Beth" is actually Elizabeth Winship, the well-known author and advice columnist for the *Boston Globe*.)

- **Disney Fans BB** (Jump:**disney fans**). This is a BB for fans of everything Disney—from cartoons to theme parks to collectables.

- **Games BB** (Jump:**games bb**). The main games board, with topics for all different types of games.

- **Music BB** (Jump:**music bb**). This takes you to the main music board, from where you jump to the individual Music 1 and Music 2 BBs, as well as Prodigy's other music services.

- **Out of Our Minds** (Jump:**out**). An online poll specifically for younger Prodigy members.

- **Pets BB** (Jump:**pets bb**). Prodigy's board for pet owners, with topics ranging from cats and dogs to ferrets and reptiles.

- **SI for Kids BB** (Jump:**si for kids bb**). The official board for the Sports Illustrated for Kids online magazine.

- **Teens BB** (Jump:**teens bb**). The board for Prodigy's teen members, with topics like Fashion, Hobbies, and Relationships.

- **The Big Help BB** (Jump:**big help bb**). This is the official board for The Big Help, an online service created by Nickelodeon and dedicated to encouraging kids to make a difference in the world.

- **The Club BB** (Jump:**the club**). A bulletin board just for pre-teens, with topics like Power Rangers, Baby-Sitters Club, Fashion, Schoolwork, and Pen Pal Requests.

- **U to U** (Jump:**u2u**). Nickelodeon's online interactive lab linked to their daily *U to U* TV show.

Carmen Sandiego, the Baby-Sitters Club, and other online stories

Prodigy offers a variety of online "stories" for kids of all ages. These range from the pre-school point-and-click pictures of the Sesame Street area to more involved games and tales from the Carmen Sandiego and the Baby-Sitters Club areas.

Just look at the stories available on Prodigy:

- **Carmen Sandiego** (Jump:**carmen**). An online "edutainment" game based on the bestselling *Where in the World is Carmen Sandiego?* software. You have to decipher the clues to figure out just where in the world Carmen has gone this time.

- **The Baby-Sitters Club** (Jump:**baby-sitters**). This is a full-featured area all by itself. Click on the appropriate buttons for this month's story, Ask Ann (questions and answers), Date Reminder (an online scheduler and datebook), Tips & Tactics (200 articles on how to be a better baby-sitter), Who's Who (notes from all the members of the club), Hotline (online questions to one of the BSC members). A *terrific* area for pre-teen and teenage girls.

- **Twisted Tales** (Jump:**twisted**). A fun little game where you supply a random bunch of words, and they're inserted into this week's story— the result is some pretty funny nonsense!

- **Reading Magic** (Jump:**reading magic**). An online book (changed monthly) for younger children. At various points in the story you can choose to take different paths by clicking on objects on the screen.

- **Sesame Street** (Jump:**sesame**). An online play area for preschoolers, based on the famous *Sesame Street* characters. Click on the various pictures to hear sounds and see animations.

As you can see, this area contains a wealth of activities for kids of all ages. I was particularly impressed with the Baby-Sitters Club, Sesame Street, and Carmen Sandiego areas.

Kids' very own online magazine: *Sports Illustrated for Kids*

Sports Illustrated for Kids is a very popular magazine among the young crowd. Now your kids can read an online version of this magazine on Prodigy—just Jump:**si for kids**.

As you can see in figure 28.5, SI for Kids has both major news stories and regular features. The regular features include The SIFK Challenge, Letters to the Editor, This Month In Sports, and Olympic Info. You can also go directly to the SI for Kids BB (Jump:**si for kids bb**).

This is a great area for children even vaguely interested in sports. The SI staff do a great job in writing to a younger audience, and kids really seem to love this magazine in its printed form. The electronic version is similar but different to the regular magazine, and certainly worth a look from your kids.

Fig. 28.5
Sports Illustrated for Kids—an online magazine for the younger set.

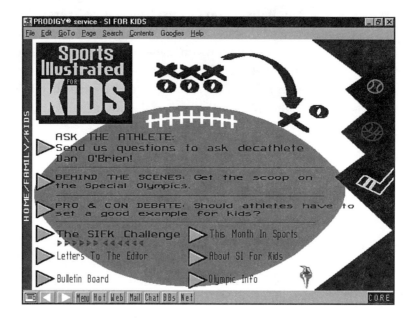

Finding family interests on the Internet

The Internet has a fair number of resources of value for the entire family. Let's start our family vacation on the Net with some family-related newsgroups (Jump:**newsgroups**):

- **alt.missing-kids:** A group devoted to finding missing children

- **alt.parenting.solutions, alt.parenting.twins-triplets, alt.parents-teens, alt.support.single-parents**, and **alt.support.step-parents**: Five groups devoted to parenting issues

- **misc.kids.computer, misc.kids.consumers, misc.kids.health, misc.kids.info, misc.kids.pregnancy**, and **misc.kids.vacation**: Six more groups devoted to parenting issues

Now let's look at a few Web sites for families (Jump:**www**):

- **Children Accessing Controversial Information** (**http:// mevard.www.media.mit.edu/people/mevard/caci.html**), a site devoted to discussion of protecting kids from bad stuff on the Net

- **Family Medicine Internet Sites** (**http://mir.med.ucalgary.ca:70/1/ family**), a list of sites devoted to family medicine

Making Prodigy safe for the whole family

Prodigy does a pretty good job of running a family-oriented service. For example, automatic software at Prodigy's headquarters automatically scans BB notes for certain offensive words and phrases, and "scrubs" them off the boards. But, despite these precautions, there are still some areas of Prodigy that you might want to make off-limits to the younger members of your household.

What are these areas? Well, let's start with the live Chat sections—you can't protect against what anyone might type in real time. Some bulletin boards (such as the Lifestyles BB and the Gay/ Lesbian BB) necessarily deal in racier subjects. And don't forget the entire Internet area—the Net is totally unregulated, just like the Wild Wooly West.

So what can you, as a parent, do to protect your youngsters from these areas?

The first thing you need to do is establish multiple Prodigy IDs for different family members. This way each member of your household can log on with a unique ID—and you can instruct Prodigy to limit access to certain areas to members with specific IDs.

To add family members to your account (and you can have six household members on a single account for no extra charge), Jump:**household member**. Click on the Add/Manage IDs button,

and then click on the Assign New ID button. Type the name of the new family member and click OK. Prodigy will assign an extension to your main ID to this new member. (For example, my main ID is JESE31, and I'm assigned the "A" extension—so my personal ID is JESE31A. If I add Martha Miller to my account, she gets the "B" extension—so her personal ID is JESE31B.)

Now that every family member has their own unique ID, you can determine access to certain parts of the Prodigy service for each family member. From the Household Member Access screen, click on the BB Access button. This lets you set access for all of Prodigy's bulletin boards. You can elect to grant or deny access to any board for any family member. This way if young ones try to access boards you don't want them to see, Prodigy won't let them do it.

Other sections of Prodigy have their own access settings. For example, when you first enter the Internet area, you can set access for all of Prodigy's Internet features.

It's worth an hour or so of your time to browse through Prodigy's sensitive areas and set access for the members of your family. It's better to be safe than sorry!

- **Family World** (**http://family.com/homepage.html**), an online magazine that's a collaboration of more than 40 different parenting publications

- **Internet Health Resources** (**http://www.ihr.com/**), a collection of reliable and practical health information

- **WWW School Registry** (**http://hillside.coled.umn.edu/others.html**), a map-based listing of schools on the Web

- **alt.kids-talk**: A group where kids can leave messages for other kids; kind of like an online pen pal club

- **finet.freenet.kidlink.*** groups: Seven groups (**kidcafe**, **kidforum**, **kidleadr**, **kidlink**, **kidplan**, **kidproj**, and **response**) that cover a range of cool topics for kids

- **rec.arts.books.childrens:** A group for lovers of children's books

- **Apollo 11: Mission to the Moon** (**http://www.gsfc.nasa.gov/hqpao/ apollo_11.html**), a terrific overview of man's first voyage to the surface of the moon

- **Barney's Page** (**http://www.galcit.caltech.edu/~ta/barney/ barney.html**), a site just for lovers of the big purple guy

- **Berit's Best Sites for Children** (**http://www.cochran.com:80/ theosite/ksites.html**), a great listing of kids-related Web sites

- **Carlos' Coloring Book** (**http://robot0.ge.uiuc.edu/~carlosp/color/**), an online, on-screen, electronic coloring book! (see fig. 33.7)

- **Children's Literature Web Guide** (**http://www.ucalgary.ca/ ~dkbrown/index.html**), a listing of children's literature on the Web

- **Curiosity Club** (**http://nisus.sfusd.k12.ca.us/curiosity_club/ bridge1.html**), a great science-oriented page for (and by!) school-children

- **CyberKids** (**http://www.woodwind.com:80/cyberkids/**), an online magazine just for kids

- **ExploraNet** (**http://www.exploratorium.edu/**), the online site for San Francisco's terrific Exploratorium

- **EXPO (http://sunsite.unc.edu/expo/ticket_office.html)**, a great online arts and science exposition; exhibits include Rome Reborn: The Vatican Library, the Soviet Archive, the 1492 (Columbus) exhibit, the Dead Sea Scrolls, and a great Paleontology Exhibit

- **Global Show-n-Tell (http://emma.manymedia.com:80/show-n-tell/)**, an online forum for kids to exhibit their favorite projects, possessions, and accomplishments

- **Kids' Corner (http://www.ot.com:80/kids/)**, a collection of games and stories for kids

- **Kids Did This! (http://sln.fi.edu/tfi/hotlists/kids.html)**, believe it or not, this is a list of home pages designed by kids around the world (and some of these are simply fantastic!)

- **Kids' Space (http://plaza.interport.net/kids_space/)**, another site for kids to share their favorite stuff with other kids (see fig. 33.8)

- **Kids Web (http://www.npac.syr.edu/textbook/kidsweb/)**, an online library for schoolkids

- **MathMagic (http://forum.swarthmore.edu/mathmagic/)**, a great math site for kids, full of quizzes, challenges, and puzzles

- **Northpole.Net (http://northpole.net/santa.html)**, Santa's home on the Web

- **Planet Earth: NASA Information (http://godric.nosc.mil/planet_earth/nasa.html)**, a listing of all the NASA and space-related information on the Internet

- **Scholastic Central (http://scholastic.com:2005/)**, the Internet center for the giant children's publishing company

- **SeaWorld's Animal Information Database (http://www.bev.net/education/SeaWorld/homepage.html)**, a great site for kids interested in all sorts of animals

- **The Nine Planets (http://seds.lpl.arizona.edu/nineplanets/nineplanets/nineplanets.html)**, a multimedia tour of the solar system

- **Ultimate Children's Sites List (http://www.vividus.com/~infov/orderscontacts.html#Neat)**, a great list of kids' sites on the Web

- **Uncle Bob's Kids Page** (**http://gagme.wwa.com/~boba/kids.html**), a listing of kids' sites on the Web

- **ZooNet** (**http://www.mindspring.com/~zoonet/zoonet.html**), the place to go to find out all about zoos on the Net

While your kids are on the Net, make sure they go to Prodigy's Kool Kids (**http://antares.prodigy.com/kidscoi.htm**) and Planet Teenager (**http://antares.prodigy.com/teencoi.htm**) interest groups. These pages link to dozens of other Web sites, USENET newsgroups, Prodigy Chat rooms, and Prodigy bulletin boards.

29

Searching an Encyclopedia and Doing Your Homework Online

● In this chapter:

● What is an online encyclopedia?

● How do you use it to look up information?

● What is Homework Helper?

● How does Homework Helper work?

Facts and figures are just a few clicks away with Prodigy's online encyclopedia . . . .

Among all the other features of Prodigy, there's one very important one that may be easy to miss. That very valuable feature is an online electronic encyclopedia.

What is an online encyclopedia?

An **online encyclopedia** is just what it sounds like—a normal encyclopedia converted to electronic form and put online with Prodigy. Because the text is all electronic, it's very easy to search for specific topics. All you have to do is enter the topic you're looking for, and the encyclopedia displays all articles that match your search criteria.

Prodigy's online encyclopedia (Jump:**encyclopedia**) is a special version of *Compton's Encyclopedia*. This online reference contains more than 5,000 articles and is a good general encyclopedia for most growing families. Prodigy even has a Web-based version of this encyclopedia that includes sounds, images, and maps—making it a real multimedia experience!

Looking it up online: Prodigy's two encyclopedias

When you Jump:**encyclopedia** you see the main encyclopedia screen shown in figure 29.1. From here you actually have two choices: the standard Prodigy-based encyclopedia, or a new Web-based *multimedia* encyclopedia.

If you have a faster computer that displays graphics and plays sounds, your best bet is the multimedia encyclopedia. To access this encyclopedia, just click the Multimedia Edition button on the main encyclopedia page.

If you have an older computer, you're better off without all the fancy sound and graphics. You can use the basic encyclopedia as it appears on the main encyclopedia page.

Fig. 29.1
Prodigy's main
encyclopedia page.

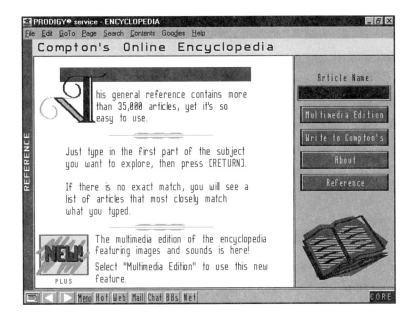

The fast and easy way: Prodigy's basic encyclopedia

Prodigy's basic encyclopedia includes a subset of the information in the multimedia version—but it's a lot easier and quicker to use.

The way you look things up in this online encyclopedia is to enter an a topic in the Article Name box on the opening screen, and then press Enter. For example, when you enter the word *england*, Prodigy returns a list of articles that match your search, as shown in figure 29.2. Click on the button next to the appropriate article to read the entire article.

Prodigy now displays the full text of the selected article. Don't forget to use the next page button to flip the pages of the entire article.

Fig. 29.2
A list of articles that matches your search criteria.

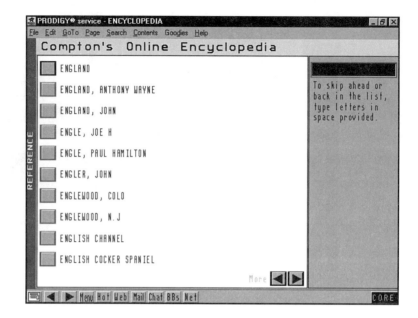

The buttons to the right of the article help you navigate through the encyclopedia. Clicking the Contents button displays the contents of the current article, so you can go directly to specific sections. The See Also button lists related articles that may also be of interest. Finally, the New Search button lets you start another search within the encyclopedia.

Information with sounds and pictures: Prodigy's multimedia encyclopedia

If your PC has enough power to run Prodigy's Web browser, I recommend that you skip the basic encyclopedia and go right for the multimedia encyclopedia. Not only does it include sound and pictures, but it also uses a much more comprehensive encyclopedia database than the basic encyclopedia does.

When you click the Multimedia Edition button on the main encyclopedia screen, Prodigy launches a special version of its Web browser and connects you to Compton's Living Encyclopedia, which is a site on the World Wide Web. Figure 29.3 shows the main screen for the multimedia encyclopedia.

Fig. 29.3

The home page for Compton's Living Encyclopedia on the Web.

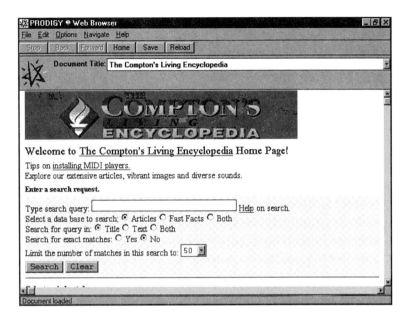

 TIP **This is a special version of the Web browser because you can't** enter any other URLs; it can only be pointed to pages of the multimedia encyclopedia.

You use this encyclopedia just like you use the basic one—by searching for a topic of interest. In this case, though, you can search through two different databases, and with various search criteria. I'll explain all the options available in the next few paragraphs.

First, you must select a database to search. You can choose to search Articles (which are complete chapters from Compton's Encyclopedia), or Fast Facts (which are summaries of articles). You might want to do a preliminary search of articles, since this type of search is the fastest. But if you want complete information, search the complete Articles.

Next, you can choose to search through Titles or Text (or Both). When you select Titles, the search engine only looks in article titles for the text you entered; when you select Text, it only looks in article text. To make sure you get all the appropriate articles, elect to search through Both titles and text.

Now you can select whether or not you want an *exact match*. Select Yes when you are searching for a precise word or phrase; select No to use operators such as AND, NOT, and OR in your search.

Finally, you need to select the number of matches you want listed, from 50 to 250. Be forewarned: selecting a larger number of matches can add a lot of time to your search.

After you enter all the parameters, click the Search button. Let's use the same example as before, and search for the word *england*. As you can see, this encyclopedia returns a *lot* of matches. Click on the main ENGLAND entry, and you're hyperlinked to the article shown in figure 29.4. As with all Web pages, any blue, underlined text is a hyperlink to another page—in this case, another encyclopedia article.

Fig. 29.4
A Web-based article, complete with hyperlinks.

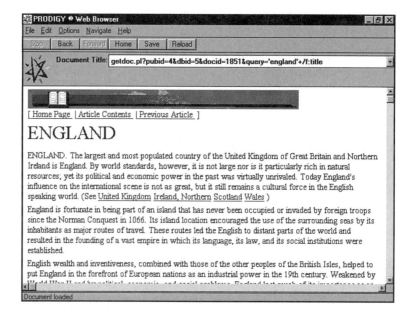

Some articles contain pictures and sound bites. For example, search for *jazz* and select the main JAZZ article. This article contains both audio clips (indicated by the musical icon) and pictures (indicated by the camera icon). Click on each icon to either play the audio clip or view the accompanying photo.

 Q&A *I have trouble playing the sound clips. What should I do?*

Go to the main encyclopedia Web page and click on the installing MIDI players link. This will give you the information you need to install an audio player on your PC.

Compton's Living Encyclopedia is a great resource for you and your family. I highly recommend it for all Prodigy members!

Another Encyclopedia on the Web: Britannica Online

Prodigy's multimedia encyclopedia isn't the only encyclopedia on the World Wide Web. The oldest and most respected encyclopedia of them all, *Encyclopedia Britannica*, is now available on the World Wide Web.

Britannica Online (as the Web-based version is called) is available as part of Time Warner's Pathfinder megasite, at **http://www.pathfinder.com/ pathfinder/favorite.html**. You'll need to access Pathfinder from this URL, and then click on the Britannica Online link. This will lead you to Encyclopedia Britannica's main page, where you can register for a free trial of Britannica Online.

Britannica Online is a fully searchable version of the main Encyclopedia Britannica database, enhanced with additional data from *Merriam Webster's Collegiate Dictionary* and other sources. Britannica Online works much the same as Compton's Living Encyclopedia; you enter a search phrase, select a database to search, and then wait for a list of all matching articles.

Britannica Online is a great online resource, but I'm not sure how much better it is than Prodigy's multimedia encyclopedia (Compton's Living Encyclopedia). You owe it to yourself to try both to decide which is best for your family's use.

The best tutor around: Homework Helper

One of Prodigy's newest services was designed to help your children prepare reports, do research, and otherwise complete various types of homework. This service is called Homework Helper, and it's a must for any school-aged child.

You get to Homework Helper with Jump:**homework**. Once there, you need to enroll (yes, it costs extra money to use Homework Helper!), and then download and install the special Homework Helper software to your personal computer. Once all this initial stuff is out of the way, you can begin looking things up in the large Homework Helper database.

CAUTION   **Homework Helper only works with the Windows version of Prodigy.**

Homework Helper is nothing more than a very large database of books, encyclopedias, dictionaries, reference works, photographs, magazines, newsletters, reports, newspapers, newswires, maps, and public radio transcripts. The Homework Helper software lets you query and browse this database to obtain just the information you need.

The nice thing about Homework Helper is that you don't have to learn any obscure database commands. All you have to do is enter a question—in plain English—and specify which parts of the database you want to search. Homework Helper does the rest of the work and returns a list of items related to your question.

Enrolling in Homework Helper

Homework Helper isn't free; it costs you $9.95 per month. This charge includes up to 50 hours of use; additional hours are billed at $2.95 an hour.

To enroll in Homework Helper, click on the About HW Helper button on the main Homework Helper screen. When the next screen appears, click on the Enroll & Pricing button. Next, you'll see a screen that describes the pricing plans, click on the Enroll Now button. Finally, you'll see the main enrollment screen. Select the members of your household you want to enroll, and your desired pricing plan. Click on OK to confirm the enrollment.

Downloading and installing the software

You need to download special Homework Helper software to use the Homework Helper service. Go back to the main Homework Helper screen and click on the Download button. Next, you see a screen of instructions; read the instructions and click on the Download Now button.

Now you see a special Download dialog box. This box tells you how much time it will take to download the software, and where the files will be downloaded to—which directory on your hard drive, that is. The default directory is your C:\PRODIGY directory, which you can change if you want—although there's no need to.

Click on the DOWNLOAD HOMEWORK HELPER SOFTWARE NOW button to begin the download. Then go get a cup of coffee or something, because it does take a while to complete the downloading (about 17 minutes at 14,400 baud).

Once Prodigy is done downloading the software (Was the coffee good? Did you have a second cup?), you need to install the software. Just follow these simple steps:

1 From the Windows 95 Start button, select Settings, Control Panel.

2 When Control Panel opens, double-click on the Add/Remove Programs icon.

3 When the Properties window appears, select the Install/Uninstall tab and click the Install button.

4 When the Install Program runs, type the following command line: **C:\PRODIGY\HHSETUP.EXE**.

5 Click the Finish button, and Homework Helper's installation program now starts. You're asked if you're ready to install Homework Helper; click Yes.

6 You're asked for the location of your Prodigy software; make sure C:\PRODIGY is entered and click OK.

7 You're asked where you want to install Homework Helper; make sure C:\HWHELPER is entered and click OK.

8 Now the installation begins. A bunch of stuff flies by on-screen pretty fast, and it's done in a matter of seconds. You're asked if you want your AUTOEXEC.BAT file automatically updated; answer Yes.

9 Your installation of Homework Helper is now complete—click OK.

That's all there is to it—you're now ready to use Homework Helper!

Looking it up with Homework Helper

To start Homework Helper, make sure you're on the main Homework Helper screen (Jump:**homework**), and click on the Use HW Helper button. Your normal Prodigy screen minimizes to an icon, and you see the new Homework Helper screen (see fig. 29.5).

Homework Helper (HWH) now has to connect, through Prodigy, to its main database. This takes a second or two, and is done automatically. When it's connected, HWH gives you a welcome message.

Click here to print the current article

Click here to cut selected text

Click here to copy selected text

Click here to paste text into the current document

Click here to use HWH's online dictionary

Click here to use HWH's online thesaurus

Click here to save the current article to disk

Fig. 29.5
The opening screen for Homework Helper.

Click here to access HWH's help system

Click here to begin a new search

Click here to spell check the current document

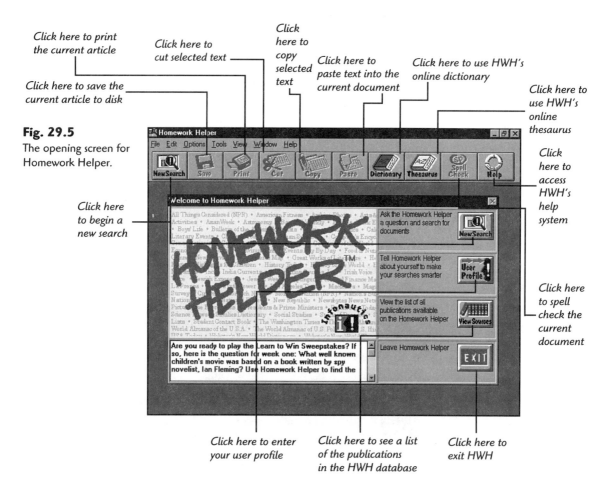

Click here to enter your user profile

Click here to see a list of the publications in the HWH database

Click here to exit HWH

Now it's time for the fun to begin. To begin your search, click on the NewSearch button. When the Query window appears, enter your question in the What do you want to know? box, and then select the items in the database you want to search.

HWH displays an error message that says Your access to Homework Helper has been disabled. **What is wrong?**

You downloaded the software but didn't enroll in the HWH service. Jump:**homework** and click on the Enroll button to complete your enrollment.

HWH displays an error message that says Unable to connect to server. **What is wrong?**

For some reason, Homework Helper is unable to connect to its database server. (HWH uses a database that is separate from the Prodigy service, and must connect to it via Prodigy's lines.) There could be several causes of this problem. It's possible that the HWH service is not working at this time—which means you should try using HWH at a later time. It's also possible that HWH has not been installed correctly—you may need to repeat the installation procedure.

Which parts of the database should you search? It all depends. If you're looking for a map, then by all means select only the Maps button. But if you're not sure *where* the information you want will ultimately be found, click on the All button.

When you're done entering your query, click on the Search button. For my example, I asked HWH "What is a jazz band?" After a minute or so of searching, it listed 150 separate items that matched my query, as shown in figure 29.6.

Fig. 29.6
HWH displays all the
items that match your
query.

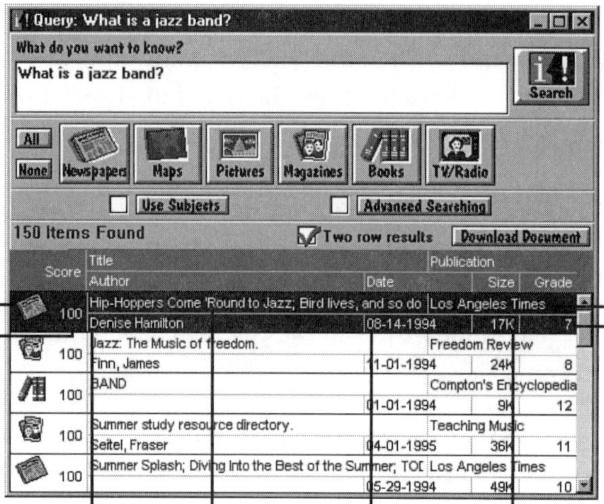

The type of item
(book, magazine
article, newspaper
article, etc.)

The score for
this item

Where the item
was published

The grade (reading
level) of the item

The author
of the item

The title of
the item

When the item
was published

The file size
of the item

Q&A

Why did I receive the message No items were found?

HWH lets you down when one of two things happens. First, it's possible that
HWH really can't find any items to match your query. It's more likely,
however, that your query is stated wrong. Try rewording the query and
searching again—it's always best to keep your questions brief. In fact, if you
keep getting low or no matches, try simplifying your query—you're probably
asking too complicated a question for HWH to properly answer.

Q&A

I'm getting too many matches to my query. How can I get a shorter list of items?

There are several ways to produce a shorter, higher-quality list of articles.
First, you can ask a slightly more detailed question. Second, you can narrow
the list of sources that you search. Third, you can narrow the list of subjects
that you search with the Use Subjects button. Finally, you can narrow the
parameters of your search with the Advanced Searching button.

Each item is assigned a score by HWH. This score attempts to recognize how
closely each article matched your query. A score of 99 would likely be a
better match than a score of 90.

The top item on my list is an article titled "BAND" from Compton's Encyclopedia. I want to read this article, so I highlight it and click on the Download
Document button. HWH downloads the document to my computer, and a

new window appears that contains the text of the selected document. From here you can scroll through the entire article, or click on the Go To Best Part button to go to the part of the document that HWH thinks best matches your query.

If this article fits the bill, you can use HWH's tools to either save the article to your hard disk, print a copy of the article, or copy selected text to paste into another document—such as a report you may be writing with your word processor.

If this article doesn't do the job, you can return to the listing of items and select another article for downloading.

TIP **HWH also includes an online dictionary and thesaurus. Access** these features by clicking on their buttons on the HWH toolbar.

Q&A ***HWH displays an error message that says*** A communications problem has been detected regarding your session to Homework Helper. Please exit Homework Helper and try again. ***What is wrong?***

Some sort of communications problem has prevented Homework Helper from processing your request. You'll need to exit Homework Helper and start it up again. (This error sometimes occurs when the HWH service is very busy.)

Q&A ***I can't find the list of items that matched my original query—where did it go?***

It didn't go anywhere, it's just in a separate window—which is probably hidden at the moment. Pull down the <u>W</u>indow menu and select the query you're interested in. This will move that results window to the "top" of the screen.

Make Homework Helper smarter

There are several ways to make Homework Helper work a little smarter.

The first way is to create a user profile for yourself. This helps HWH better target its searches in the future. Begin by clicking on the User Profile button.

Fill in as much information as you can, and then click OK.

Next, you can fine tune the "magnification" of HWH's searches. This determines how hard HWH searches through its database. Just pull down the Options menu and select Power Setting. When the Power Setting dialog box appears, move the slider left or right to decrease or increase the power of HWH's searches, and then click OK.

You can also choose to make your searches more selective by turning on or off various subjects in HWH's database. Click on the Use Subjects button, and you'll see the Subjects dialog box, listing various subjects. Pick the subjects that you want to *exclude* from your search and click on their buttons. (An "off" will be displayed on all buttons turned off.) HWH will then only search through those subjects still turned on.

There are other ways to limit the range of your searches. Click on the Advanced Searching button to display the Advanced Searching dialog box. Here you can select to search only certain date ranges, publications, authors, and/or titles.

TIP **You can discuss Homework Helper with other Prodigy users on the** Homework Helper BB (Jump:**homework bb**). This is a good place to get any questions answered, or find solutions to any problems you're having.

30

Playing Games Online

⬤ **In this chapter:**

- **Learn about sports and strategy games**

- **Play games with the Prodigy computer**

- **Get hints for your favorite computer games**

- **Talk to other gamers on games bulletin boards**

- **Find games resources on the Internet**

Prodigy is a great place for gamers to gather—and play!. .

If Prodigy is like a small town, you'd expect to find an arcade at the end of this online Main Street, filled with kids with too much time on their hands, dropping virtual quarters in to the online equivalent of pinball machines and video games. Well, Prodigy has lots of games on line, and you'll find lots of kids "hanging out" at this online arcade

Exploring Prodigy's Galaxy of Games

Prodigy offers a variety of games you can play online, along with lots of games-related news and information. Most of Prodigy's game-related resources can be found on the Galaxy of Games (Jump:**game center**), a focal point for all gaming activity on Prodigy (see fig. 30.1)—or accessed directly via JumpWords.

Fig. 30.1
Prodigy's Galaxy of Games.

 TIP   **Since new games are constantly being added to Prodigy,**
Jump:**games** to see a list of the most current games.

Run your own team with sports and strategy games

Prodigy offers several types of strategy games. You can find simple board games (like Chess), more complex "adventure"-type games (like Rebel Space), and even fantasy sports games (like Fantasy Football). Check out these sports and strategy games on Prodigy:

- **Baseball Manager** (Jump:**baseball manager**), online rotisserie baseball

- **Fantasy Football** (Jump:**fantasy football**), online rotisserie football

- **Guess-a-Move Chess** (Jump:**chess**), where you're presented with a chess challenge and you have to guess the next move

- **Rebel Space** (Jump:**rebel**), an online adventure game

- **Sports Illustrated for Kids Challenge** (Jump:**sifk challenge**), a sports trivia quiz for kids of all ages

Some of these games cost money to play; some of them (the fantasy sports games, in particular) can take several weeks or months to play. If you're interested in these sorts of games, Prodigy probably has something you'll like!

Play against the Prodigy computer

Prodigy offers a number of simple "point and click" games you play against the Prodigy computer—or, in some cases, against other Prodigy users. They're a great way to spend a little time between more taxing Prodigy activities.

Check out the following games:

- **AJ Dakota** (Jump:**aj dakota**), where you try to move—tile-by-tile—from the lower-left corner of the screen to the upper-right corner, without having the "ceiling" collapse on you

- **Boxes** (Jump:**boxes**), where you try to "surround" the other player's tiles (you can play this game either against the computer or another Prodigy user)

- **Carmen Sandiego** (Jump:**carmen**), an online version of the popular children's game

- **Fill in the Blanks** (Jump:**fitb**), where the object is to guess the letters that are missing from five words on-screen—kind of like *Wheel of Fortune* (you can play this game either against the computer or against up to three other Prodigy users)

- **Frantic Guts** (Jump:**frantic**), an online trivia quiz

- **MadMaze** (Jump:**madmaze**), where you turn left and right to find your way out of a maze

- **Match It** (Jump:**match**), where you turn over sets of boxes to try to find matching words

- **Police Artist** (Jump:**police**), a game of visual memory where you try to reconstruct a face from parts like eyes, nose, mouth, etc.

- **Square Off** (Jump:**square**), a math game where you try to form equations that equal a specific number

- **Thinker** (Jump:**thinker**), a game of deduction where you try to figure out a sequence of four colors

- **Twisted Tales** (Jump:**twisted**), a fill-in-the-blanks storytelling game

- **Yearbook** (Jump:**yearbook**), where you try to guess the year in which a series of events occurred

Prodigy calls some of these games Quick Games, and some Fun/Humor games. Whatever they're called, they're fun to play!

Learn the secrets of the masters with *Computer Gaming World's* game hints

Prodigy, in cooperation with *Computer Gaming World* magazine, offers an online database of hints to popular computer games. Just click the Game Hints button in Galaxy of Games to access the database; the hints are categorized by Adventure/Role-playing games and Strategy/Sports games. You search for hints by the name of the game, and the hints are often quite comprehensive.

TIP **Click the Game News button in Galaxy of Games to read game** reviews.

Talk to other gamers on the Games bulletin boards

Prodigy has four bulletin boards for hard-core gamers:

- **Games BB** (Jump:**games bb**), covers a broad variety of gaming topics, with topics on computer games, arcade games, board games, card games, and fantasy games

- **Role Playing Games BB** (Jump:**rpg bb**), for RPGers of all types, with topics on Magic: The Gathering, Star Trek, Star Wars, Dungeons & Dragons, and other fantasy and sci-fi games

- **Trivia BB** (Jump:**trivia bb**), with all sorts of trivia questions and discussions

- **Video Games BB** (Jump:**video games bb**), targeted at cartridge game players, with topics for all the major video game platforms, including Nintendo, Sega, Atari, 3D0, and CD-I

 TIP **Jump:trivia to see all of Prodigy's trivia-related resources in one** place.

These BBs are great places to hang out and exchange messages with other Prodigy members who share your gaming interests. Heck, you can even pick up a few tips and tricks from the "old timers" on these BBs!

Playing games on the Internet

As if you couldn't get enough games and gaming info on Prodigy, you can always venture out on the Internet for even more game resources.

Newsgroups for gamers

Let's start by looking at game-related newsgroups (Jump:**newsgroups**). The following newsgroup areas contain lots of games-related groups:

- **alt.games.***: There are newsgroups in this area for just about every major game, including Descent, DOOM, Mortal Kombat, and Tie Fighter

- **comp.sys.ibm.pc.games.***: This area includes groups for major PC-compatible games, like Flight Simulator

- **comp.sys.mac.games**: One newsgroup for all Mac-compatible games

- **rec.games.***: This is the main gaming area on USENET, with dozens of newsgroups for traditional games like Bridge and Chess, state-of-the-art Internet MUDs, exciting trading-card games, and all the major videogames

Games on the Web

Newsgroups offer great interaction with other gamers, but you can find more cool stuff at key game-related Web sites. Fire up Prodigy's Web browser (Jump:**www**) and take a look at these sites:

- **Cardiff's MUD Page (http://arachnid.cm.cf.ac.uk/User/Andrew.Wilson/MUDlist/)**, a comprehensive list of Net-based MUDs and MOOs

- **coNsOLe wORlD (http://arachnid.cm.cf.ac.uk/Games/)**, a good site with lots of videogame information

- **EA Online (http://www.ea.com/)**, the Web home of Electronic Arts

- **Fantasy and Other Role-Playing Games (http://www.acm.uiuc.edu/duff/index.html)**, a compendium of information for RPGers

- **Game Bytes (http://sunsite.unc.edu/GameBytes/)**, an online gaming magazine

- **Gamer Connection (http://www.mcp.com/brady/connect/)**, a great place to exchange gaming tips and meet other online gamers, sponsored by BradyGAMES

- **Games Domain (http://wcl-rs.bham.ac.uk/~djh/index.html)**, with links to hundreds of Net-based game sites, walkthroughs, home pages, electronic magazines, and MUDs

- **MUDs (http://draco.centerline.com:8080/~franl/mud.html)**, lots of info about MUDs and MOOs

- **Nintendo Power** (**http://www.nintendo.com**), Nintendo's supersite on the Web

- **NUKE** (**http://www.nuke.com**), perhaps the best site on the Net for games of all shapes and sizes

- **Outland Online Games** (**http://www.outland.com/**), a place to play graphical, real-time games with other Internetters

- **Sega Web** (**http://www.sega.com/**), the official Sega site on the Web

- **Yahoo's List of Game Sites** (**http://www.yahoo.com/Entertainment/Games/**), a really big list of game-related resources on the Internet

- **Zarf's List of Interactive Games on the Web** (**http://www.cs.cmu.edu/afs/andrew/org/kgb/www/zarf/games.html**), a very comprehensive list all sorts of different Web-based games—from online chess to trivia quizzes, to MUDs and MUSHes

In addition to these sites, check out Prodigy's Trivia interest group (**http://antares.prodigy.com/trivicoi.htm**). This page lists dozens of Web sites, newsgroups, bulletin boards, and Chat groups for "triviots," and is worth visiting.

Visiting Que on the Net

Macmillan is on the Net via a very large World Wide Web site called the Macmillan Information SuperLibrary. You can get there by entering the URL: **http://www.mcp.com/mcp/**.

As you scroll through the home page, you'll see all the many things you can do. Just take a look at this list:

- Go to the home page for any Macmillan publishing imprint by clicking on the logos on the main screen. For example, you can go to Que's home page by clicking on the Que logo next to the big library.

- Find out **What's New**—new book releases, special offers, contests, and even employment opportunities.

- Read the latest copy of the **SuperLibrary Newsletter**, complete with articles from some of Macmillan authors and a monthly column from yours truly.

- Enter an online **Bookstore** and browse through thousands of titles, many with tables of contents and sample chapters. From this bookstore you can hyperlink to other online booksellers, search a list of all the booksellers in the U.S., and even order directly from us, if you want.

- Sign up for notices of upcoming books at the **Reference Desk**.

- Download hundreds of shareware, freeware, utilities, and demo programs from the **Software Library**.

- Learn a little bit about us from the **Macmillan Overview**—which includes home pages from Macmillan employees, as well as pictures of Macmillan kids!

 TIP The MCP site is a part of the larger Macmillan Information SuperLibrary site, which features information on a variety of general reference topics, from travel to pet care. You can access this larger site at the following URL: **http://www.mcp.com/**.

Que on the Web

In addition to the main SuperLibrary section, you can go directly to Que's section in the SuperLibrary (**http://www.mcp.com/que**). Here you can find lots of information specific to Que books, including announcement of upcoming releases. See figure A.1 for a glimpse of Que's main page.

Fig. A.1
Que on the Web.

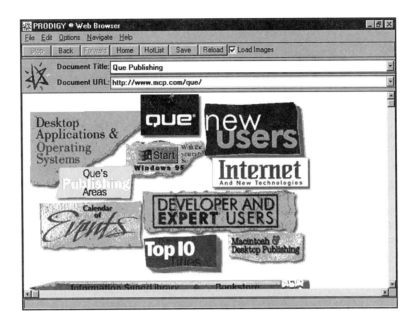

Communicating with the author (that's me!)

I've created a special *Using Prodigy* page that constantly updates the contents of this book (**http://www.mcp.com/people/miller/prodtop.htm**). I also have a Web page on the Macmillan site (**http://www.mcp.com/people/miller/**), and several Web pages on Prodigy's site (**http://pages.prodigy.com/IN/jese31a/index.html**).

If you want to contact me, the best way to do it is via e-mail. I appreciate your comments about this book (or anything else, for that matter); your

feedback on the previous edition helped to make this one better. You can contact me at:

- Prodigy address: **jese31a**

- Internet address: **mmiller@mcp.com**

Please feel free to drop me a note and tell me how you liked this book, or if you have any questions. I can't guarantee that I'll be able to answer all messages personally, but I'll do my best!

Thanks for reading the book—I'm looking forward to hearing from you!

Index

C

call waiting, disabling, 23
Calvin and Hobbes
  Archive (Web sites),
  286
Cameron's Moto Page,
  300
Canada BB
  Politics/Separation
    topic, 295
  Travel topic, 297
Canada Net Pages (Web
  financial sites), 227
car reservations,
  243-247
Careers BB
  Travel topic, 296
  see also jobs
Carlos' Coloring Book
  (Web sites), 316
Carmen Sandiego online
  game, 313
categories
  AP Online feature, 182
  Computer Support
    Center, 297-298
  Online Personals, 106
CBS Television: Eye on
  CBS (Web sites), 287
celebrities, information
  about, 284-285
Center for
  Innovative Computing
  Applications
  (Web sites), 258
Chat, 88-99
  BB, 99
  configuring, 90
  excluding guests, 94
  Instant Messages, 98
  nicknames, selecting, 89-
    90
  Pseudo area (adult), 97
  restricting access, 91
  rooms
    Auditoriums, 88
    creating private
      rooms, 94-95
    jumping from, 18
    Member rooms, 88
    Prodigy rooms, 88
    selecting, 90-91

sending private
  messages, 98
sessions, 93-94
special events
  checking
    calendar, 96
  participating in, 96
  transcripts, 99
threads, 93
window, 92
Cheezy 80s (Web sites),
  287
Children Accessing
  Controversial
  Information
  (Web sites), 315
children's activities
  bulletin boards
    Ask Beth, 311
    Big Help, 312
    Club, 312
    Disney Fans, 312
    Games, 312
    Music, 312
    Out of Our Minds, 312
    Sports Illustrated for
      Kids, 312-313
    U to U, 312
  games (Carmen
    Sandiego), 313
  Internet groups, 316
  Kids Zone, 310
  stories
    Reading Magic, 313
    Sesame Street, 313
    Twisted Tales, 313
  Teen Turf, 311
Children's Literature
  Web Guide, 316
CIS (CompuServe
  Information
  Service), 68
City Guides service, 241
City.Net (Web sites), 249
ClariNet news
  (Internet), 184, 200
classified ads,
  see Online Classifieds
clicking, 12
Club (children's BBs),
  312
CM 4/CM 6 error mes-
  sages, 23

codes (HTML), 156
Collecting BBs, 293
collecting bulletin
  boards
  Adult Trading Cards, 294
  Collecting, 293
  Comics, 294
  Hobbies, 294
  Memorabilia topic, 294
  Trading Cards, 294
  Wine, Beer and Spirits,
    294, 298
Collecting Resources
  (Web sites), 300
College and University
  Home Pages (Web
  sites), 151
columns (computer
  software), 253
Comedy Video service,
  280
Comics BBs, 294
commands
  Edit menu
    Copy, 61
    Paste, 61
    Snapshot, 183
  File menu
    Exit, 58
    Print, 182
  Goodies menu
    Sounds, 39
    Tool Bar Setup, 10
  Help menu
    (Contents), 50
  Navigate menu (Global
    History), 145
  Options menu
    Advanced Options,
      150
    Power Setting, 332
  Path command, 31
  Reservations menu
    (Flight Reservations),
    244
  Search menu
    commands, 181
  Weather menu
    Int'l Weather, 191
    US City Forecasts,
      190-191